driftless run

A CROSS COUNTRY JOURNEY THROUGH CRISIS, COMMUNITY, AND ENDURANCE

jeff rich

LITTLE CREEK PRESS
MINERAL POINT, WISCONSIN

Copyright © 2025 Jeff Rich

All rights reserved. No part of this publication may be reproduced, distributed, or transmitted in any form or by any means, including photocopying, recording, digital scanning, or other electronic or mechanical methods, without the prior written permission of the publisher, except in the case of brief quotations embodied in critical reviews and certain other noncommercial uses permitted by copyright law. For permission requests or other information, please send correspondence to the following address:

Little Creek Press
5341 Sunny Ridge Road
Mineral Point, WI 53565

ORDERING INFORMATION
Quantity sales. Special discounts are available on quantity purchases by corporations, associations, and others. For details, contact info@littlecreekpress.com

Orders by US trade bookstores and wholesalers.
Please contact Little Creek Press or Ingram for details.

Printed in the United States of America

Cataloging-in-Publication Data
Names: Jeff Rich, author
Title: Driftless Run. A Cross Country Journey Through Crisis, Community, and Endurance
Description: Mineral Point, WI Little Creek Press, 2025
Identifiers: LCCN: 2025902952 | ISBN: 978-1-955656-96-2
Classification: SPORTS & RECREATION / Running & Jogging
SPORTS & RECREATION / Cultural & Social Aspects
BIOGRAPHY & AUTOBIOGRAPHY / Sports

Book design by Little Creek Press

Thank you to my friend, Morgan Lynn Haun, for creating the scene on the title page.

For my parents, Betty and Dick,
who were always there.

TABLE OF CONTENTS

PROLOGUE 1

RUNNERS' KEY 5

One: REMEMBRANCE 9

Two: THE GRIDIRON GANG 12

Three: THE PEARL 26

Four: THE WINDS OF CHANGE 36

Five: THE WINTER BLUES 45

Six: THE NEW FAMILY 48

Seven: MISFITS AND MASOCHISTS 60

Eight: THE CRUCIBLE 70

Nine: RUN FOR THE HILLS 78

Ten: AWAKENING 85

Eleven: THE YOGI 97

Twelve: TRIBULATION 104

Thirteen: RENEWAL 117

Fourteen: A COHESIVE TEAM 137

Fifteen: ADVERSITY'S RAIN .156

Sixteen: SKIN IN THE GAME .167

Seventeen: FALLEN 173

Eighteen: RESURRECTION 183

Nineteen: CHASING THE WHITE WHALE 201

Twenty: LIVING IN DOUBT 215

Twenty-One: DAWN 236

Twenty-Two: BREAKTHROUGH 243

Twenty-Three: THE MATRON 278

Twenty-Four: LEGACY 282

EPILOGUE 291

WHERE ARE THEY NOW? 296

ACKNOWLEDGMENTS 300

ABOUT THE AUTHOR 304

PROLOGUE

It is the early 1980s, and the farm crisis has gripped the dairy farm communities of southwestern Wisconsin's Driftless Region. The local economy is suffering, and socio-economic change is underway, straining the traditions of the past. It is a time without cell phones or the Internet when small-town teenagers search for ways to connect and fit in. This is a story about a group of young athletes from two of these communities struggling to succeed under difficult circumstances. It is also the story of two novice coaches—Gary Brone and Arnie Miehe—leading those teenagers and pioneering their programs in the old but obscure sport of cross country. Both are in unfamiliar territory as they begin. They will encounter challenges on and off the course that threaten their self-esteem. But their pursuit of excellence will bring them face to face.

The story is told from my perspective, as I experienced it as a teenager on one of those teams. Other than a few names that have been changed, the events are true. My path to cross country was accidental, and I did not realize how transformative the journey would be when I started. It seemed like a simple enough sport. Run fast and you win. Run slowly and you lose. But on rare occasions, life offers us a glimpse into the possibilities beyond our everyday limits. In those special moments, circumstances arise that seem too magical to believe. Sometimes the best gifts come in small, ordinary packages. Life sets a messy table in front of us, but in the middle of that mess lies opportunity. It is where character can be forged, and dreams can be achieved if we are willing to accept the hardship.

From the time I was born, my father coached athletes in basketball, football, and track and field. As soon as I could walk, I observed these sports from the bleachers, sidelines, and locker rooms. Before I was old enough to play, I was with my dad on the bench as an equipment manager and in the huddles during timeouts. That early experience gave me a deep interest in athletics and an appreciation for each sport's strategy and artistry. At first, I sought the praise and stature bestowed upon the best athletes, but over time I became drawn to the lessons instilled through sports and their value as a guide for young people. If not sidetracked by a participant's selfishness, athletics can serve as a working model for building virtue. Athletics' worth comes from those lasting traits the participants gain during the struggle and that they can reapply fruitfully on their life's journeys.

I found the sport of cross country to be the most instructive for those lessons. The physical demands on the individual are merciless, yet success depends upon the sacrifice of others. The sport is steeped in humility, with the least talented having the most influence on the outcome. Cross country's objective is simple, and accountability is clear, making it difficult to escape the sport's lessons.

Cross country originated in England during the early nineteenth century. Teenage students created the game of "hares and hounds" at school to mimic their fathers' sports of hare and fox hunting. The running term *harrier* has its roots in those field sports, as do *the pack, the field*, and *steeplechase*.[1] The game of chase was also a form of hide-and-seek, utilizing open country, woodlands, hedgerows, streams, and other natural obstacles to hinder pursuers. It was as much a sport of tactics as it was of skill or endurance. The sport evolved into its modern version by the turn of the twentieth century. Cross country was adopted as an event in the Olympic games in 1912 and was eventually integrated into the modern pentathlon. By the 1980s, it was beginning to take hold in the small, rural districts of western Wisconsin.

Since then, cross country has become popular as a high school and college sport in the United States. Despite this broad adoption, it still

---

1. Roger Robinson, "The Origins of Cross-country," *Runner's World*, September 13, 2009, www.runnersworld.com/advanced/a20800271/the-origins-of-cross-country/.

exists in relative obscurity in the public eye. For those who have never participated in the sport, it is difficult to relate to the experience. Other than the start and the finish, it can be an inconvenient competition to witness. The drama during a race is more internal than external. Trials felt by the athlete remain unseen by spectators. While appearing to be an individual endeavor, cross country is most notably a team sport. It is rarely covered in print or on television. The sport's stars are not featured in advertisements selling products. While an often overlooked sport, cross country offers some of life's best lessons through its purity and sacrifice.

I have never written a book before and never held a dream of authoring anything beyond a technical paper. But after four decades, the craving to capture the thrill of participating in a pioneering program, the challenges of the times, and especially the lessons learned, have forced my hand. I am compelled to share the story with you and to honor two coaches who have helped countless young people on their journeys through life.

A NOTE TO THE READER

This story is narrated from two perspectives:
a first-person account of events by the author as well
as a simultaneous, third-person account of the opposing
team's journey. Though unconventional, this storytelling
approach provides a more compelling view of parallel events.
Visual aids (team logos) are included to assist the
reader with significant shifts in perspective.

RUNNERS' KEY

COCHRANE-FOUNTAIN CITY (C-FC) PIRATES

CLASS OF 1985

Paul Abts "Cud"

Scott Adler "Ardie"

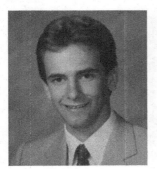

Jeff Rich "Smiley"

Guy Todd

CLASS OF 1986

Mark Brone "Space"

Dan Lettner

DARLINGTON REDBIRDS

CLASS OF 1985

Troy Cullen "Culley"

Doug Dunham

Tom Evenstad "Evie"

Jay Stauffacher

Brian Whalen "Helmer"

CLASS OF 1986

Bob Cullen

Todd Johnson

James Schuetz

CLASS OF 1987

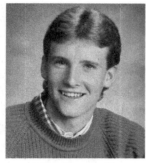

Kirk Evenstad

Dave Hirsbrunner "Hirsh"

Dale Kelly

Kent Ruppert

To what ends do we strive if not for those that are shared?
—Jeff Rich

CHAPTER ONE

REMEMBRANCE

August 30, 2015

The sun was at its zenith on that August day as I meandered north on the Great River Road toward my roots. Despite the radiant sky, my mood was gloomy as my mind hearkened the echoes from earlier years, trying to find a happier place. On my left was the Mississippi River, its immense and timeless waters flowing south, visually marking my journey back in time. I knew those waters well, and with the window cracked open, my senses intensified the memories. On my right were the hulking bluffs of Wisconsin's Driftless Region, standing guard over the great valley. The plants had reached their peak growth by August, and the hardwoods were clothed in vibrant leaves. But hints of the approaching fall were present. Along the road, the goldenrods were bowing their yellow heads, and the milkweed pods were erupting in tufts of white. Red and orange accents were beginning to decorate the sumac, forming my path on either side of the road.

When I entered Fountain City, I turned left and drove past the ball diamond where I'd coached the Little League team thirty-one years earlier. Though the sun was prominent, summer ball was over, and the field was void of life. A line of vehicles was parked along the road leading up to the bike shop, and I searched for a spot to park. Getting out of my car, I could see a crowd gathering next to an immense canvas tent pitched between the shop and railroad tracks along the river. As at most memorial services, relatives, friends, and community members had gathered to honor a life well-lived. But the crowd was unusually large, even for a small community where most of the inhabitants were like family. I began to recognize faces, though they were more creased than I remembered. Retired teachers, classmates, school board members, kids I'd coached in Little League, patrons and matrons of the community were all there, spanning several generations.

"Hi, Jeff!"

Turning around, I saw Karen Stettler standing in line. She had been a grade ahead of me in school, and I had not seen her in over twenty years.

"Karen! How are you?"

"I'm fine, but I wish we had a better reason for getting together."

I agreed and gave her a hug.

"I think we'd all prefer to be somewhere else right now," I said. "I can't wrap my head around it. But it is still so good to see you! It's been too long."

We began sharing our life milestones, bridging the decades of absence, covering weddings, children, and careers. It went on like that for nearly an hour, standing under the warm sun and catching up with old acquaintances as the two of us inched forward in line.

By the time we reached the shadow of the tent, beads of sweat were rolling off my head and dripping down my spine. I loosened my tie and ducked underneath the shelter. Once my eyes adjusted, I could see rows of folding chairs lined neatly within and a continuation of the line around the shaded perimeter. Tables, covered carefully with photographs, were placed along the path, and people were scouring them as they stood in line.

I began combing the images and noticed several black-and-white photographs from the 1960s.

"Oh my. Look how attractive they were!" Karen exclaimed.

"Yes," I could only reply. "Don't they look wonderful?"

The shots were of Gary and Judee Brone, in their youth, on a boardwalk in New York City. They were both gleaming with the smiles of happier days. Their faces were recognizable to me, but it was from a time long before I'd known them. Farther to the right, on the same poster board, were their wedding photos. Then came the baby photos of their boys, Mark and Jesse. The line moved forward, and I noticed the albums sitting on the table. A photo of Mark as a high school freshman, suited up in his football uniform, grinning from ear to ear, immediately jumped out at me. Suddenly, my mind carried me back in time to the summer of 1982 when I'd first met Mark on the gridiron. We could not imagine it then, but football would forge our path into cross country.

CHAPTER TWO
THE GRIDIRON GANG

August 3, 1982

The whistle shrieked, and fifty breathless bodies pounded against the earth. In an instant, the mass of flesh was upright, and the staccato chop of cleats resumed. Coach Ken Wagner blasted the whistle, and in another instant, the players' stained shirts turned ninety degrees to the right and then swiveled back to face forward. The next whistle repeated the twist on the left side. Knees lifted rapidly, and the team drummed their legs until the sound of the whistle commanded them to drop onto their chests and repeat the drill.

From the sidelines, an onlooker could barely see the goalposts through the thick fog. Had it not been for the sounds, the players could have been apparitions in the early light of that August morning. But behind their facemasks, brows were wet with sweat, and grime was collecting on their arms from the collisions with the dirt. At that time of year, the afternoon sun and suffocating humidity punish those who labor in it. The nights were growing longer and cooler with the approach of the autumn equinox. The result was a heavy fog covering the drowsy river valley before the sun had peeked above the bluffs to the east. Coach Wagner had his team starting two-a-day practices at dawn for the upcoming high school football season.

As head coach for the Pirates, he was determined to get his team prepared to improve on its 3-6 record from the previous fall. He was on a mission to purge weakness.

To my right, Hugh Martin was chopping on the practice field during the "up-downs" and was short of breath from the effort.

He glanced at me briefly. "When's he going to stop?"

I slurred back through my mouthguard. "Not much longer."

We were about the same height, but I was forty pounds lighter. Next to him, my sophomore frame looked slim. But the work was not as hard for me. Hugh was a senior captain whose thick, muscular build made him an imposing running back. He could outsprint most of the squad despite weighing over two hundred pounds. Colleges were recruiting Hugh for his prowess, and although he was a good sprinter, endurance was not his strong suit. I had learned to appreciate his strength the previous fall when he had leveled me with a "decleater" in the middle of the field. His facemask had crashed into my helmet's ear hole as I pursued a ball carrier, and I'd blacked out momentarily. After getting to my feet, I wobbled through the rest of practice with my ears ringing and my mouth babbling gibberish. We had recently started spending more time together, running through ball exchanges and passing routes during the summer. In addition to starting on defense, I had been the team's quarterback since the prior season. That distinction occurred less for my ability than the team's deficiency. Team depth was so poor that, at times, a freshman or sophomore with some level of skill would be tapped to play varsity. Since then, Hugh and I had developed a rapport, and I had earned his respect.

To my left, I could hear Scott Adler slurping breaths through his mouthpiece. Scott and I had been friends since we met in the second grade. His mom had been our Scout den mother; we attended swimming lessons together; we joined band together; we had the same catechism classes; and we had been Little League teammates. He was of average height and weighed about 135 pounds. Although small for a linebacker, Scott had uncommon physical strength and was densely muscled. He was looking forward to getting some time in the varsity lineup during the upcoming season.

Directly behind me, the Jackals chopped their cleats into the tattered sod and twisted at the whistle. "Jackals" was my private name for the gang of upperclassmen who bullied the younger kids. Some had athletic talent, and some did not, but they all had a thirst for viciousness and carried full-grown ferocity in their bones. Teenage boys will attack another just to boost their illusion of strength within their peer group. After puberty, many suddenly occupy bodies with impressive strength, where there had been little but a couple of years earlier. This awakening presents an advantage to move up the pecking order of dominance, and some leap at the chance. The Jackals would not think twice about playing dirty, and they never missed an opportunity to pounce. Their black helmets and white facemasks enhanced their image as grim reapers on the field. The Jackals resented that I had started on varsity before them, and we were not friends. For the time, we tolerated each other out of necessity as teammates. But I would not turn my back on them, particularly when coaches were absent, and I did my best not to provoke a mutiny.

Hugh was our go-to guy on offense. It was common for him to carry the ball more than thirty times during a game while we ran our triple option. Opposing defenses would key in on Hugh, and if he did not have the ball on a dive or pitch, his role as a decoy would free up a receiver or allow my feet to get to the edge. But Hugh was a leader in title only. Like the other senior captains, he was not a natural leader, and his off-field demeanor was genial. On the other hand, the Jackals had gifted leadership in the Machiavellian sense. They drew their power through cunning manipulation and fear. They were intelligent enough to execute their deeds when hidden from the eyes of adults. The Jackals set the tone for the team when the coaches were absent.

Mark Brone was chopping his feet far back in the group with the other freshmen. Most of them barely weighed a hundred pounds and lacked coordination. As boys, still holding dreams of the NFL in their heads, they were oblivious to the train wreck coming their way. They were the sacrificial lambs upon the altar of "manhood," and the Jackals were famished.

It was difficult at a high school of our small size to field a football team. The offense and defense used eleven players each, and then there were needs for special teams. Injuries during the season further depleted the ranks. Some were farm kids who were expected to help with chores and whose parents would not let them play. So, for rural high schools with enrollments under three hundred students, only half of whom were boys, fielding a team was challenging. Nearly one-third of the boys in the high school were needed for sufficient depth.

Anyone with some ability was encouraged to be on the football team, and the lure of the Friday night adulation from fans, cheerleaders, and the local media held an attraction for most boys. The macho image also compelled them to join. Like gang membership, the pressure was strong and particularly hard for teenage boys to resist. The trial by fire was an unspoken expectation for becoming a "man" in the culture of the time.

Like his classmates, Mark's growth spurt was just beginning, and he had entered the two-a-day practices at five feet, six inches tall, with little more than a hundred pounds on his frame. But that had not diminished his enthusiasm, and he was still bigger than some. He had waited eagerly for this moment. For years, he had been amassing a sizable collection of football cards. Roger Staubach, Kenny Stabler, and Fran Tarkenton looked down from the bulletin board on his bedroom wall. His mother, Judee, encouraged him to dream big and to always do his best.

The whistle shrieked once more. Wagner yelled, "Bring it in, guys," and the squad started clapping in rhythm.

"Good job! Take a knee."

The team knelt and removed their helmets, revealing fifty dripping mops. As if choreographed, each of the players wiped sweat from his brow with his shirt.

"Second practice starts tonight at six o'clock, so get here early so we can have a full workout before dark. We've got a lot of work to do before the scrimmage next week. Tonight, we'll run our mile to see what kind of shape we're in. By next week, we'll begin full contact drills. There isn't much time, so I expect all of you to pay attention and give your best effort. Captains, make sure that we're ready to go by six. All right! Hit the showers!"

The group immediately sprinted to the water spigots on the exterior walls of the school. Cleats hammered on the pavement, creating a clatter as each member scrambled to quench his thirst. The rush was so earnest that a couple of freshmen slipped or were pushed to the asphalt in the race. There had been no water breaks in the two-hour morning practice, and the humid conditions had sapped the entire team. It was a trial of toughness—and a common practice in the 1980s—to go without water. The manager's kit had salt pills that were distributed by request. Still, Wagner wanted his crew to harden themselves for the season in the heat. He didn't need his kids vomiting during drills from a belly full of water.

"Ahhh!"

The outburst came from the day's first victim. His head had been kicked into the cement block wall as he reached his mouth toward the spigot. The freshman had boldly attempted to drink first, and a Jackal had put him in his place.

"Get the f*** out of the way! You freshmen get to the back of the line, and don't let me find any of you little shits trying to cut in front of me again!"

The skinny kid had no recourse for an appeal; the coaches were nowhere in sight. He sheepishly fell back to the end of the line, with blood dripping from his hairline. Instantly, the Jackals swarmed the spigot and drank in order of dominance. They swallowed feverishly and splashed the excess over their heads until they were satiated. The freshmen learned quickly from the example at the spigot. They flipped their helmets upside down and put a finger underneath to plug the hole. Then they'd fill their crude vessels and lift them above their heads so they could gulp the contents earnestly as they walked to the locker room—sweat, grime, and all. The adaptation was not only a faster way to get water; it reduced the chance of getting your head knocked into the wall by the pressing crowd.

While the freshmen waited their turn at the spigot, I jogged to the fountain in the gym. One year of experience had taught me to avoid the melee outside. After swelling my stomach with water, I walked down the stairs and pushed through the doors to the locker room. Once inside, my nose met with the odor of sweaty socks and Stickum, which had saturated the walls for years. The warm scent of freshly laundered towels competed for my attention, and I picked one out of the bin next to the doorway and carried it to my locker. Alex Van Halen's drumbeat throbbed off the walls as "Runnin' with the Devil" covered the chatter of dozens of players preparing to shower. The coaching staff had a separate office, and the door was closed while they discussed the players' performances in private. As soon as I removed my cleats, the screaming began.

This time, the cries were coming from another skinny freshman, that day's second victim. Other than being small, he had done nothing wrong. A couple of Jackals had cornered him in the shower. It was one of their favorite tortures for hazing the new class, and they called it "scouring." The Jackals would turn on two adjacent showerheads, one cold and the other to its hottest setting. Then they grabbed their victim and flung him back and forth under the streams, shocking him with the stinging contradiction. The jolt was so tremendous it took your breath away, and the kid's screams subsided after a few seconds. I was out of view, sitting on the bench near my locker, but I could visualize his pinched face and pink torso being tossed back and forth. As I removed my T-shirt, I heard the Jackals laugh hysterically from within the shower room.

"Look at that hairless freak!"

The rest of the upperclassmen paid little attention, and those who did said nothing for fear of putting a target on their backs. Hazing was considered a rite of passage. It happened in every high school to some degree, but it was an all too common sight at small high schools struggling to field a team. Fourteen-year-old boys were thrown into combat with seventeen- and eighteen-year-old brutes as if they were physical peers. Their immature bodies were punished throughout the season during practices. They were the fodder for the upperclassmen seeking to be men but who were mentally still children. At larger schools, the greater numbers meant that freshmen played with freshmen on a separate squad, sophomores made up the junior varsity, and the varsity was comprised mostly of upperclassmen. That segregation did not stop bullying completely, but the physical maturity was more balanced. If the senior class or captains had strong convictions, hazing would not be tolerated. This was the case the prior year when I was a freshman. That senior class would not allow the Jackals' behavior to get out of hand, although there had still been attempts.

When the torture finally ended, victim number two wiped the tears from his wet face and tried to regain his breath. As humiliating and stinging as scouring was, he had been spared the worst treatment that could be unleashed upon a freshman. After a few days, most learned to seek refuge until the upperclassmen had finished their showers, only entering afterward. But none of them were safe until the Jackals had dressed and gone home.

When I stepped into the shower, I saw the kid trying his best to pull himself together. His eyes would not meet mine as his crouched figure shuffled toward the lockers. I had not attempted to stop the assault, and I was ashamed of it. I knew that it would have been futile, and an attempt would surely have brought retribution down on me. Plus, I was expected to command the Jackals on the field, and the fragile truce that I'd achieved with them would be destroyed if I intervened. I knew how those freshmen felt. The Jackals had made several attempts at bullying me while we were in junior high. Each time, I had evaded the conflict or diffused the situation. During my freshman year in football, I had ascended quickly enough to varsity that the seniors provided me some cover. My father was also a teacher, so the Jackals had limited opportunities to attack me without being noticed by a staff member or for fear of getting benched. It was an advantage that others did not have. My lack of action gave me a cowardly feeling that ate at my gut. If I had gone to the coaching staff to report the bullying, I would have been shunned by the whole team. It would have been even worse for one of the freshmen to do so. Young men were expected to grin and bear the treatment. I vowed to myself that I'd change things when I became a senior. But doing the right thing often meant doing the difficult or unpopular thing. Doing the right thing might lead to banishment, and my desire to succeed in football was paramount. So, I buried my objections.

"Kev, are you about ready to go?" I asked my brother, who was just toweling off.

He was always the last one to get dressed. Kevin was also a freshman, but unlike Mark, he had a November birthday and was already pushing six feet in height. That fact and his fierce temperament helped him sufficiently dissuade the Jackals.

"Ya, Smiley, I'm comin'!" he said, using my nickname.

"Dad's waiting in the car and wants to be at the job before noon," I barked back.

Our father had formed a painting business years earlier with two other teachers as a way to make ends meet when no checks were coming in during the summer. My two brothers and I occasionally worked with him to earn a little spending money and to help him complete some additional jobs before school started. Kev and I would have preferred to go home and rest after practice, but on that day, we were headed to Cochrane to scrape and prime a house instead. In the spring of 1982, Ken Wagner had asked my dad to join the football coaching staff as the defensive assistant. Dad had opted out of that role the prior season when I was a freshman, even though he had been an assistant for many years before that. He had anticipated that I might play on varsity, and he had even asked Wagner to keep me on junior varsity for my first season, but to no avail. He understood the scrutiny that came for a coach's kid. He did not want the jealousy or pressure placed on me if he was coaching. He kept the head basketball position that year and made sure I did not play on the varsity as a freshman. He had three sons coming up in the ranks and was looking to avoid trouble with the bleacher perception of favoritism. Our father wanted us to earn our roles if we were going to play for him.

By five o'clock, we were finished with our work and on our way to the school for the second practice of the day. The air was steamy, and the sun was still high enough to keep the temperature around ninety degrees. Kev and I each lifted duffel bags out of our family's 1969 beige Plymouth Fury and walked into the locker room to get dressed. The Fury was our second car, but my brothers and I loved the 440 cubic-inch V8, which roared when a foot pressed on the accelerator.

We were still without pads for the evening practice. Wagner's plan was to run drills with our helmets and cleats. After that, the skills position players would run some basic passing routes. At sunset, he'd start the mile run.

"Did you get to the pool this afternoon?"

I looked down the bench and saw Scott knotting his laces and looking back at me. His perpetually broad smile exposed his upper gum.

"Nah, we had to paint a house today," I responded. "Probably won't finish it until this weekend. What'd you do?"

"I was baling hay up on the ridge in that damned heat. I bet I drank five gallons of water."

"What are you going to do with the money?"

"Get a car. Can't get my license until next June, though, unlike some people."

Scott was alluding to my August birthday and the fact that I was already driving with a permit.

"Well, it doesn't help much to have your license when you don't have a car of your own, like me," I said. "Maybe you can buy that car, and I'll use it to cart you around."

Scott laughed, and we donned our helmets before trotting up the steps and out the door.

When we turned the corner toward the practice field, I could see a small group of freshmen fleeing in front of the Jackals. They made it past the track and bolted into the cornfield behind the opposite end zone. The Jackals were screaming at them and calling them cowards. The captains were already lined up for calisthenics. They had started leading the team through the drills before the coaching staff left the locker room, but as was often the case, the Jackals were running their own show. The freshmen hid themselves in the corn successfully, and the Jackals gave up the chase to take their place on the chalk lines for the drills. After a few minutes, the coaches trotted onto the field, and Wagner took over barking commands at the team.

"Time for leg lifts. Get on your backs!"

The response was a communal groan. By this time, even without pads, the humidity was saturating the players' T-shirts, and everyone knew what was coming. The abdominal muscles would have fled if they could have. Each kid was in for an agonizing fifteen minutes of core work, lifting his legs and holding them at various heights and angles for excruciating amounts of time. It was an essential exercise for avoiding injury in the sport. But the core work during the first week of practice left the players stiff and aching by the next morning, seizing them like old men.

About this time, the freshmen rashly chose to emerge from the cornfield to take their places toward the back of the group. They did not get far before Wagner erupted in an angry rant.

The rest of the team stood mute and watched the reprimand. During the spectacle, I looked over and noticed the glee on the Jackals' faces. In the end, the freshmen ran laps on the track and paid a price for the mayhem.

As the sun started to set, Wagner blew the whistle and signaled for the team to circle him.

"Okay, it's time for our mile run. I want to see what kind of shape you guys are in. We need to be able to play all out for four quarters, and this will tell us how much more conditioning we need. The faster you finish your four laps, the less work you'll have to do in upcoming weeks. You freshmen better put in some effort on this, or I'll make you run another mile!"

While I was listening, I recalled the same event the previous season when two players had walked off the field. They were among the biggest kids on the team, standing well over six feet tall and with thick trunks. They were farm kids who were solid contenders for a position on the line. They could toss bales of hay all afternoon on the farm, but they were not tough enough to handle the mile run. The pair strolled back to the locker room and handed in their gear. Wagner's sieve worked. The linemen who made it through were not large, but they were fierce and in shape. A mile run seemed like nothing to me. I could not get their choice out of my head. *How could they quit over something so trivial?*

Running had never seemed hard for me. Despite beating most of the football team in Wagner's mile, I did not think I was particularly good at endurance races. A few of my classmates, like Guy Todd, were smaller and more gifted at long distances. At that time, I thought of myself as a sprinter. But my mother and father had both run when I was young, and I had watched their example. My dad quit smoking when I was twelve, and he replaced his cravings with running. I had accompanied him on some five-mile runs around our home, and it introduced me to the strenuous but gratifying workout that comes from running. During junior high, my mother had entered me in several 5K runs at local festivals, and we ran in those events together. It was certainly a challenge to run a few miles, but it was something I viewed as fun, not scary. So I was naturally confused as to why others would be overwhelmed by the thought of running a mere mile. But I was just starting to understand the impact of body size in football— and in distance running.

After the mile run, the practice ended. The group trotted off the field toward the locker room, repeating the race to the spigots from the morning but with less violence than before. I could see a Jackal ahead of me, sneaking up on freshmen and rapping their helmets from behind with his chinstrap. The Jackals made sure they got to the locker rooms first so they could wet some towels. When the freshmen approached the showers, they'd crack those whips and brand their victims. A number of the freshmen skipped the evening shower and waited for their parents to pick them up outside the building. It saved some time and was an unspoken method for avoiding the gauntlet.

Despite the hazing, some kids wanted to play football but were not allowed to. They were expected to assist with chores on the farm, especially during the fall harvest and spring planting seasons. Small family dairy farms were still plentiful in Wisconsin at that time. Roughly half of the students at the high school lived or worked on dairy farms. It was hard work with cows needing to be milked twice a day, every day, and the chores to sustain the operation were endless. Despite the hardship, in many ways it was a good life, creating tight family bonds and an attachment to nature.

But by the early eighties, the farm crisis had begun, and the small family farm in Wisconsin was beginning to decline. It was the end of an era that would span the next several decades and result in a much smaller number of farms that became huge mechanized dairies. Families needed large amounts of capital to support the operation, and in the early eighties, the U.S. prime interest rate was in the double digits. It loaded most farmers with debt and little profit to show for the toil and risk. Banks were foreclosing on family farms in droves. Suicides among farmers were spiking, and operations that had been in families for generations were folding from low milk prices and the crushing debt required to operate. If they could cover their debts, some farmers sold their dairy cows and switched to raising cash crops, beef, or poultry to lower their expenses and stave off foreclosure. Others doubled down by purchasing failed farms to maintain profitability on slimmer margins through increased volume. Midwest states with agriculture-based economies especially felt the pressure. It was not discussed openly, but we could see the stress on the adults' faces. The chronic worry never left their eyes. School finances were also impacted. Much of the educational budget in Wisconsin was funded through property taxes levied on farmers.

One effect of slashed budgets was the discontinuation of sports. Rural districts tended to be large geographically. Bus fuel and equipment costs needed to support a sport were "wants" not "needs." Hard decisions had to be made. Baseball was dropped during my freshman year in high school, limiting opportunities for those of us interested in a summer sport. Middle school sports had become mostly intramural, and I remember wondering if varsity sports might be discontinued altogether. It was no surprise that some kids did not get the opportunity to join a team. During that time, the parents and coaches of the district started a booster club to help fund sporting opportunities and limit the financial burden on those who wished to participate.

The Cochrane-Fountain City School District (C-FC) was formed in 1958, consolidating the school districts of Cochrane and Fountain City into one system. The Cochrane School District included the Village of Cochrane as well as Buffalo City, which by the 1980s had populations of roughly five hundred and one thousand, respectively. Fountain City also had roughly one thousand residents. The C-FC School District covered roughly 150 square miles, enveloping the southern third of Buffalo County. For students who could not drive to practices or sporting events, the district would provide buses to drop off participants following an after-school practice. This was an added expense for the school, but it helped with participation in those days, especially for kids whose parents had evening milking chores and could not sacrifice the time to pick up their children from practices.

By 1982, the consolidated district had been in place for several decades. Nevertheless, there were echoes of the rivalries between the communities before the consolidation, when they had been opponents. Some parents still held past grievances from that time, although those thoughts were not vocalized. The students of the eighties did not hold these same views. Still, they were indirectly affected through their parents' social circles and by the distance separating the communities of the district. During school events, adults grouped in the bleachers by tribal cluster. Most adults in Fountain City either worked at the Army Corps of Engineers, where the enormous Thompson dredge was docked, or made the short drive to Winona, Minnesota, to work. In Cochrane and Buffalo City, the main employment was at the oat mill or the power plants in Alma. Both communities had churches for the common denominations, sponsored separate Little League teams for their youth, and had their own community pools. Kids who were not yet old enough to drive a vehicle were limited to a circle of friends within the mile or two that they could bike, inhibiting the bonds and connection needed to form strong teams by the time they were in high school. On top of that, there had been several episodes of large groups of athletes who had been caught at drinking parties and penalized with suspensions. Drugs were beginning to infiltrate rural districts as well. More and more kids were turning to this type of activity for social acceptance rather than make sacrifices for the rewards from athletics. All of this contributed to a general cloud over the sports programs in the district.

A yearbook aerial photo of Cochrane-Fountain City High School in the early 1980s.

During the second week of practice, our team was wearing full pads on the gridiron and hitting the sleds. Save a few, the freshmen looked too small for their gear. The equipment they donned were the worn leftovers from a decade earlier and not suitable for the varsity. Some of the pants and jerseys had holes or were patched. Helmets were marred from previous battles and had throwback grilles attached to the front. But the sparse school budget required their use. The view was comical as the freshmen's helmets bobbled loosely on their heads and their baggy pants hung below the knees, barely suspended by belts high on their waists. The shoulder pads on the freshmen jutted out in awkward lumps while their gangly arms protruded underneath. Seeing them run through drills was like watching geese take flight from water—and just as noisy.

Classes started the third week of August, and the heat persisted. The school was not air-conditioned, and the box fans were running on high as I made my way to the locker room after the final bell. Each year brought a fresh feel to the school. Everyone had a new locker as they gained seniority. The scent of fresh wax hung in the air. The students had new jeans, new shirts, new sneakers, and new binders. Girls had new hairstyles to complement their summer tans. Even the faces seemed new as students transformed into adults. I pushed through the doors of the locker room to don my gear and noticed a freshman brushing past me in the opposite direction. He did not look up. He was still in his street clothes, but his head and shoulders were soaking wet. It was an odd sight, and as I sat down on the bench in front of my locker, I saw one of the Jackals beaming.

"What happened?" I asked Scott, who was sitting next to me.

"Swirly," Scott uttered without turning.

It suddenly made sense. A swirly was the ultimate disgrace to a young man and the torture the Jackals savored the most. The coaching staff had not yet entered the locker room for practice, and the Jackals had pounced. The victim was caught in an unlucky moment in the bathroom. The Jackals grabbed him and forced his head into a dirty bowl while flushing the toilet. The kid struggled but could not overcome their numbers. The porcelain bowl was fractured in the conflict, and there was water all over the floor. When the coaches showed up, everyone claimed that the mess was already there when they entered. Other than a new work order for the custodial staff, things carried on as usual.

CHAPTER THREE
THE PEARL

That same week, 160 miles to the southeast of Fountain City, Arnie Miehe was starting his first season as the cross country coach for the Darlington Redbirds. A year earlier, he had been running the Redbirds' football team through two-a-day drills as an assistant football coach. Now, he found himself as the leader of a struggling program in an obscure sport, looking to attract numbers and ascend to excellence.

Darlington lies on the southern edge of the Driftless Region, nestled in a valley on the banks of the Pecatonica River. It was first settled in 1836 by Jamison Hamilton and called Centre for a time. Early settlers burrowed for minerals in the area, and lead mining prospered. In the 1850s, the railroad came through, the population grew, and the community became the Lafayette County seat. The small city was renamed Darlington in 1869. Alfred Ringling, of the famous Ringling Brothers Circus, got his start in Darlington as a harness maker.[2]

By the 1980s, the economy of Darlington, with a population of roughly 2,300 residents, was focused around the area's rich soil, and dairy farms covered the rolling landscape. In the center of town is a statuesque courthouse built around the turn of the twentieth century. The building towers from the top of Main Street, which descends

---
2. https://en.wikipedia.org/wiki/Darlington,_Wisconsin.

The LaFayette County Courthouse at the top of Main Street in Darlington. Photo by Jeff Rich.

five blocks south to the river, between century-old structures. The community is called "The Pearl of the Pecatonica."

In the early eighties, the high school belonged to the Southern Eight conference with larger Class B districts. At the time, Darlington was considered the doormat of the league athletically. The school was the one that most of the other teams in the conference marked a "W" next to on their schedules. Darlington had not won a conference title in any sport in ten years and had never advanced any team to a state competition. The high school paralleled C-FC in many ways, including a losing culture. It was also a culture in which every able-bodied male was expected to play football in the fall. However, unlike C-FC, Darlington had a cross country program that had been launched in 1968. Prior to his retirement, the team's coach for the first fourteen seasons approached Arnie to see if he would be willing to lead the program.

Arnie Miehe was raised on a dairy farm near the small town of Belmont, not far from the southern border of Wisconsin. Although he was modestly built, he was an excellent athlete with quick feet. In the 1970s, the popular TV show *Green Acres* featured a pig that also had the first name of Arnold. By the time Miehe was in junior high, the older kids had branded him "Arnie the Pig," which he despised. When Arnie was in eighth grade, his track-and-field coach had noticed his talented feet and lined him up against the varsity's star distance runner to test his prowess. He handily defeated the team's best runner and became known as "Arnie the Runner." He discovered that he had a gift for running and, even more, that he craved winning. But at that time, speed was viewed as a means toward autumnal victories on the gridiron rather than something to be squandered on a cross country course with nerdy peers. The football coaching staff took notice, and expectations were set for him by the time he was in high school. Arnie's legs made him an ideal candidate for running the high school football team's wishbone offense, which depends upon deception and speed. Arnie became Belmont's quarterback.

Yet the call to compete as a runner still beckoned to him. The lure of distinction was too much to resist, so he asked his track coach to enter him in a cross country invitational in nearby Platteville while he was still Belmont's quarterback. He won the race and set a new course record. Upon his return, he asked the football coach if he could run cross country as an additional sport and was immediately rebuked. Football was king, and community pride was integral to the team's success. Community members did not look favorably on a gifted athlete who gave up football to pursue a running career. Arnie conceded and finished his high school career on the gridiron. But he did not forget his dalliance with distance running, and he went on to excel at the two-mile event in track during the spring seasons, qualifying for the state meet in that sport.

After high school, Arnie attended the University of Wisconsin–Platteville, a few miles from his home, and played quarterback for the football team during his first year on campus. But his yearning for distance running did not relent, and he quit football to join the university's cross country squad as a junior. The

Coach Arnie Miehe in 1983. Photo courtesy of Arnie Miehe.

competition at the college level was much more intense, and the experience gave him an appreciation for what it was like to run in the back of the pack. He also came to love running for running's sake, not just because he was good at it. While he was working on his degree, Arnie was hired as an assistant football coach at his hometown high school. He continued to balance the dichotomy between football and cross country in a world that did not accept both. By early 1980, he was on the faculty in nearby Darlington and coaching football because that role was posted along with the teaching position.

When Darlington's retiring cross country coach petitioned Arnie to take his place, it rekindled Arnie's hunger for the sport, and he jumped at the chance. In the fall of 1982, he became the head cross country coach for the Redbirds.

During the spring and summer, he had campaigned to recruit a core group of kids he could use as a foundation for the program. Arnie knew that he would eventually need good runners to be successful. He would need gifted athletes who might otherwise play football. He vowed to himself that he would not build his team from "football rejects" but compete to attract kids to his program on its own merits. Arnie's initial strategy was to recruit popular kids to form a nucleus for recruitment within the student body. His theory was that if he could recruit leaders first, the best runners would follow.

He had his eye on Troy Cullen. Arnie was a track-and-field coach and had witnessed Troy run an eight-hundred-meter race in 2:06 while he was still in junior high. The young man was a naturally gifted athlete who also played football, basketball, and baseball. But there was no doubt that he was meant to be a runner with his spectacular stride. He stood around six feet tall with sandy hair and a strong, chiseled face. It was apparent that he was going to lead Darlington athletics during the next four years. Troy was one of those kids to whom the other boys gravitated. He was a leader and immensely popular in school. As luck would have it, Arnie had an ace in his pocket for recruiting Troy. Troy's older brother, Todd, was a senior runner on the cross country squad. They both went to work on Troy and convinced him to forgo football and join the cross country team instead. Arnie had found his lightning rod.

By the time practice started in August, Arnie had fourteen boys on his squad. All but two were underclassmen. Among them were freshmen James Schuetz and Bob Cullen, Troy's cousin. Both were

Darlington High School. Photo courtesy of Arnie Miehe.

physically immature and weighed under one hundred pounds. Troy also had a number of his classmates join the team with him, including Jay Stauffacher, Doug Dunham, and Tom Evenstad.

Living three blocks from one another, Tom and Troy were close. Homer and Katie Evenstad had six children. Tom and Kirk were the youngest. The family owned a five-hundred-acre dairy farm with one hundred milking cows, but they lived in town. Through sixth grade, Troy and Tom had attended Holy Rosary Catholic School together, not far from the courthouse. Where one was found, there was the other. Tom was a good student and popular with his peers. He had been on the football squad his freshman year, playing running back and linebacker on the junior varsity. The varsity and JV football teams had been crushed by opponents the entire season. At the last JV game in Mineral Point in 1981, the Redbirds squad had been throttled 60–0. That kind of humiliation, week after week, year after year, impacts a young athlete's psyche. There is no joy in losing, and a young athlete's identity suffers. On the bus ride back from Mineral Point, Tom had decided to join Arnie's inaugural team the following fall. He wanted to be with Troy doing something fun together, and he was sick of losing. He had kept that secret to himself until he could no longer hide his intent. After the first cross country practice in August, Tom stepped out of the locker room at the same moment the football coach, Gary Ringen, walked by.

"Hey, Evie," Ringen said. "Not going out for football?"

Tom's eyes dropped, and Ringen continued: "Hate to see you go, but good luck!"

Tom felt guilty for not telling his coach earlier, but Ringen liked the young man and still treated him with respect. Both moved on. Suddenly Tom found himself in a predicament. He was a strong kid, which fit well for football, but he was only an average runner. Like all small towns, football was king in Darlington, and the shadow of shame for quitting the sport was tough to shake.

There was another recruiting "first" in that inaugural season under Miehe's leadership. In his first year coaching track in 1980, Arnie had worked with a small freshman girl named Ann Smith, who had never competed in a sport before but showed early promise as a distance runner. She was a quiet farm kid who had grown up milking cows. Despite her small stature and blonde hair, there was a toughness that had come from the work ethic she'd developed doing chores. Arnie encouraged her to consider going out for cross country. She became the first and only girls' cross country runner at Darlington as a sophomore. By the time Ann was a senior in 1982, she was the captain of a full girls' squad and held the records for the distance events on the Darlington track.

On the first night of practice, freshman Bob Cullen sat on the floor of the gymnasium stage searching the faces of the other kids who had assembled in front of Arnie. Bob was next to his older brother, Mike, who was a senior captain for the team. But Bob was anxious, and he did not see any other freshman boys on the stage. Moments later, his classmate James Schuetz walked in accompanied by his older brother, Jeff, and Bob sighed in relief.

During the workout, James Schuetz found himself running at his brother Jeff's side, struggling to keep up. Arnie had sent the squad onto their high school course to drill the route into their brains. Although James was a farm kid accustomed to hard work, he had not yet had his growth spurt. In contrast, his junior brother carried enough sinew on his bones to start at fullback for most football teams.

Between gulps of air, James looked over to Jeff and asked, "Is this how fast we'll be running during races?"

Jeff glanced at his little brother. "Oh, no," he responded with a sly grin. "We're just getting started."

Miehe liked to run with his team. Still a young man in the early eighties, he was talented enough to run a 5K in under 16 minutes. So when practice began in August, he was often able to set the pace on long endurance runs with his crew.

One day, the Redbirds were putting in miles around the community golf course. The terrain served as a good model for many of the racecourses they'd encounter. James found himself struggling to keep up and fell further back after each hill he encountered. In the middle of another steep climb, the heaviness in James's legs nearly stalled his progress. At that moment he felt a firm hand in the middle of his back, pushing him up the hill. Then an encouraging voice rang in his ear.

"You're stronger than you think you are!"

Arnie knew that the mind must master the body in order to overcome the suffering in a race. He stressed the mental aspects of the sport with his kids and reminded them that anything was possible if they believed they could do it.

One of the most challenging routes the Redbirds used was a six-mile workout they named "Larson's Loop." It did not take James long to realize what his brother had been talking about.

Larson's Loop started at the high school and went southeast on County Highway K through the rolling countryside. The first few miles made a general descent over several tributaries and into the banks of the Pecatonica River Valley. The team eased into the run and picked up speed as they approached Red Rock Road near the river.

By August, the blue flowers of chicory and the white lace of wild carrot replaced the dandelions that had blanketed the ditches along those roads in June. Grasshoppers were plentiful and flitted erratically off the shoulder of the road. Finches, sparrows, and bluebirds coasted over the runners' heads.

Alfalfa fields intermingled with countless acres of corn and soybeans. Milk trucks passed by the team, transporting raw product from the bulk tanks to the dairies. A perpetual breeze above the valley carried the scent of cow manure from the pastures and barnyards. Growing up in the presence of dairy cows, one could never completely escape the scent of manure. Once accustomed to the aroma, it was not offensive. Manure had a reassuring familiarity as the soil's fuel for the next cycle of growth. Beef cattle dotted the landscape and stretched their necks beneath the fences to reach more succulent greens. When Arnie's squad passed, the cows pulled up and stared back at them with thoughtless eyes, chewing their cud. The sweet smell of silage seeped from the concrete silos where the chopped corn was stored. It was mixed with the scent of freshly mowed hay lying in the fields. Elevators perched on haymows atop barns. Dairy cows pastured on the wooded hillsides and open fields, carving narrow dugways into the terrain. The muffled pulse of tractors plying the landscape bestowed a heartbeat to the scene before them.

After reaching the banks of the river, the loop turned left again toward County K, and the team began a steep, undulating climb out of the valley. The pace slowed, and the labor intensified as the group struggled to ascend from the basin.

Once on top, the terrain gave Arnie's crew a chance to stretch out their strides and shake their hands to release the tension from the climb. His squad came out of oxygen debt, and the pace increased again. The younger runners and those who had not logged miles over the summer struggled to recover and suffered over the last couple of miles to the school.

Although Darlington had started a cross country team fourteen years earlier, the health of the program that Arnie inherited was anemic. It was not a winning tradition. Getting enough kids to easily field full teams for both the girls and boys in Arnie's first season was a surprise. Remarkably, the Redbirds had enough boys to field a full junior varsity team as well. While Arnie was pleased with the results of his initial recruiting class, he knew he needed to establish systems and routines to keep the program moving forward. Those systems and routines were essential to attracting support for the program, both in the student body and in the community. They had to be fun, engage a broad group, and develop excellence.

Arnie didn't waste time. Over the summer he started the Mile Club. To become a member, each runner needed to log a minimum of two hundred miles in the ten weeks of summer break. The roughly twenty miles per week was enough to establish a solid aerobic base prior to practice beginning in August. Those kids who exceeded the two-hundred-mile mark made the club, got their photos in the local paper, and were acknowledged at the end of each season in Arnie's annual cross country yearbook, distributed to each member of the team.

On the first night of practice, Arnie held a cookout after the team finished their training run. It was an easy way to welcome new kids and helped to build relationships through food.

During the last week of August, Arnie organized the inaugural alumni run. He placed an ad in the paper inviting former runners to come back and race the high school teams on the home course. A traveling trophy was awarded afterward, and in 1982, the men's alumni team beat the varsity 36–41. It was the first cross country meet for eleven of the Redbirds runners, and it gave them the chance to gain race experience before competing against other schools.

Early in the school year, Arnie organized the first junior high and grade school meets to introduce younger kids to the sport of distance running. The races were age appropriate, with shorter distances, but the kids jumped at the chance to compete. The results were printed in Darlington's local paper, the *Republican Journal*.

The evening before the Redbirds' first race, Arnie pulled the door handle at East Catherine Street in Darlington and held it open while his team marched through the entrance of Lafayette Manor. Like most coaches, Arnie planned light workouts the day before a race, but this time he added a twist. He wanted to provide his runners with a new perspective on life and instill gratitude. There had been some grumbling within the squad that the workouts were demanding too much, that it was becoming torture. The kids' eyes were wide as they hesitantly stepped past their coach. Their noses were greeted by the scent of the cafeteria, mixed with a hint of rubbing alcohol, during the walk down the hallway. Each one had an assignment to engage a resident in bingo, checkers, conversation, or to push a resident in their wheelchair for a stroll outside. The building was a county-owned nursing facility, and Arnie had set up a visit for his team. A variety of ailments afflicted the residents of Lafayette Manor. There were stroke victims, dementia patients, elderly residents with physical disabilities, and even younger ones stricken with other afflictions. The kids engaged the residents, and after more than an hour, Arnie summoned his team back to the facility's courtyard to begin their workout.

Members of the Darlington High School cross country team stroll through the garden with residents at Lafayette Manor. Photo courtesy of Arnie Miehe.

After returning from their run, the group gathered in the parking lot for some final instructions. The setting sun's rays stretched over Lafayette Manor behind Arnie as he spoke to his team. From the picture window in the commons room, several of the residents were waving to the kids who had just visited them.

Arnie turned around, and his voice lowered to a soft tone.

"I've heard some of you complain about our workouts. You have nothing to complain about. You are not suffering—not really. Those people in that building are suffering more than you are. Each time you feel like you are ready to give up during a race, I want you to think about them. What would these people give to be in your shoes, running with their lives ahead of them and nothing but blue skies over their heads? You are blessed to be able to run. If I could, I would paralyze each of you for a week so you could feel what it is like not to have the use of your legs. But I can't do that. This is as close as I can come to helping you understand how grateful you should be. You are lucky. What you are able to do with your legs is a gift, and you will not have that gift forever. Think about that the next time you feel like you want to quit."

He closed the practice, and the squad dispersed to their cars.

CHAPTER FOUR
THE WINDS OF CHANGE

On the first Friday in September, we found ourselves running pre-game drills at Whitehall, a school with a strong football tradition and a team that was expected to contend for the conference title. The previous week we had lost a defensive battle in the season opener by six points. Our offense had struggled, and as a young quarterback, I was lacking in confidence and making plenty of mistakes. I did not relish the quarterback role as much as playing in the defensive backfield, where I could dish out the hits. I had a knack for defense. I could read opposing quarterbacks and instinctively understood where the ball was going. I made reliable tackles, forced turnovers, and elevated my status in the position quickly. My aspiration was to play defense in college. But as anyone who has played the position knows, quarterback was another matter. With the seemingly infinite reads, plays, and options, my poise suffered. I was still learning how to hold onto the ball when taking a hit. I had to accept some blame when the offense faltered. The team needed me to be better, and I loved football enough to sacrifice my ego.

But that night in Whitehall had a fresh feel to it. It was a new week and a beautiful evening for high school football. As our squad took the field, the pep band was blaring Chicago's "Make Me Smile," and the cheerleaders stoked the venerating crowd gathered for the rivalry. Halide lamps illuminated fresh chalk, and the goalposts gleamed with a new coat of paint. The scents of cut grass, coffee, and popcorn merged over the bleachers. Moments earlier, the sun had retreated below the horizon, casting tinted beams above the assembly. The announcer's voice crackled from the loudspeakers, and the whistle commanded the ball to sail off the tee. Our team's fortunes fared much better during the first half than they had a week earlier. Our defense held the Norsemen's offense scoreless and allowed only a few first downs, matching Wagner's expectations. But the big surprise was the offensive productivity. Blocking was crisp, turnovers were absent, and penalties were minimal. My reads were going smoothly, and receivers were hanging onto the ball. Hugh had gained big chunks of yardage on the ground, including a touchdown, and I had thrown a pass for another. We'd found a rhythm on offense, and things were finally starting to come together. Our kicker missed an extra point, but we went to our bus at the break, leading 13-0. Wagner was calm and complimentary in his halftime speech.

Things changed in the second half. Whitehall made adjustments on defense and found a new level of intensity as the game proceeded. Yards became harder to find. Several of our upperclassmen had been drinking at a party the night before and had not shaken their hangovers. They became fatigued in the second half, missing tackles and assignments. One of them puked through his facemask on the field before being burned for a touchdown pass on the next play.

We lost 13-14.

Wagner's tongue-lashing was even worse than the one the previous week. He was livid with his defense. He had not anticipated the group's apparent lack of endurance, particularly the poor tackling, in the second half.

"We will not be embarrassed like that again this season during a second half. Do you call that tackling? On Monday we're going back to full contact on all of our drills. For everyone! I want to see if you can hit somebody next week!"

I didn't pay too much attention. I had played one of my better games. Running extra sprints in practice was not a concern for me, unlike some of the others.

Coaches generally frowned upon tackling skills position players during practice. Like most teams, our coaches usually had those players wear colored mesh pullovers on top of their jerseys as a signal to the defense, prohibiting contact when they were vulnerable. The risk of injury was too great over a long season, and those skills players could not be easily replaced. I tended to like contact, and I had become accustomed to taking a lot of hits as a quarterback. It was an expectation of the position, and I didn't give it a second thought. On Monday, there were no colored pullovers for the skills players.

Toward the end of practice, I was leading the varsity scrimmage with the first-string offense. After receiving the snap from the center, I sprinted to the right side of the line on an option play. The second-team cornerback came at me for the tackle, forcing my read and pitch to Hugh. Our bruising back ran with the ball around the edge and up the field untouched. I never saw that. The collision occurred with my cleats dug into the sod and my left leg fully extended. The impact on the thigh was not noticeable—only the screeching bite within the knee as my torso lurched abruptly over my leg. At that instant, it was unclear to me what had just happened. The top and bottom of my leg came oddly unhinged and had gone in different directions for a split second. My knee was shrieking in pain as I lay on the field. Once lifted off the ground, I was placed on the sideline with my leg elevated on my helmet and wrapped in a cold pack. Within a few minutes the joint was engorged with fluid, nearly paralyzing it, and the pain ebbed into a more tolerable ache. Even then, it seemed deeper than other injuries I had suffered, more to the core of the leg and how it functioned.

Several coaches looked it over, ultimately concluding that it was just a bad sprain. There was no suggestion of a fracture or obvious need for medical treatment. Old-school culture still reigned on the football field. Back then, trips to the doctor weren't made for sprains, for getting your bell rung in a collision, or for dizziness in an August practice without water breaks. Instead, it was all part of forging a player into one who could contribute despite pain and discomfort. Plus, there was my own denial and determination to get back in the game. Football was central to my aspirations. Playing through pain was a personal expectation. Concussions, jammed fingers, bloody noses, and ankle sprains had not stopped me before. In my stubborn rationale, the same approach seemed valid for playing football with a sprained knee.

During the following days, the coaching staff kept me at quarterback through a constant cycle of cold packs and aching whirlpools in ice. Lateral movement was difficult, and it was nearly impossible to accelerate as I could before the injury. The knee allowed rotation on any axis and was only stable when standing or running straight ahead. Worst of all, the staff decided to bench me on defense. The injury hampered my ability to defend quick receivers. I had become a liability for the team and was unable to play my favorite position.

In late September, we hosted Augusta. It was another loss. I bruised my tailbone and had a poor game. I limped around the field when I wasn't taking hits, and I fumbled twice.

Afterward, as I was entering the locker room, Scott grabbed my shoulder pad and said, "Hey, what happened with your dad after the game?"

I gave him a puzzled look. "What are you talking about?"

"I think there was a fight. I saw a large group in the middle of the field, and the coaches were pulling your dad out of there."

I later learned that a fan had shown up drunk and repeatedly shouted at the coaching staff from the bleachers during the game. In particular, he singled out my dad. The fan felt empowered to make personnel choices for the team, and he decided that I should be benched. It didn't matter that the team had limited options at the position or that Wagner made the roster decisions. It didn't matter that I had started both ways a year earlier when my dad was not on the staff. It didn't matter that I was inexperienced at quarterback or that I was injured. He jawed at my dad from the bleachers for the entire game.

"Get him outta there!" "Your kid is awful!" "Are you stupid?"

When the clock ran out, the fan marched onto the field after my dad and started shoving. Most of us had already trotted off to the locker room. The coaches and a large group of fans were still congregated near the fifty-yard line when the trouble started. It had nearly turned into a brawl but for the fact that the other coaches and a few players intervened. It was a shameful episode, and it had a significant impact on my father. After thinking about it over the weekend, he told Wagner that he would not finish the season. He stepped down from the staff. He also notified the athletic director that he was resigning as the varsity basketball coach and that they should begin a search for his replacement, who would be needed very soon.

I went back to practice the following week as if nothing had changed. But the shame I carried as the reason for the conflict clung to me beneath my gear. My father's absence at practice was noticeable, and several teammates begged me to get him to reconsider. As an alternative, the staff let the second-string quarterback run plays with the first-string offense and had me resume my role at defensive back. On the first play from scrimmage, I leapt into the air and intercepted the ball. Upon landing, my knee gave out, and I collapsed on the turf. The rest of the team hovered over me in their grimy outfits as if expecting me to get up like I had before. But this time, the joint was locked, and there was no way I could continue. There were no cheering crowds and no championship on the line.

The next morning the phone rang in the apartment above the hardware store in Fountain City. Judee Brone walked through her kitchen to pick up the receiver.

"Hello!"

"Hello, Mrs. Brone. This is the administrative office at the high school. We're calling to check and see if Mark has been sick lately."

"No, he has been fine. Why do you ask?"

"Well, he hasn't shown up at school the last two mornings, and we're wondering where he is."

"What! What do you mean he isn't at school?"

Judee was beside herself. After hanging up, she spoke to her husband, Gary, and he calmed her down. They remembered that Mark had eaten breakfast with them that morning, and he'd been home the prior evening at his normal time. They decided to wait until the evening to see if Mark returned.

When Mark walked into the apartment that afternoon, his parents confronted him about his whereabouts.

"Mark, where have you been all day?"

"At school. Whaddya mean, Mom?"

"The school called this morning. They said you haven't been there the last two days!"

Mark was caught and finally admitted to his truancy.

"I've been down at the boathouse, fishing."

He had only been a few blocks away the entire time. Gary and Judee probed further to try to understand the reason for their son's misbehavior. He had always seemed to enjoy going to school. Mark explained that the Jackals had been harassing him in the hallways, the bathrooms, and the lunch line.

"I'm sick of going to school. I don't want to go there anymore! Mom and Dad, can we please move back to Minneapolis?"

Gary and Judee didn't have the financial flexibility to make another move. They had committed every last dollar to the hardware store. Mark had to go back to school and learn to cope with the Jackals.

My injury did not improve over the next couple of days, so my dad drove me to the hospital in Winona for an MRI (magnetic resonance imaging). As I lay on the cold table in a gown, a needle slid under my kneecap, causing an odd twinge as it was inserted deep into the joint. The technician aspirated three syringes of fluid and then injected contrast dye through the needle. The throbbing pressure of liquid forced through a syringe could not be ignored. It was unpleasant, especially for a kid who hated needles. Then the technician asked me to stand up and flex the joint briefly to make sure the dye was distributed well enough to provide adequate images. That caused the knee to squish audibly, like boots in mud.

The test revealed tears in the meniscus cartilage, and a week later I was in surgery. Before my discharge, the surgeon entered my room and examined the knee in front of my parents.

"Jeff, there was a lot of damage, and I removed the medial meniscus to reduce your chances of having the knee lock up in the future."

Without cartilage, nothing was left to cushion the bone from normal wear and impacts.

He went on. "While I was in there, I also noticed that your anterior cruciate ligament (ACL) had ruptured. The withered ends had already been absorbed by your body. There was nothing left for me to reattach."

"When do you think I'll be able to get back on the football field?"

The surgeon paused, glanced at my parents, and drew a breath. In 1982, surgical techniques to graft an ACL were experimental, and there was no option for my leg.

"Jeff, your knee is going to be very unstable. I'm sorry, but you need to stop playing football or you'll damage the joint even more than you already have."

I could not speak after hearing his words. My parents' eyes held no answers, only sorrow, and I could not stop the tears from falling. The news that my football days were over was hard to swallow at sixteen years of age while still harboring childhood dreams. Before the surgery, no one had prepared me for the possibility that I might not play football again. I had held a football in my hands since I was two years old. There had been potential to pursue my dreams with that path. I had presumed that the surgery would fix my leg, and after some time on crutches, I'd be playing again.

The same self-centered, ungrateful questions of a person going through the stages of grief went through my head. Like so many other teenagers, my focus was on myself and my problems, not on others. The gift of two athletic legs had been suddenly taken from me, and my self-esteem struggled mightily with the loss. At that age, I measured myself and others through the lens of athletic prowess. My value hinged on whether I could excel at a skill or win a contest. Athletes were my role models. I emulated their behavior and pursued their examples of achievement. My happiness revolved around my success in sports. From the outside, my struggle was not noticeable. Underneath, I had lost a portion of my physicality, and it affected my self-worth. I felt as if my birthright had been stolen from me, and I became driftless. I did not have the term in my vocabulary, but I had been thrust into an identity crisis.

Football had been my favorite sport, and it was the game for which I had been best suited to use my athleticism. In the end, football's gift to me was a damaged leg that would send me on a new course. Life was about to teach me some lessons through an injury that would be with me for the rest of my days.

Leaning on my crutches, I watched from the sidelines as our team finished the season with a 2–7 record.

The 1982 Southern Eight conference meet was held in early October, and the Darlington Redbirds were in a position to accomplish something the school had not achieved in any sport for a decade—a conference title. Darlington's first four boys finished in the top thirteen at the meet and were waiting by the chute for their fifth runner, Bob Cullen, to cross the line. The freshman was good enough to hold the fifth spot on the varsity. Still, at roughly five feet, two inches tall, and weighing ninety pounds, he was struggling to compete against the older kids. Bob's brother, Mike, a senior co-captain, gazed on the course after exiting the chute, still gasping for air. Arnie stood next to him, along with the other Redbirds varsity runners. Each crossed his fingers, waiting in anticipation for Bob to cross the line. The wait for a team's fifth runner can be agonizing. Seconds seem like hours as opponents funnel through the chute, stacking up points. Arnie turned to Mike, who was still grimacing and holding his hands on his hips.

"How far back do you think he is?"

Mike simply shrugged his shoulders.

Bob was a straight A student, and even at that young age, he was dedicated to his craft. But his body had not yet caught up with the maturity of his character. After another minute and forty seconds, Bob floundered into the chute, utterly spent. It wasn't enough, and the Redbirds fell short by nine points, placing second. Bob fought back tears after realizing he had not run fast enough to give his team the conference title.

The autumn of 1982 marked many firsts for the Darlington Redbirds' cross country program. Both the girls' and the boys' teams achieved winning records in dual meets. The boys also won their first invitational ever, bringing home a trophy for a sparse trophy case. They went on to qualify for their sectional meet, finishing in fourth place. It was by far the best season in the program's history.

There were a couple of notable individual achievements as well. The students elected Ann Smith as Darlington's homecoming queen. She also qualified for the sectional and placed ninth as an individual to finish her career. Troy Cullen, although only a sophomore, qualified for the state meet in Kenosha and placed twenty-first. He was the first runner from Darlington to ever compete in a state cross country championship.

Arnie took care to record each accomplishment, large or small, and communicated them to the school and community. His squad had been successful and established themselves as winners. The program's cornerstone was set in place that first season, and Arnie planned to frame the walls with his underclassmen.

CHAPTER FIVE
THE WINTER BLUES

Bill Clark was the new head basketball coach who had been hired after my dad resigned. While Clark did his best, the team's unity disintegrated soon after practices started. The talent pool of seniors was even weaker for basketball than it had been for football. By Christmas, the team was winless.

My recovery from surgery took several months, but I was able to play varsity basketball for the last half of the season. It did not take me long to discover how impaired I had become on the court. My left leg had been my strongest limb before the injury, but I could no longer jump solidly off it or make crisp lateral cuts. To help stabilize the knee, I had been fitted with a custom brace. The monstrosity had a heavy steel frame with multiple straps to hold it in place. It cramped my calf muscle, and I limped up and down the court while wearing it. I had a ball and chain attached to my body where there had once been a motor. It was noticeable from the bleachers, though no one spoke of it in front of me. The kid from the previous year was diminished. Like a broken toy on Christmas Day, unable to meet expectations, I moved from point guard and became an undersized post player.

Despite the struggle in my head, I knew there was nothing anyone else could do to fix my predicament. I replaced my deficit with discipline. I worked to adapt through proficiency and will. I learned how to ignore the pain. When I felt weak, I wore determination on my face to feign strength. The changes yielded some fruit, but I should not have been playing basketball. It caused more permanent damage to the joint, and for my entire career, I had a swollen "grapefruit" knee. Even so, I could not bring myself to give up basketball. It was my family's first sport, and it was unthinkable for me to quit if I could still walk.

The season crawled along at an agonizing pace, loss after loss. I was in the starting lineup after the holiday break, but that made little difference. We ended with a record of 1–18. I was happy when it was over. The bad experience prompted Clark to resign, and he migrated to better coaching pastures.

By springtime, my dad was looking for new pastures as well; the post-game episode on the football field had soured his outlook on our school. He had been a faculty member and coach at C-FC for a decade, and my youngest brother, Greg, would be an incoming freshman as I began my junior year. Dad anticipated more trouble, but he was not ready to give up coaching basketball. He had dedicated himself to the sport. I had witnessed his countless hours teaching kids the game, writing practice plans, reading books, reviewing film, attending coaching clinics, and assisting at camps. My father began interviewing with other schools.

There was a break between the winter and spring sports seasons, sometime after St. Patrick's Day and before Easter in most years. On the cusp of track season, Bob Cullen was striving to improve himself, putting in some miles whenever he could. As a freshman, he had performed well enough to capture the fifth spot on the varsity and had clocked times under twenty minutes. But he was not satisfied after failing to secure the conference championship for his team the prior fall. His brother, Mike, was graduating, and Bob wanted to fill the gap. Arnie had noticed Bob's potential and encouraged him as the track season approached. Bob's dedication to his craft was visible to the community. He could be seen on the streets of Darlington on those early spring mornings in 1983, running along the Pecatonica River.

For those who look for it, the end of winter is a hopeful moment, hinting at renewal. Bob could see it on his runs. The sun was stretching north in the sky, and the daylight was lingering well into the evening. The thaw was underway, with winter still clawing to hold its grip during the night. The nocturnal battle created a layer of fog in the dark when the warming temperatures of the thawing earth met with the frigid sky. On some of his morning runs, Bob witnessed the sun rise to a glorious hoarfrost. The tiny needle-like, crystalline formations of frozen fog attached to any exposed surface. Trees and fields were caked, as if sugar had been cast over the landscape, surrounding him with trillions of twinkling prisms at first light. It was as fragile as it was beautiful. As the sun's power overtook the sky, the frost would wilt before it, turning the trees into soaked sentinels standing in the snow on the river's banks. The sunlight resurrected winter's icy corpse by noon, transforming it with hints of life. Blades of grass pierced through the white cloak among the patches of earth that emerged on the landscape. Glimmering rivulets snaked from puddle to pond as the meltwater descended to the river. Bob's shoes kicked up spatter from the wet streets on the route. The smell of damp sod and crop residue permeated the crisp air. The rebirth was not limited to the landscape. Bob was transforming himself into a formidable runner.

CHAPTER SIX

THE NEW FAMILY

They called it "government cheese," and the square orange slice looked back at me from my plastic plate. After Ronald Reagan signed the farm bill in 1981, the federal government filled warehouses around the country with the stuff. It was given to schools, military cafeterias, welfare recipients, food banks, and the elderly in an effort to stabilize the milk market after the government had provided subsidies to dairy farmers. The supply of milk had burgeoned, creating a huge surplus. The government purchased the milk and made cheese to maintain a stable price. Our school received the free stuff and distributed it to us. I was perpetually hungry at that age, so I snatched the slice off my plate and inhaled it.

The spring sun shone through the cafeteria windows as several hundred teenagers murmured over their institutional rations. The clinking of silverware and clonking of plastic trays reverberated off the cement block walls, adding to the din. The mixed scents of dish soap and stew from the kitchen spilled into the room. After choking down a paltry serving of stew, Mark Brone approached my table and asked me to join him in the library before the end of lunch hour. When I stepped onto the carpeted floor, Mark was sitting at a table near a microfiche viewer. Scott was next to him with two more of my classmates, Guy Todd and Paul Abts.

Mark had joined the track team and was enjoying the co-ed

experience at the practices and meets. He held some promise as a runner, and that realization inspired him to consider an alternative sport for the upcoming fall season. Mark had had his fill of the football scene at C-FC the prior fall. He had been looking to belong to a clan that did not want him. He had been seeking fun in a culture that fostered exclusion and fear. Mark had initiative for a kid his age, and he was motivated to build something from scratch. He was leading the venture on his own, and he had not yet turned fifteen.

As I took a seat next to my classmates, Mark made his pitch.

"My dad said that he would coach a cross country team this fall if we can get enough of us to sign up. We need at least five runners, but seven would be better since that is a full team."

We had all heard of cross country, since our school had made an unsuccessful attempt to start the sport in the late seventies. Although none of us were familiar with the history, the Wisconsin Interscholastic Athletic Association (WIAA) had held its first state cross country championship many decades earlier, in 1913. But seventy years later, it was still an obscure sport at small schools, and none of us knew the rules or how the scoring for a meet worked. We did not know why a team could run with five but still have two more on the squad in a race.

Mark went on. "I've had enough of those jerks in football. Who else do you think would be interested in running? I'm trying to see if there are enough girls for a girls' team. Karen and Heidi Stettler said that they'd like to run. What do you guys think? Would you join?"

I had met Mark's dad, Gary, several times. Gary and his wife, Judee, owned the old hardware store in Fountain City. They had recently moved back to the area after more than a decade of living in New York City and Minneapolis. They were noticeably different to my teenage eyes and appeared as throwback flower children from the sixties. They were friendly to speak with but somehow didn't fit in with the culture of rural western Wisconsin. The Brones had two boys, Mark and Jesse. Mark was older and a year behind me in school. From time to time, I would see Gary running on the roads in the area to keep in shape, and I'd seen the Brones pick up Mark from sporting events in their yellow Volvo station wagon.

"I'm going to talk to Dan Lettner and see if he would join us, too," Mark continued. "What about you, Cud?"

The dictionary defines *cud* as the regurgitated stomach contents a cow chews for a second time as part of its digestion cycle. It was a disgusting nickname, but we all used it for Paul Abts. None of us knew how it originated, but the poor kid had endured the moniker since we were in grade school. Paul lived on Hill Street in Fountain City, not far from Mark's home, and hung around his place frequently. He was about five feet, five inches tall and weighed around 110 pounds. He had sandy hair, a sly grin, and a nose for mischief. Paul was a naturally gifted runner but undersized for football. Mark had seen him race in track meets and knew he had potential as a cross country runner. It was no coincidence that Mark had made his first request with Paul. They hung out together nearly every day, and it was a safe bet for an affirmative answer.

"Yeah, I think I'd like to join," Paul said.

"How 'bout you, Guy?" Mark gazed across the table.

Guy Todd was the most prolific distance runner the school had seen since its inception. Every track coach in the conference knew his name, and he was threatening school records each time he stepped on a paved oval during the spring. He stood about five feet, eight inches tall and was about ten pounds heavier than Paul. Although modest in stature, Guy was a skilled wrestler and had surprising strength when challenged. We didn't have a nickname for Guy; he was too cool for such things. He was handsome, and we watched the girls' heads turn as he passed them on a street or in a hallway. Guy was warm and smiled easily, but he was generally soft-spoken and of few words. There was a quiet intensity behind his blue eyes. He wasn't a vocal leader but led through his deeds in a contest.

"Sure," Guy said, "but let me think about it overnight."

It did not take him long to decide to join.

Mark turned to me and blurted, "How 'bout you, Smiley?"

The nickname was bestowed upon me years earlier in Little League while I was at bat, facing the sun and squinting. The kids in the dugout inferred a smile, and ignoring the name had not made it go away. It had stuck, thanks to my brothers and Mark, who took every opportunity to provoke me if they could. I had no plans for the fall season other than mowing lawns and shooting baskets.

"Sure! Count me in, Space."

Space was the moniker I threw back at Mark in retaliation—short for space cadet— mocking his teenage antics.

For Scott, Mark's proposal created a dilemma.

"I don't know, Mark. I got some reps at varsity linebacker last season, and I have a good chance to be starting at that spot this year. The guys are counting on me to be there this fall, and I'm finally going to get a chance to play on most of the snaps."

Mark knew that Scott liked to run 5Ks in the summertime to stay in shape. But having tasted the limelight, abandoning his teammates was not something Scott considered lightly. He was not a quitter, and his loyalty was strong. Scott also knew that the Jackals might seek retribution if he left. Scott was popular with his peers, and his status was likely to suffer at a point in life when image and self-esteem reigned supreme. It wasn't an invitation most teenagers would accept.

"I'll think about it some more," Scott said.

Scott always grinned when he spoke, making it difficult to read his intent. He also had a habit of mumbling his responses, making it hard to discern what he had said. The combined effect was that we did not know if we could take him seriously.

"Okay, Ardie," Mark said. "We'll give you some more time to come to the conclusion that you're joining us in the fall."

Ardie was a nickname we occasionally used for Scott since his dad's first name was Arden.

The shrill pitch of the bell rang from the hallway, and I closed the conversation.

"We gotta go. We can talk more about this later."

Scott and I chatted about the opportunity on our walk through the halls. After entering the classroom, we sat down facing the cement block wall, and he flipped the power switch on the new Commodore 64 that we shared for our assignment. The monitor flickered to life and stared back at us with its green display as the 5 1/4-inch floppy drive booted up. We opened our books and started hammering on the keys to complete our Computer Methods assignment.

Mark persuaded as many students as he could and worked to build interest in the new venture. The late 1970s attempt to launch a C-FC cross country team was led by elementary phys-ed teacher and assistant basketball coach Rich Abts. But after a couple of seasons, the farm crisis pinched the school's budget, and the administration dropped the program, along with several other sports. Mark's campaign was not going to find support in the head office.

By midsummer Mark had recruited five girls who were interested in forming a team for that first year. They were led by incoming senior Karen Stettler and her sophomore sister Heidi, both of whom were talented distance runners. Junior Mary McCamley, sophomore Becky Lettner, and freshman Tracy Duellman were also committed to joining.

In the sport of cross country, the first five runners on a team count for the overall score in the competition. Each runner accumulates points based on their order of finish. As an example, the first-place runner scores one point. The runner who comes in fiftieth place scores fifty points. Like golf, the lowest cumulative score wins the team contest. Faster runners score fewer points. The sixth and seventh runners on the team serve as tiebreakers in the rare event there is a tie between two teams' first five runners. The sixth and seventh runners can also impact a race by outrunning any of the top five runners from other teams and adding to their team score. It helps to have good sixth and seventh runners in the likely event that one of the first five runners is injured, ill, or just having a bad day. The girls would only have five runners and would need to manage without a backup if the new sport was approved.

By June, the pool in Cochrane was busy with swimming lessons during the mornings. In the afternoons, it was open to the public, and Scott had a season pass. He tried to get to the pool for a short time each day in between his jobs. On opening day, I strolled along the edge of the water with my beach towel and spotted him sitting on the concrete near the diving boards. Scott spoke as I sat down.

"Thought you might be mowing lawns today."

"Naw, I did that this morning so I wouldn't sweat as much. It's time to cool off now. What about you? Don't you need to hay today?"

Scott smiled. "First crop isn't ready to cut yet, so it will be a bit. Besides, I was sweating plenty this morning."

"Why was that?"

"I put in a ten-mile run."

My eyes widened as Scott leaned back onto his elbows.

"Really? I thought you were going out for football this fall. Why are you putting in a long run like that?"

"I'm going to enter Grandma's Marathon in Duluth next week."

"What!? Are you nuts? Why would you do that?"

"I don't know. Just thought it might be a fun way to test myself."

"Scott, you just finished track season and that takes a toll. You haven't been logging the kind of miles you need to run a marathon either."

"I know, but I think I'm in pretty good shape, and I feel good, so I thought I'd try it."

"Isn't there an age limit? I mean, can you enter the race at fifteen?"

"Turns out there's a guy from Winona who signed up who now has a conflict and can't go. I'm going to use his name and registration."

"How are you going to get up there without a car or driver's license?"

"Already got that figured out. I'm hitching a ride with another runner from Winona."

My voice was sarcastic, although I knew Scott would follow through with his folly.

"Well, good luck. Nice knowing ya. Just so you know, twenty-six miles is a lot farther than ten! The first guy that ran a marathon in Greece collapsed and died when he finished."

Scott enjoyed running and had an early passion for endurance sports. He had an excellent work ethic and the pain threshold of a martyr. Scott averaged seven-minute miles over the 26.2-mile course along the shore of Lake Superior. He returned from the race as if it had only been a 5K fun run.

By midsummer my dad had offers to become the head basketball coach at two other schools in northern Wisconsin. Both offered a higher salary. My parents took my brothers and me on trips to visit the schools and get a sense for the fit. But some new developments were pushing back on our plans to move. Upon Clark's departure, the athletic director prodded my dad to pick up the varsity coaching duties at C-FC once again. He had had some winning teams in the previous decade, and the results of the prior season, without him on the sidelines, had sobered the clan in the bleachers.

After the spring semester there had been another change. Ken Wagner resigned as head football coach and accepted a position with another school. A former student teacher, Nate Lewis, was hired as the new football coach at C-FC. Lewis was well-liked by the students and staff. The culture on the football field was likely to change in the fall and possibly offer a better experience for my brothers.

During those summer days, not knowing fully what my future

would bring and keeping it to myself, I had been pressuring Scott to join the cross country team. We would see each other regularly in Cochrane and chat about it. I carried some guilt since I did not disclose my uncertain future at the school. I guess I was trying to keep my options open, or perhaps in my subconscious, I wanted to stay.

After a great deal of deliberation at the kitchen table, my parents decided to keep our home and remain at C-FC.

Soon after, on an evening in mid-July, Gary Brone trotted up a flight of stairs to the second-floor conference room of the Fountain City State Bank. The building was in the middle of town at the intersection of North Main Street and Highway 35, a short walk from Gary's home. The bank prominently displayed the Swiss coat of arms on its facade and was a site commonly used for the high school's booster club meetings. Gary had been placed on the agenda, and he asked for some initial funding to support an inaugural season. Since the school athletic budget had evaporated, Gary needed the booster club's help to get started. He offered to volunteer his time as a coach for the team if the school's athletic department would offer the sport and provide busing to the races.

Gary and Judee Brone in the early 1980s with sons Mark and Jesse (holding the family dog). Photo courtesy of Mark Brone.

Gary was likable, and the booster club members quickly warmed to him while they listened to his plea for support. He made a convincing pitch and was granted five hundred dollars in funding to pay for the entrance fees to the invitational meets the team would enter. It was seed money, with no commitment beyond the first season, and it was contingent upon filling both a girls' and boys' team with participants for the fall.

Gary Brone was raised in New York State. He arrived in Winona, Minnesota, in the 1960s to wrestle at Winona State University. Although he stood nearly six feet tall, he was not an imposing figure with his slender, wiry build. Gary earned a social sciences degree from Winona State before he married Judee and moved to New York City. After some time spent in multiple states as a counselor, the couple returned to the area to raise their family in Fountain City.

Gary was also a marathoner and knew how to train for distance running. For a man of forty years, he was in stellar shape. Fitness was a way of life for Gary. He was quick to smile and would engage in conversation with anyone about nearly anything. It was a good skill for a hardware retailer.

Judee Brone admires her husband's medal after Gary finished a marathon in the early 1980s. Photo courtesy of Mark Brone.

Even in a group, no one could fail to pick out Judee Brone. She brought sunshine with her into a room. Her curly blonde hair and blue eyes were always accented with bright lipstick, colorful scarves, painted nails, and a cheery voice that rang off the walls. She decorated her space in a similar fashion. Judee was a good cook and quick to offer food to anyone who popped in for a visit. She had a passion for the arts, and in later years she would direct plays at the historic auditorium across the street from their hardware store on North Main.

Like many young couples, Gary and Judee were of modest means and undertook various jobs to support their family. At the time Gary started coaching the cross country team, the Brones were living above the hardware store. The store was in a century-old building situated on the corner of North Main and the steep Fountain City dugway. It was located two blocks from the tracks and the river.

Tom and Kirk Evenstad were haying nearly every day that summer on their farm near Darlington—or at least it seemed that way. Each of them rose early in the morning to milk, but the other chores on the farm were not waived. Rain was in the forecast for the next day, and hay was lying in the fields. It left them with little time or energy to log miles and join Arnie's Mile Club. But the farm work kept them lean. It was another hot summer day, and both boys were driving John Deere row crop tractors. Each had a kick-baler attached, launching bales into the wagons they were towing in the field. They finished their final pass at nearly the same moment and parked near the elevator. Kirk hopped off his tractor and climbed into the haymow. Tom snatched the sixty-pound square bales off his wagon and started dropping them on the elevator. Kirk grabbed them off the floor in the haymow and stacked them in their proper place. Tom was sweating in the sun outside, but the temperatures were well above one hundred degrees in the haymow, and dust had blackened Kirk's nostrils. They worked silently as a team and in harmony, each one knowing the other's role and anticipating the next step in synchronicity. It was an efficiency gained from endless days of repetition with the same tasks. No wasted motion, no wasted time. Once the wagons were emptied, Tom unhitched them and parked the tractors. In a few minutes, Kirk finished up and joined his brother in the car to drive home. They had plans to meet the guys and play some basketball before the evening milking. The Evenstads had a paved court with two hoops in their backyard on Lucy Street, and it was a common place for pick-up games with their friends. When they arrived home, Troy and the crew were already shooting baskets.

Upon my parents' decision to stay, seeds of hope sprouted in my head. I had not recognized my desire consciously, but the possibility of a new opportunity with a new sport boosted my outlook. Suddenly I had something to look forward to, something to which I could devote my energy. As with a pugilist, distance running had always been a way for me to stay in shape for other sports, nothing more. But in the summer of 1983, I found a new purpose for my running. I began transforming my body from one that could withstand the brutality of football to one that could endure a footrace over a significant distance. The streets along the river near my home in Buffalo City became littered with my tracks. I shed weight from the effort and found my stride.

I discovered that the best time of day for a training run was the early morning. The biting insects were less active, and the temperatures were tolerable. At sunrise, the pavement was painted with condensate, and the echoes of my footfalls seemed louder than they would at a later hour. The lean muscle and swiftness of youth made it easy in those days. My mind wandered, and I was not consumed with any pain from the labor. Flexible legs reached ahead without difficulty, carrying my weight and pulling me forward with grace. The workouts were not the jarring torture that comes from such exercise at a more advanced age when elasticity has fled the body, and arthritis seizes the joints.

My runs began by heading north along the river. The white strobe beacons from the two stacks at the power station in Alma were in view. Rising seven hundred feet, they stood like sentinels above the fog-laden valley, exhaling their breaths of condensing gas over the peaks of the bluffs. If there was a breeze aloft, its direction could be judged from those plumes. But most summer mornings were calm, and the columns remained vertical.

Next to the river, the dense air tasted of raw fish and wet wood. The surface of the slough was usually placid and stained silty brown, providing the backdrop for a visual feast. Lime-colored algae caked the backwaters, occasionally suspending the white carcass of a fish or carved with black rivulets from the muskrats that inhabited the marsh. Blue damselflies and green darners skimmed over the surface. I spied egrets and herons hunting the shallows with their keen eyes peering from statuesque frames. Turtles sunned themselves on logs jutting above the water's surface. Kingfishers dropped from branches overhanging the water's edge, plucking their prey from under the surface and returning to their perches. More rarely, a beaver slapped the water's surface, annoyed by my intrusion. Everything was green and vibrant, a complete departure from the windswept, icy desolation of winter. By late summer, the tepid water in the sloughs nourished a thriving biome of diversity. The organic mire would not decay until late September when daylight fled and temperatures cooled. I was fortunate to grow up next to the river, and running on those summer mornings was not just good for building endurance; it was good for my soul.

Afterward, I removed the elastic sleeve from my left knee. The short sleeve provided a little support as the joint recovered from the wound that stalked me. Most days, the knee was fine. It was healing well by the end of summer, showing less swelling and only radiating moderate pain from the workouts. My range of motion had returned after the basketball season ended. The purple scar was fading and becoming more pliable with the skin. When I was running, the linear motion did not cause the knee to give out, giving me a sense of freedom from the injury. It was something I could still do, much like I had before, and it made me feel like an athlete again.

But I was still unsure where my running might lead me or if I would get the chance to compete in the fall. Mark's recruiting campaign fell short of the five boys needed to launch a cross country team. My appeals to Scott had also failed, and we were out of time. In the first week of August, Scott and Dan Lettner started two-a-day practices on the gridiron, along with my brothers. My window of opportunity was closing.

As Tom Evenstad opened the door of the gas station on Galena Street in Darlington, the bell jingled above him. His brother, Kirk, was in tow. Bill and Betty Cullen owned the 76 station near the Pecatonica River. It was a tiny place with a single lane for filling cars. Todd and Troy were usually there working, and it was a common spot for Troy's friends to gather. The Evenstads had walked downtown to catch up with Troy and see who was around.

Hearing the bell, Troy looked up from behind the desk and welcomed them in. "Hey, Evie. What's up?"

Tom removed his sunglasses and looked back at his friend. "Thought we'd stop by for some Mountain Dew and candy bars."

Tom walked over to the pop machine with his quarters, and Kirk scanned the shelves.

"Kirk! Are you going to come out for cross country practice next week?" Troy asked.

Kirk looked back at him and nodded. He knew that he had enough athletic ability to play football, but the choice to go out for cross country had been forming in his mind for months. Kirk tossed a couple of candy bars on the desk and smiled at Troy. As an incoming freshman, it was a boost to his self-esteem to have a four-sport letterman speaking with him.

Before school ended in the spring, Arnie had pulled Kirk aside and encouraged him to think about joining the team. Kirk had seen the fun that Tom and his peers were having together in the sport. He also had a handful of classmates who were ready to join him. They'd felt the magnetism.

Like most younger brothers, Kirk measured himself by whether he could beat Tom at any contest, and the Evenstad boys were constantly competing. But they were not enemies, and each respected the other. Tom was two years ahead of Kirk in school and had always held the upper hand when they played games in the backyard. But Tom had noticed that his younger brother was becoming hard to catch and thought he might have some potential as a runner. He had been recruiting him to join the team.

"Well, if you're going to join us," Troy said, "I hope you've been putting in some miles. Arnie's workouts are no cakewalk."

The pop machine clunked, and a can rolled into the pocket at the bottom. Tom bent over to retrieve the soda and walked over to hand it to Kirk. He then turned to Troy and winked.

"Culley, he's been haying with me all summer."

Troy turned back to Kirk and grinned.

"It's a different kind of shape. You'll be sucking wind."

Troy knew what was coming and that he'd be sucking wind, too. He had been playing baseball all summer and had not logged many miles. Although he was a gifted runner, running was not his passion—winning was.

CHAPTER SEVEN
MISFITS AND MASOCHISTS

As two-a-day practices commenced, C-FC's new football coach, Nate Lewis, liked what he saw from Scott. He had added sinew over the summer, and he had a nose for the violence of the sport. That hard work delivered benefits. Scott earned starting varsity positions at linebacker and offensive guard. But during the first week of practice, Scott was working through the conflict in his mind that had been needling him for several months and that he could no longer let fester. Scott was a cerebral kid, not particularly goal-driven, but he was analytical. The roots of his future profession in engineering were already showing. Despite his coach's endorsement, Scott surmised that he was undersized, with marginal skills that were just good enough to start for a poor team. Like a typical engineer, he deliberated until the last minute to make a difficult choice. He mulled over each possible angle, every risk and benefit. His calculus ultimately concluded that he was a better runner than a football player. At the end of the first week of practice, he walked into Lewis's office.

Lewis looked up from his desk as Scott closed the door behind him.

"Coach, I've made the decision to quit football and join the cross country team."

Lewis drew a breath and sat back in his chair.

"Sit down for a minute, Scott."

Scott took a seat as his coach asked.

"I know you like to run, but we have plans for you. Have you considered how many kids would love to be in your position right now? The coaching staff has picked you to start on both sides of the ball. It would be a shame to walk away from an opportunity like that. Most kids never get that chance."

Scott sighed and cast his eyes toward the floor. "Yeah, I know, Coach, but I've given this a lot of thought, and it's what I want to do."

Scott's affable personality could leave a listener with the mistaken impression that he was not strong in his conviction. Lewis sensed this possibility and tried to provoke some doubt in the teenager. He leveled his gaze at Scott.

"You can run with friends for the rest of your life, but the opportunity to put on pads and play on Friday nights won't come again."

It took him long enough to make decisions, but once Scott made up his mind, he didn't waver.

Scott answered with a smile. "I'll live with that." He walked out of Lewis's office and handed in his gear to the manager.

Dan Lettner had similar doubts during two-a-days. He took the same path as Scott and quit football to join the cross country team.

During the second week of August, formal cross country practices began in Darlington. It didn't take Kirk long to realize what Troy had been talking about at the gas station.

One of the Redbirds' first training runs of the season was named the Great Holland Road Run. Holland Road ran due west from Darlington, and the workout was a grueling seven-mile test of will. It started near the Evenstad farm and was run with the rising sun at the runners' backs. Many of the kids had never covered a distance of that length nor trained on hills before the test. Holland Road was straight as an arrow on the map but had dozens of repeating undulations. The topographical roller coaster meant that runners could never see beyond the next hill. Arnie would deliver a pep talk to his crew before the workout.

"What you are about to do is something that many of you have never done before. You're going to be tested to your limit. I want you to focus on the next hill in front of you and think of nothing else until you reach the finish. Don't think about how far you have to go or how far you have come. Just concentrate on conquering the next obstacle in front of you. We'll have a ride there to take you back to town when you are done. Whatever you do, don't give up. Don't let piles of dirt beat you today or in any of our races. You are living beings. Don't ever be defeated by a lifeless pile of dirt in front of you!"

The crew started on a steep downhill slope, and within a minute, they were climbing a precipitous grade of over one hundred feet. As Kirk reached the top of the first ascent, the next ravine came into view before him. There was no time to stretch out his stride and recover from the climb before he was extending his hips on the next descent. Kirk's respiration and spirits had not yet recovered from the first slope when he was immediately confronted with the next steep "pile of dirt" in front of him. Establishing a consistent cadence was impossible. Each climb became more difficult in Kirk's mind as the workout progressed.

"Focus on the next hill!"

The words reverberated in Kirk's brain as he remembered Arnie's instructions. Anticipating the next hill would have overwhelmed him in the midst of his suffering, so he did his best to focus in the moment on the challenge before him and not think too hard. Troy and the older kids were out in front, but all of them were gasping for air. Mile after grueling mile, the undulations continued until, finally, Kirk could see the van parked ahead, near the blue Harvestore silos that marked

Looking west on Holland Road, Darlington, Wisconsin. Photo by Jeff Rich.

the end of their torture. By then, pride kicked in, and there was no way that he was going to quit within sight of his goal.

The runners trickled in and sucked air for minutes after reaching the finish. The workout had been rough, but the accomplishment filled each kid with a new sense of confidence. The test was a passage into a new mindset, one viewed through the lens of perseverance.

Anything was possible.

Arnie's numbers were flourishing by the start of the 1983 season. Twenty-one boys and fourteen girls had gone out for cross country. Six starters were returning on the boys' team, and five starters were back for the girls' team. Both had achieved the necessary depth to field full JV squads.

Arnie needed help coaching all the kids who had joined the team. He approached the school board and requested the funding for an assistant coach. The success from his first year and the growth in numbers convinced the school's leadership to grant the request. Arnie knew who he wanted as an assistant. Ann Smith had graduated in the spring and was starting in the fall at the University of Wisconsin–Platteville. Arnie asked her if she would have time to help him with the team. Ann had the respect of the younger kids, and she knew Arnie needed the help. She agreed and started driving from campus each day after she finished her classes.

During one of their August training runs, Arnie turned onto Main Street, leading the boys' squad through the downtown on their way back to the school. Troy and Tom were in the group, shirtless and dripping with sweat under the intense sun. As they passed the Midway Bar, several patrons were sitting outside with beers in their hands, watching the young men run by.

"Run for gay rights!" one of them heckled in a booming voice.

Without breaking stride, Arnie turned his head and belted back, "Anything for you, pal!"

Troy and Tom looked at each other and would have laughed had it not been for their lack of breath. That moment illustrated to them that Arnie did not care what others thought about his team's quest. He wasn't going to let bullies hold sway. The only opinions that mattered were those within the team. They were becoming a unit and had work to do to bring the community along with them on their journey.

With Scott's and Dan's defections from football, C-FC had just enough numbers to field a boys' and girls' cross country team in 1983. In the final hour, Mark's campaign crossed the goal line, but Gary was starting with sparse supplies. There were some shorts, tank-top jerseys, and cotton sweats available with "Track & Field" printed on the front. They would not be needed until the spring, so Gary commandeered the outfits for the fall season. The school also had marker flags and a measuring wheel that could be used for setting up a course. But that was it, and there was no money allocated for anything else.

Gary was new to coaching. Despite his marathon experience, all he knew about the sport of cross country was that his brother had been on their high school team back in New York. At that time, he wondered why his brother had joined the obscure sport, which seemed like a lot of pain for little glory. Gary had only agreed to coach the team to support his son. His experience as a counselor was reflected in his method. He emulated the style that his high school wrestling coach had used with him. Gary's approach was nurturing, and he bolstered self-confidence in us. He was easygoing, but it would be a mistake to say that he was not personally committed or driven for success. He prepared workout routines and expected everyone to show up for practice on time. Gary made sure he communicated with us regularly and brought us together to form stronger relationships. He established goals and was focused during competition. But he was not the barking drill sergeant most of us were used to, and he was never profane. His approach was more art than science. At times, he took a laissez-faire approach to practices or even with his instruction at meets. His focus was on building confidence within each of us and fostering relationships between the team members. Gary wanted to build mutual aspirations and the trust of a family. He wanted each runner to step up and lead when there was a gap, even if that meant filling the role of player-coach during a practice, race, or an outside activity. He did not need to motivate us to run. We had chosen to leave our previous endeavors to join the team and were already seeking something different. Gary also knew from his stopwatch that he had some reasonable talent to work with, so perfecting the craft of running was not going to be his biggest obstacle.

Creating a winning culture was another matter. Success depended upon a culture in which team members expected to win and reached for bold, risky goals. Just as importantly, a winning culture fostered support when a teammate needed help. He wanted us to sacrifice for one another when our mutual success depended on it. That is a key difference between running as an individual versus running as part of a team in a cross country race. Each teammate suffers during the same race on your behalf, for everyone's shared benefit. That comes with the responsibility of reciprocal sacrifice. The amount of pressure from that responsibility can be intense, and a poor performance cannot be hidden from teammates. It is particularly painful to bear when the contest is consequential to the team's goals. There would be no easy races and no clemency through excuses. Our teenage minds had not yet come to that realization, but Gary understood it. His methods cultivated cohesion in his squad for that hardship. He focused on building solid relationships. Gary wanted to understand each of us, the challenges we faced, and what our motivations were underneath the surface. Getting at that stuff took observation and trust, helping us fit into our natural roles on the team. It was the reason we most often called him Gary rather than addressing him as Coach, not out of disrespect but out of closeness.

At first, the team met in various locations to begin with some longer training runs. Those longer runs cemented a base of endurance and made sure that anyone who had not been putting in the work over the summer could be brought up to the minimum expectation. Gary had given us literature laying out the workout routines he planned to use in the training. He asked us to read the material and familiarize ourselves with the concepts. It was awkward at first, giving up the habits of the past and training for a new sport that had been thrown together in a matter of a few months. The new routines felt foreign, especially for those of us who had played football in other years. We were a bit disoriented by the unfamiliar situation we found ourselves in. Each of us had joined the team not knowing what we were really pursuing. Several wanted an alternative to football, and some were looking to keep in shape for their winter sport. Others just wanted to belong for social reasons. Whatever the reasons were for our involvement, we all liked to compete. We were working hard, but we were still without intention, driftless runners in that sense, lacking a goal to orient us. We worked intensely in those early days of training. Our team shared competitiveness and determination. We were driven from within. All of our team members were from middle-class or lower-middle-class households. None of us had much money or were accustomed to fine things. Most worked part-time to earn a little income for a few possessions. When privation is experienced firsthand, the outcome is often a fierce determination to change your circumstances. We were not starving, but we were all craving something.

Gary asked us to show up one morning at the school, halfway between Cochrane and Fountain City. I stepped out of the car and approached my teammates, who were clustered at the end of the parking lot near the idle fleet of buses. Mark was weaving and cutting back and forth with his hand stretched out in front of him. He was shouting, "Can't touch this!" at Dan, in between taunting grunts and squeals as he sprinted through his zigzagging dance of evasion. The rest of the group was rolling with laughter while Dan's fury painted his face crimson.

"I'll get you, Brone!"

The show had started when Mark walked up behind Dan, licked both of his index fingers, and stuck them in Dan's ears. If Dan had caught him during his moment of rage, Mark would have paid the price, but he was too quick, and he flaunted his grin during the antics. It was a common prank, and Dan never had any hope of catching him. Thus, he was frequently Mark's target for provoking a diversion with a predictable outcome. We watched the comedy for a minute or so until Dan breathlessly gave up his futile pursuit. Mark kept a safe distance until Gary had started practice, and the agony of the workout erased Dan's anger. We were working hard but having fun along the way.

One advantage C-FC had in the late seventies and early eighties was a paved track. Many other small schools had cinder tracks or no track at all. Gary planned to use that advantage during our interval training. The track allowed him to closely observe the runners as we made laps, monitoring our level of effort and precisely measuring the intervals and cooldowns. On the track, he was able to use the stopwatch to accurately measure progress against goals. It revealed any slack in effort from a member of the team or the team itself. It made it easier for Gary to stay in the middle of the workouts and reduced some of the inconsistency caused by the elements.

Interval training helped the body more efficiently manage oxygen. During extended exercise, such as running, the body needs to produce energy through metabolic processes that require the breakdown of glucose. When oxygen is plentiful and the body is not in "oxygen debt," the lactic acid threshold can be managed below the extreme fatigue level. This is called aerobic (with oxygen) exercise, and it was how our long, steady endurance runs improved. But intense efforts, such as maintaining a sizzling pace in a race, running up steep hills, or sprinting toward a finish line, will put a body into oxygen debt. The lactic acid levels will skyrocket soon after. In this condition, the body does not have oxygen to use for converting glucose to energy and must burn the glucose through other processes called anaerobic (without oxygen). When the metabolic process switches to an anaerobic state, it creates a plodding, numb heaviness that crashes over the body and gives the slow-motion sense of oncoming paralysis. In other words, it was agonizing when we had "hit the wall," as we used to call it. Methods such as running intervals could be used to improve oxygen efficiency and avoid this effect.

Interval training involved short periods of intense sprinting, followed by periods of slow jogging when the body could recover from oxygen debt and clear lactic acid waste. These episodes of sprinting and jogging were repeated many times during such a workout. Usually, the intervals were arranged in ladders, starting with a 100-meter sprint, 200-meter, 400-meter, and so on, until reaching a grueling 800-meter sprint. Then the ladder would step back down again and end with a 100-meter sprint prior to a final cooldown. The jogging intervals that followed each sprint in the ladder were usually as long as the sprint itself. It was tough work, and it was hard to hide a poor effort if you were having a bad day.

The football team's practice field was in the center of the C-FC High School track. The cross country squad began interval workouts on the track, and shortly after the season started, the two teams crossed paths. Teenage boys can be expected to provoke one another, and there was friction during those encounters. Juvenile tribalism will sink to name-calling and bullying when life experience is short or a weak mind's rationale cannot justify a desired outcome. The insults

The 1983 C-FC cross country team before an interval workout early in the season. From left to right: Todd Farrand, Karen Stettler, Jeff Rich, Tracy Duellman, Dan Lettner, Heidi Stettler, Paul Abts, Becky Lettner, Scott Adler, Guy Todd, Korey Klink, Mary McCamley, and Mark Brone. (Note: Farrand and Klink did not return to the squad after the 1983 season). Photo courtesy of the *Winona Daily News*.

and expletives were always initiated by the Jackals, concealed behind their black helmets and white masks. They had greater numbers, and there was no reason for us to attack them for the sport most of us had once participated in. It is a common conflict at small schools, even today. Cross country teams are often filled with kids who are smaller or not physically well-matched for football. They are frequently cast as the nerds or misfits who cannot pass muster for the other sport. That was not true of our 1983 boys' team, but it was—and still is—a common projection passed along by those with low self-esteem. The Jackals started the treatment toward us, and it tended to occur just out of earshot of the coaching staff, conveniently providing plausible deniability. The new sport was viewed as a threat, potentially stealing athletes away from an already thin depth chart for football. The Jackals started shouting at us during our laps, calling us "grass fairies." Soon it became profane, and our ears were treated to "There go the fairy motherf*****s," or "Keep it up, you cross country c***s." Lockers in the shower room would get penned with lyrical gems. Most of the football team did not act this way and had higher standards of conduct, but the Jackals felt it was acceptable to serve insults to us as underclassmen.

It irritated me. Most of them had watched from the sidelines while I started for the team the prior two seasons. Many among them could not have endured the torture we were going through each day in practice. They were the same kids who whined about Wagner's mile a year earlier. But I had a valid reason for not playing football. It was harder for Scott, who would have been starting that season. He and Dan were viewed as traitors, even though they were representing the same school in a new sport. We did not take the bait, and it never got physical. We were usually too winded to shout back anyway, and there was an unintended benefit from the treatment. It gave our team a chip on its shoulder, and we became determined to silence the Jackals with our results.

CHAPTER EIGHT
THE CRUCIBLE

A few days later Gary had us logging miles in the valley, and I could see an irksome yellow speck ahead of me despite the stinging sweat blurring my view. Our footfalls were scraping over the pavement as we pursued our hare under the heat of the sun. The initial week of practice had been relatively uneventful. Our team put in some easy miles to build our base of endurance and started the interval training on the track. We had generally come together as a group with a new routine. Rather than barking at his team, Gary used the workouts and his kids' personalities to "break them down and build them up." One of his tools was his yellow Volvo station wagon from the early seventies that he drove to the practices. By the second week, he had started to lead us down the road with his beater. It soon became the object of our contempt. We learned to hate that car.

Gary would occasionally run with us on our long endurance training routes. It was natural for him since he was a marathoner and in excellent shape for his age. It also gave him a close assessment of the capabilities of each member of his team. But during the second week of training, he wanted his squad to increase the pace for an extended distance. Even with his level of fitness, it would be too much for him to run at that pace and still coach effectively over those miles. After age thirty, the body struggles to replicate the speed and resiliency of pure youth, so Gary devised a plan for us to trail behind

JEFF RICH

him on our training runs while he drove his Volvo. At first, it made sense to us and was not upsetting. He would tell the team to meet him at a corner or a specific point about a mile ahead on our route, and he would give us new instructions when we caught up. He did not tell us how far we were going to run, only that we were building our base. We expected the runs to be longer than our races would be. At the time, high school boys' cross country races were five thousand meters, roughly three miles, or one league in the old vernacular. The body needed to have a reserve to call upon deep into a competition, and aerobic capacity was built by training over distances longer than the race itself. On the other hand, we did not expect the workout to be the multiple-hour, twenty-mile training run that was required for marathons. It would be somewhere in between, and we did not know if he intended four miles or perhaps six miles for the run. As we came alongside, Gary started moving the Volvo forward and called out the first-mile split from the stopwatch.

"Seven-thirty. Pick up the pace and meet me up the road another mile."

We answered his call, and at the next rendezvous, he uttered, "Seven minutes. You're doggin' it! Pick up the pace, and I'll see you another mile ahead."

We were normally compliant, so we accepted the instruction and strode down the pavement without protest. The increased pace caused us to labor more intensely. Nearing the three-mile point, we anticipated that the apex of our workout was close and coasted the final yards to the Volvo. We expected to turn around and head back to our starting point, which would make our run a full six miles for that morning.

"Six-thirty. Better, but you're still not working hard enough! Run another mile."

As Gary drove off, Mark exclaimed, "What the hell is he doing?"

Gary kept repeating this process and would not tell us when we would turn around despite our inquiries. Each time he wanted a faster pace, and he knew he would get it from the group of kids he had out on the floor of the valley, toiling in the sun.

Each of us was fiercely competitive, not only to eclipse one another in a contest but to better our personal record. We often acted like siblings, looking to best one another and establish the pecking order in the pack. The friendships were strong, but we persisted with these little rivalries. However, there were never any lasting grudges among the boys on the team. One minute we could be punishing each other in a trivial competition, and the instant after finishing the contest, we would be the best of friends again. Oddly, that flexible and resilient attribute turned out to be an advantage. We pushed each other harder in training, which benefited the entire group while never losing sight of the big picture or respect for one another.

Guy was quiet but intense, and he had enough talent to bury us in the dust behind him. He would not be denied the lead for long, and Guy certainly wasn't going to let any of us beat him. He could not bring himself to allow that, not even in a training run. Scott had the unrelenting tenacity of a wrestler who would punish his opponent in competition. I was a coach's kid, and to say that I was driven was an understatement. So, if Gary asked for an increased pace, he was going to get it, and we were going to torture one another while attempting to take the lead. None of us wanted the shame of being the caboose, either. Gary had already perceived these traits within his team and had begun to leverage them to the advantage we would need.

We started to feel some significant discomfort from what had become a six-minute-mile pace, deep into the workout, under the climbing sun of that August morning. A six-minute-mile was brisk but not difficult for us in those days unless we were asked to string several of them together in the middle of a long run. Breathing was labored, sweat stung our eyes, and our cheery chatter turned into short utterances, then no talk at all. The pace was too fast for wasted breath on talk. It was replaced by the sounds of deep respiration and our footfalls, which converged into a rhythmic cadence.

Then a voice shattered the tedium.

"There goes the happy hippie and his dirty banana!"

The outburst had come from Mark, and although the lack of breath made laughter costly, it was hilarious to us. We began taking turns throwing vulgar insults at our coach and his yellow jalopy. It made us feel better amid the agony, and it became a contest of who could hurl the most creative obscenities. After a few minutes, the suffocating effect of the workout reclaimed control, and the expletives sunk to the four-letter sort.

At the five-mile mark, Gary waited on the shoulder and shouted another instruction when we approached.

"Turn back toward the high school and meet me there."

It should have been a moment of relief, but by that point our competitive nature was working against us. We would not relax the tempo and kept pressing one another for the lead. It went on for the rest of the trip back to the school, a punishing pace with obscenities flying from our mouths when we had breath in our lungs to expel them. It did not occur to us then, but our mild-mannered coach had created a common enemy for our team, uniting us early in our journey. We all liked Gary immensely and, out of respect, would never swear in front of him, but when we saw him pulling out his Volvo for a practice run, the cussing would start like Pavlov himself had planned the workout.

Gary used the Volvo a few times each season to prepare us for racing. Using the technique too much or too deep into the season when trying to peak for key races or nursing injuries was detrimental. But early in the season, it increased mental toughness. Not knowing when the suffering was going to end was hard for our psyches to overcome. We were mentally tough kids, mostly, and could endure pain for short periods, particularly if we knew when it would end. But Gary knew we needed to develop another level of toughness for the racing we were about to face.

Each of us was familiar with the five-thousand-meter (5K) "fun runs" that we had entered at summertime community festivals. At a little more than three miles, a 5K is a relatively easy run if it is jogged at a modest pace. It is not intimidating for most distance runners. That changes if you are fighting to lead the pack in a race or when your teammates are depending on you during a critical contest. In cross country, you cannot escape the responsibility to your teammates. Yielding the pace for your own physical comfort while others suffer on your behalf results in unbearable shame. Each time we competed, we would be put in that self-imposed crucible. We were discovering the difference between racing and jogging a 5K early in our training, and it was as stark as night and day.

An average time for a high school boys' cross country runner to cover five thousand meters over uneven terrain is about twenty minutes. That is not a long time, but you can suffer an eternity in that span when you are in respiratory distress. Each minute becomes a month in the mind, and the physical torture can be tremendous, even without injuries. The torrid pace required to stay at the front of a race creates a suffocating inferno within the rib cage. The rapid flow of air chafes the throat, and the diaphragm can cramp. Muscles in the legs and arms fill with lactic acid when the cells begin to run out of oxygen. The intense cardiac effort can create the taste of blood in the mouth from elevated pressure within the pulmonary capillaries. Soon, a plodding heaviness ensues, and the limbs defy the brain's commands. If the runner suppresses the anguish and attempts to push through it, hearing and vision can become affected. Lacking oxygen, the brain spirals toward collapse.

Even if a cross country runner can ignore the physical torment, the mental battle is worse. The mind is in a constant argument with itself during a race. Like two sides of the same coin, a runner's internal voice flips between *I can* and *I can't*. Both voices serve a purpose. The *I can* allows runners to achieve more than we think is possible, accepting risks, and pushing through resistance. The *I can't* saves runners from rash choices that could cause irreparable harm.

The test becomes how long an athlete can handle the mental crescendo of argument, like two screaming toddlers creating an increasing din of anguish. We all have our limits. Even champion marathoners will, at some point, yield to the flip-flopping tantrum, unable to put up with it any longer. They must then relax the pace or quit altogether. Each race becomes a test of parsing the truth within one's mind. If you have exceptional resilience, you can push yourself to the point of passing out and collapsing. But that also defeats your primary goal and can have serious consequences. Contemplating this torture before a contest can cause an anxiety attack, so one finds distractions to avoid thinking about it.

Mental toughness is fundamental to the sport of cross country and is perhaps its defining characteristic. A graceful stride, slender build, and disciplined training can increase metabolic efficiency to shorten the suffering or mute the mind's voice. But ultimately, it comes down to your pain threshold and how much screaming your mind can take within itself. I've always been intrigued by the variety of physiques at the front of the race in distance running. While it is common to see the efficiently graceful, diminutive body type at the front, it is not uncommon to see a person with a broader frame or eccentric stride setting the pace, likely transporting an ultra-tough passenger brain.

Gary knew his team needed to build mental and physical toughness to withstand the stress of the crucible. The Volvo served well for that purpose—and for expanding our vocabulary.

Early in our training, Gary had our team meet in Cochrane for a morning run in the valley. The Cochrane pool held swimming lessons before opening for the public free swim at noon. Gary had arranged for us to use the pool before the morning lessons to have our squad do some high knee sprints in the shallow end of the pool as a speed training skill. He intended to improve strength and sprinting speed without the unwanted impact of running on pavement. For those of us on the team, it was a novel cross-training opportunity with the benefit of dipping into the cool pool after a long run. The shallow water workout went according to Gary's plan. When he finished those drills, he gave our team fifteen minutes of free time to dive off the boards and swim. We did not hesitate and quickly plunged into the deep end of the pool. Without saying a word, Guy followed along with the rest of us and jumped off the board. After a moment, there was a commotion on the surface as Guy struggled to keep his head above the water. Gary and the rest of us were caught off guard. Growing up next to the river, most of us learned to swim at an early age. Cochrane and Fountain City both had public pools and offered lessons to youngsters. But Guy was a farm kid, and like a lot of farm kids, he lived too far to bike to lessons easily. Guy was a cool dude, and we had never seen him look out of control. He was our best runner and too competitive to reveal any vulnerability. But he could barely save himself in the water, and we had to shepherd him back to the edge of the pool. The incident ended our practice, and Gary never took us to the pool again.

Darlington had a whole crop of young runners who were showing some early potential. Todd Johnson was a tall, skinny kid who had not gone out for a fall sport as a freshman and decided to join the cross country team as a sophomore. He was still maturing physically and was the kind of kid that many coaches would have dismissed early in high school. After joining the squad, Todd found himself in the mix of a lively JV group.

Todd knew Kirk Evenstad had potential as a runner, but Kirk wasn't the only talented kid in the freshman class. Kent Ruppert, Dale Kelly, and Shawn Hauser were at the core of a strong JV unit. They were all little squirts. Ruppert was the smallest, standing four feet, ten inches tall and weighing less than ninety pounds. But their hearts were as big as life, and they liked to have a good time. The movie *Risky Business* had landed in the theaters by August, and it was a huge hit. One of the freshmen's favorite pranks was to grab a bunch of brown paper towels from the dispenser in the bathroom and stuff them in the floor drains. Afterward, they turned on the showers and flooded the locker room floor. Then they'd run and slide across the slick surface, imitating Tom Cruise dancing to Bob Seger's "Old Time Rock & Roll." It was a good impersonation, apart from sunglasses being their only article of clothing.

As a junior, Tom Evenstad's times were improving, but he was struggling to break into the varsity lineup. The younger kids looked up to Tom for leadership on the JV squad. One evening, after finishing a tough workout, Tom pushed through the doors to the locker room. Seger's hit was blaring as he entered, and he almost slipped on the floor. Tom's face flushed hot. He had seen enough of the antics from his underclassmen. The locker room was a disaster, and Tom was sure that Arnie would catch hell for letting his crew get out of hand. He marched across the floor and grabbed his brother by the throat, shoving him up against a locker. Kirk's sunglasses slipped off his face and revealed a wide set of eyes, stunned by his brother's reaction.

"Kirk! What the hell are you idiots doing? Shut off that box and clean this up!"

The boom box went silent, and the other kids stood mute with their mouths agape. After a moment, Tom's anger evaporated, and he released his brother from his grip.

"Don't let me find any of you doing that ever again! You need to think of how your actions reflect on all of us, especially Coach Miehe."

Tom turned and walked to his locker. The freshmen didn't waste any time and went to work cleaning the floor in silence.

Locker room antics. From left to right: Todd Johnson, Kirk Evenstad, and Kent Ruppert. Photo courtesy of Arnie Miehe.

CHAPTER NINE
RUN FOR THE HILLS

I pulled into an open parking spot on North Main Street and noticed my teammates standing in a circle on the sidewalk. The boom box speakers cast the yearning lyrics to Rick Springfield's "Jessie's Girl" as I approached. Guy twisted his torso with a hop and kicked something off the sole of his back foot. The colorful bag arched toward Mark, who slid his toe forward to keep it from hitting the ground, shooting it back up in the air near Paul. Paul caught the fabric sack in front of him on the instep of his foot and passed it to Scott but missed high. As I walked up to their circle, I made an attempt at a save, but the bag skipped off my foot and fell to the ground. Mark gave me a mocking look.

"Smooth one, Smiley!"

My teammates were adept at Hacky Sack, but I had not mastered the game. The contortions made my left leg squawk whenever I joined in with them. Hacky Sack had become a popular pastime with teens in the early eighties and was something we'd do to entertain ourselves before a practice or meet. It required focus and dexterity and kept us limber. There were many days when we tossed the sand-filled bag around with our feet while waiting for a torturous workout to begin. We had shown up in Fountain City to battle with the hills, and it was common for us to start from the hardware store on North Main.

JEFF RICH

Gary forged our bodies with hill work. We were blessed to live in the best part of Wisconsin for running up hills, or perhaps more appropriately, cursed. Within the school district, we could not walk more than two miles without bumping into a steep limestone bluff. These small mountains were spared from the last glacier eleven thousand years ago, creating the spectacular backdrop of the Driftless Area. The telltale drift left from glaciers is absent, unlike the rest of Wisconsin. Limestone bedrock dominates the region. The glaciated plains of the Upper Midwest could not form a starker contrast to the Driftless Area. The colossal sheets of ice tilled the earth, grinding the surrounding landscape into ordinary, predictable conformance. But the Driftless lingered, feral and puzzling. Shadowy caves dwell beneath the bluffs' peaks, and frigid streams meander through the valleys. The Driftless stands alone, encircled by unfamiliar terrain, lost in time.

The bluffs rise five hundred feet above the valley floor and are creased with ravines called coulees. The name came from the early French missionaries and trappers who paddled into the Upper Mississippi River Valley during the seventeenth century. The coulees are veiled by hardwood canopies of oak, ash, hickory, walnut, and black cherry. County roads drape over the bluffs' contours like asphalt ribbons. Most of the roads in the area were paved to support the tanker trucks hauling milk. On daily runs, those trucks carried the economic lifeblood of the state to the dairies that processed it for the markets. In spots, the roads have gradients up to 15 percent. It was into those hills that our team would run.

Some of the highest peaks and most challenging slopes were along the river near Fountain City, settled in 1839 by Thomas Holmes. For a time it was called Holmes' Landing. It had a natural harbor and abundant hardwood forests that made the location a good spot for riverboats to take on firewood for their boilers. Later it was named Fountain City after a fountain in the center of town that harvested a natural spring from the limestone. The fountain has been upgraded and is still there today. Starting in the 1850s, several breweries operated in the city. Caves in the limestone offered natural cool storage for the product. By the mid-twentieth century the breweries had disappeared, but the recipe for the original Fountain Brew survived. Fountain City is a picturesque community, particularly when viewed

Eagle Bluff towers above Fountain City as viewed from the Mississippi River, October 2021. Photo by Jeff Rich.

from the top of a surrounding bluff or the waters of the Mississippi. On the north side of town is Eagle Bluff, which dominates the scene. Its west-facing slope cascades toward the harbor where the Corps of Engineers facility once maintained the Thompson dredge. Eagle Bluff's south slope plunges to Highway 95 at its floor, which is also called the Fountain City dugway.

Sheer cliffs crown the peaks of the bluffs above the community. The city is steep and offers the impression of a terraced Alpine village. Many of the buildings were constructed of brick with limestone foundations and adorned with stepped gables, typical of the mid-nineteenth century. From Hill Street, the highest north-south street in the city, a person with a good arm can throw a stone and hit the river just across the tracks. Historic St. Mary's Catholic Church stands prominently on Hill Street and is easily seen from the river. One block to the west, below that church, is North Main Street. The hardware store, the auditorium, Abts' grocery, and the popular Monarch Tavern were all located on North Main. Farther south on the same street, near the bank and namesake fountain, was the Corner Store. My parents would take my brothers and me there when we were in grade school. We would sit on bar stools and be served an ice cream soda that would fizz and froth at the tops of our glasses. Artisans' studios and craft shops are sprinkled throughout the community as they are in many river towns. Immediately to the north of the hardware store is the dugway that intersects the Great River Road one block to the west. On that corner sits the Golden Frog

Supper Club. "The Frog" was built in the 1870s and has retained its original floor and other furnishings. Each Friday locals gather for the weekly Wisconsin fish fry, complete with deep-fried cheese curds. In my youth, the place was packed with adults washing down their battered cod with brandy old-fashioneds and fueling a blue haze of smoke.

The hill workouts started at the hardware store, often on Saturday mornings. On many days, we ran south through the streets of Fountain City for our warm-up until we reached County YY. We then turned to the east and attacked "the beast." Heart rates shot up immediately, and oxygen debt set in soon afterward. We had to discipline our minds for the rest of the climb. YY was long enough that it did not pass quickly, and the road ascended roughly five hundred feet over about a mile. Lungs were stretched to their capacity. Diaphragms heaved, and it was not uncommon for a runner to develop a stitch in his side, adding to the discomfort. On the hills, we focused on pumping our arms more vigorously to "pull" and "push" ourselves upward. It felt like we were in slow motion, and we were miserable the whole time. We hated YY as much as we hated the Volvo.

On other days, Gary had us run shorter but more intense "hill repeats" on the streets of Fountain City. Since the community was

Looking south on North Main Street, Fountain City, Wisconsin. Photo by Jeff Rich.

narrowly strung along a steep bluff, the streets perpendicular to Highway 35 ascended nearly one hundred feet in three blocks. The gradient was extreme, and those narrow lanes could be perilous for vehicles in the winter. Gary treated these workouts similarly to the interval training on the track, but it forced us to focus on the techniques of hill running. We ran south from the hardware store for a half mile, then turned and stormed the hill. We pumped our arms and legs furiously as we ascended the slope. Once on Hill Street, we ran for several blocks to recover. Then we'd turn toward the river, descend another block, and storm the hill again. We repeated the routine in a serpentine fashion through the city. Repeatedly we sprinted up the precipitous streets, eyes fixed on the pavement, legs driving against the earth. As time went on, we became a small swarm, moving in unison up and down those hills.

It looked easier than it felt. Newton's second law of motion states that the force required to move an object of constant mass is directly proportional to that object's acceleration. In other words, we were the objects, and the acceleration was gravity, applied equally to each of us. His mass determined the force required for each runner to move up the hill. The heavier the runner, the harder he was going to have to work to maintain the pace of a smaller runner on the same ascent. Dan, Mark, and I were the heaviest, weighing between forty and fifty pounds more than Paul. Guy and Paul flew up those hills. Scott was the middleweight in our group and had excellent upper body strength, which gave him an advantage on climbs. In competition, he seemed to relish watching a hill grind his opponents into submission. It was hard for all of us, but the heavier runners suffered tremendously on hills just to keep pace. My longer stride gave me an advantage on flat terrain, but my teammates tormented me on those hills.

Gary intuitively knew how important hills were to our sport. He preached hills to us.

"Never let a competitor pass you on a hill. It will defeat you mentally. I want you to pass others on the hills. If you are going to get passed at all, the flats are better, and you might recover and move up on the opponent shortly afterward. But at all costs, do not get passed on the hills. No matter how tired you feel, just put one foot in front of the other and get over the top. For gosh sakes, we're going to be the best hill runners in the state! Look at where we live!"

It was a common pronouncement, and it came out with such enthusiasm. He was always smiling when he said it, as if he expected us to be excited by the words. That was his standard pep talk before a punishing workout.

Despite the agony, we all recognized the importance and strategic benefit of hills in a race. Hills were a reality in cross country, and the techniques for conquering them were not something we picked up while running on a flat oval track. Like it or not, Gary was molding his team into hill runners and preparing us to exploit the opportunity they provided.

There was a side benefit to the tough training regimen after it started. The intensity of the workouts would trigger a release of endorphins from the pituitary gland. Vigorous exercise can trigger their release, blocking the communication of pain signals in the nervous system. During the agony of a difficult run, the endorphins numb the pain to a tolerable level, and the mind can drift to another place while the miles pass. A runner can mercifully lose track of time. Once the suffering is over, the residual endorphins' presence in the bloodstream gives the runner a sense of euphoria, called a "runner's high" that might last for hours. That is often why runners become addicted to running. After a time, it was as if our subconsciouses were seeking that high, turning us into masochists.

The former Fountain City Hardware building. Photo by Jeff Rich.

The hill workouts finished at the hardware store, and we gathered in the Brones' upstairs apartment afterward. If it was a weekend morning, Judee had hot chocolate and pancakes ready for us. Or she would make egg-in-a-hole by carving the center out of a slice of bread and frying an egg in its center. On weekday training runs after school, we might stay for a pasta supper and devour piles of spaghetti. The training regimen created insatiable appetites, and we swallowed embarrassing amounts of food. Calories were an afterthought, and we lost weight during the season despite never missing an opportunity to eat. The Brones' kitchen became familiar to each of us and was a place for camaraderie. Judee asked questions of each kid and sprinkled smiles within the group. We would sit around the table and share the laughs of youth, having cleared the punishing run from our minds, endorphins coursing through our veins.

CHAPTER TEN

AWAKENING

Arnie was setting high goals for the upcoming season with his boys' team. They had nearly won their conference meet in 1982 and had also been competitive in their invitationals. Six of the squad's starters were returning. The team was focused on winning the conference title and at least one invitational during the season.

The alumni meet on August 27 provided a good omen as the boys defeated the alumni squad by three points. But they ran into some difficulty in September with other teams in their region that had also improved from the previous season. Boscobel, the defending state runner-up, had returned their best runner with a complement of solid underclassmen. Fennimore was ranked third in the state coaches' poll. Darlington faced both schools early in the season. The Redbirds were competitive but were denied the invitational victories they were seeking.

The teams' struggles continued when they faced Platteville in a dual meet. The Hillmen were the second-ranked team in the state in the larger Class B division. The Redbirds had improved but lost by twelve points. Bob Cullen was still running in the fifth spot for Darlington as a sophomore, and James Schuetz had ascended to fill the seventh spot on the varsity.

Arnie's team's progress was evident to him, but they were running into stiff resistance. Troy Cullen was establishing himself as a remarkable runner, and the seniors, Jeff Schuetz and John Lange, were very competitive. Arnie could feel that they were on the cusp of a breakthrough if his younger runners could continue their progress.

Our first contest on the 1983 schedule was a dual meet against a small school named Arkansaw, located an hour's drive north, near the confluence of the Chippewa and Mississippi Rivers. During September, several other meets were "duals," competing against one other team. Often, the teams that visited our course were other Class C schools with even smaller enrollments than C-FC. Districts such as Arkansaw, Gilmanton, and Taylor had enrollments of fewer than two hundred students. Sometimes those schools were too small in numbers to field a football team, but they offered cross country as a fall sport. Even though the smaller schools had fewer students, they often had better cross country teams since their best athletes had only one fall sport option. Arkansaw was a member of another conference and had a strong cross country program. It was a good test for our first meet.

In previous years, a five-thousand-meter course had been laid out on the C-FC property. The course looped twice around the campus. It started in the center of the school grounds, near the football field, and wrapped around the elementary playground adjacent to Highway 35. It then turned east along the red pines of the school forest and again south toward the paved track before returning to its origin. The surface was fair with a couple of short climbs. All of it was framed by a bluff covered in mixed hardwoods and red cedar trees behind the school. The bluffs of Minnesota could be seen across the sprawling valley to the west. The course was scenic, particularly in the autumn evening sunlight when the races were held.

SEPTEMBER 2, 1983

It was on such an afternoon when Arkansaw lined up next to us behind the chalk line, wearing their orange jerseys. The gun cracked, and we bolted forward in a rush, eager to test ourselves.

Once on the course, the colored marker flags guided the competitors along the route. Blue flags directed the runners straight ahead, red flags for left-hand turns, and yellow flags for right-hand turns. Most course officials would spread a chalk line in the center of the race lane throughout the course, but not always. It was important for runners at the front of the race to pay attention, particularly if they had exceptional talent and were running by themselves. A release of endorphins and a lack of competitive pressure could cause the mind to wander, triggering a runner to miss a flag or take a wrong turn. Some courses included multiple loops or partial loops that could magnify the confusion. It was not uncommon to have a lead runner lose time while retracing an errant turn on a course.

Guy established himself at the front of the race immediately, and the competitors quickly separated on the course. After the first mile, it seemed like the run was not a competition at all. With only thirteen runners in the race, the distances between consecutive participants became several hundred meters. It felt foreign. In most sports there were other contestants in proximity or within physical contact. Even in summertime 5K events at the local festivals, you had dozens of other runners nearby.

Is it red for a right turn? "R" seems to make sense for a right turn. Or is it yellow for a right turn?

Mark was second-guessing himself as he ran alone on the course. The feeling of detachment had him bewildered while he tried to remember. He did not want to get disqualified in his first race and struggled to keep the next runner in view so he could confirm the route.

While Mark pondered his next turn, Scott, Paul, and I had each other to rely upon. It turned out that we were evenly matched during a race, and Scott and I fell in behind Paul.

Paul Abts was a tough kid but the smallest in our bunch. No one who saw us together would single him out. His size limited his options with other sports, but he was perfectly suited for running cross country. He was pleasant to be with—unless we were racing against him. Paul's physique was perfect for the sport, and he had a similar stride to Guy's. Paul was a gifted runner. He wasn't afraid of hard work, but his natural ability made up for his occasional lack of discipline. Besides his gifted stride, Paul's greatest attribute was his ability to dig deep and give a gutsy performance. The two of us spent a lot of time suffering side by side in races. I tended to go out fast, and Paul liked to work his way up from the back, saving energy for the end. Paul picked me up on many occasions when my mind's tantrum was getting the best of me. We made an odd couple with my bigger frame next to Paul's diminutive size. Still, there we were together, nearly every race, picking off opponents when we charged up hills. He made me a better runner.

Paul came from modest means—all of us did—but somehow, we knew that Paul had challenges that the rest of us weren't facing. He needed guidance and was searching for somewhere to belong. Paul was the youngest of four boys, and his parents were aging. His nearest brother was five years his senior, and by the time Paul entered high school, all of his brothers had graduated. Paul no longer had direction or boundaries. He found himself driftless in the void, translating into poor academic performance. As a sophomore, he started skipping his social studies class and failed the course. By the time we were beginning our first cross country season, Paul had to retake the class to compete. It was a seminal moment for him. He did not want to be that kid, the one who graduated a year behind his classmates. Paul had been showing up at the hardware store with Dan to hang out with Mark ever since the Brone family moved to Fountain City. His home on Hill Street was nearby. Those three kids were a tight-knit group, and Gary had encouraged Paul to join the team when it formed. Gary was becoming Paul's mentor, providing some of the direction and boundaries he needed to develop.

The finish was as unfamiliar and detached as the contest itself. It ended with a few punctuated claps from a handful of spectators. Guy was the first runner to cross the line for that inaugural dual meet on our home course. Scott, Paul, and I finished together, and our team captured an easy victory. It was a nice surprise for our first attempt, and Arkansaw would soon become a familiar foe.

SEPTEMBER 6, 1983

The sun shone through the window, and the vinyl-covered seat was sticking to the skin on the inside of my bare arm. I was listening to Billy Squier's *Don't Say No* album on the Sony Walkman I had borrowed for the bus ride. Right after Labor Day, our team traveled to the community of Black River Falls, roughly sixty miles east of our high school.

Sunshine spilled onto the fairways of the golf course as our bus pulled into the crowded parking lot at the local country club, where the local high school held the Tiger Invitational. Gary had worked with our school's athletic director to obtain an invitation early in the season. It was our inaugural invitational race, and it was a large, annual event with ten teams from larger Class B schools in attendance. At that time, the WIAA arranged its state tournaments into three classes. Class A comprised the districts with the largest enrollments in the state. C-FC was in the smallest classification, Class C.

A big invitational was a visual feast when high pressure dominated a cloudless sky. As I stepped off the bus, I was struck by the view. The emerging fall hues of aspen and maple ringed the course. The spectrum of colors from the large group of contestants dotting the fairways only enhanced the scene. With seven runners per team, an invitational with ten teams had roughly 140 runners, with both the girls' and boys' races. Parents and coaches lined the perimeter in large numbers. Prior to the start, squads scattered over the fairways, stretching, jogging, and scouting the route. On that particular day, the conditions were ideal for racing, with calm winds and temperatures in the seventies.

The Black River Falls course flowed over gentle hills that divided the fairways. At times, it followed the cart paths through small groves of trees on the site. A long incline at the end of the course separated the runners on the final sprint. It was a beautiful racecourse. Golf courses were usually the best grounds for a race since they had regularly maintained paths and trimmed grass. When a local golf course was not available, host schools would set up a course on their grounds. In those cases, the conditions could vary widely, depending upon the property constraints and the level of maintenance. The school sites would often have limited acreage, creating smaller loops, more turns, and fewer straight stretches than most golf courses, sometimes leading to more hazards.

The girls went first, and the start of the large race was thrilling. A long chalk stripe was laid out, and each team took their positions as a cluster in chalk lanes abreast of their opponents, creating a broad front. The official called the runners to the line and set them with vocal commands. The pistol cracked, and the colorful mass of legs and arms jumped forward and sprinted down the straightaway with a lightly thundering rumble. The group did not separate immediately; each team and each runner strove for a spot near the front. For the first several hundred yards, they clung tightly, nearly all the runners able to exist within the mob for the initial portion of the race. In those early moments, the *I can* always wins the argument with the *I can't*. By the time the runners reached the quarter-mile mark, they started to separate at the front and back of the pack. The horde soon morphed into a natural bell curve, with fewer at each end and the majority clustered in the center.

To our surprise, Karen came across the finish line in second place. She had shown all of us what was possible. Her younger sister Heidi finished fifth. Our girls' team placed fourth that day—a solid start for a squad with only five runners in its first invitational. Karen was an honor student and humble, yet she was a gutsy, gracious competitor who provided leadership for the rest of us. Off the course, Karen was warm and would disarm you as a conversationalist. We were in French class together and quizzed each other in the foreign language at practices. She excelled at mental toughness and could run with the boys. A runner with fine form, she was without equal when it came to conquering the argument in her brain during a race. Karen was our only senior in 1983, and she led by example right from the start.

Throughout the season, our girls' and boys' squads acted as if we were one team. We practiced together, traveled together, ate team meals together, and laughed together. When one team was racing, the other was strung along the course at key points to cheer their peers on. It was uplifting to hear a familiar voice when battling one's mind during a race, particularly if surrounded by opponents. It gave the *I can* mindset a needed boost. There wasn't a packed crowd in a tight space as in other sports. Since meets started immediately after the school day, the other sports teams were obligated to join their own practices and were unable to attend cross country meets. The crowds would be at the start and finish, but cheers were mostly absent for the rest of the race, the silence replaced by gasps and footfalls.

As I watched the girls run, it became apparent how different cross country was from other sports for the spectators. Once the race was underway, the throng of fans sprinted across the course to the next best spot to view the action, repeating this several times before settling along the straightaway near the finish. No other sport was like that—contestants and spectators all in motion at once.

The boys' teams lined up on the chalk, and my pulse was racing. It was not a confident moment. Standing abreast of so many runners, I suddenly realized I was among the giants in my new sport. It occurred to me that my size might be a disadvantage, unlike football. From summertime 5K runs at local festivals, we knew that we were respectable runners but also recognized that we were not as fast as the college runners and elite marathoners. The recent win in the dual meet was our only reference. We had no idea how we would measure up to a large group of competitors. When the pistol rang out, we sprinted down the fairway and established ourselves as a clutch within the mob. It was a cautious beginning, seeking security together under foreign circumstances. The pace was tolerable, and our adrenalin levels were high. The itch to compete needled us, but we had been warned to avoid the temptation of an early sprint. It was our first big race, and we had to guard against hitting the wall near the finish. We were feeling our way. Guy was the first to separate from us and make a move for the front.

Guy Todd. Photo courtesy of the *Winona Daily News*.

Guy Todd was a magnificent runner who comes along at a small high school once in a generation—or longer. One time, on an August training run around Lake Winona, Guy was dissatisfied with our brisk pace and struck out on his own. Before long, he was a half mile ahead of us on the paved trail. As we approached the south end of the lake, we could see him rounding the corner and turning back to the north on the other side.

"Look at that!" Scott exclaimed.

As we turned our heads, we got a good view of Guy across the lake in full stride, transfixing our gaze and dropping our jaws. It was a sight to behold. We all envied the God-given gifts he had been blessed with. He did not seem to run but, instead, glided over a course. I remember thinking I could place a cup of coffee on top of his head while he was running next to me, and it would not spill. He also had a perfect combination of sprinting speed and the endurance required for long-distance racing. When we watched Guy run, we knew we were witnessing the efficient stride of a thoroughbred, soothing and poetic. His mastery convinced an opponent it was easy, belying the torture of running at that speed over such a distance. During a race, his feathered, sandy mane would drift behind him, reinforcing the image of a stallion. He ran with a stoic expression on his face. He seemed relaxed, making it difficult for any runner who tried to challenge him near the front. We were not able to hear him breathing either. Most of us could not fake our way through the agony of the blistering pace at the front. The misery would show on our faces, and the struggle for air was audible. Guy would mentally defeat opponents while they searched his face for a crack in his composure. They would suffer next to him for a short time, finally succumbing to the pace and then helplessly watch him run away from them. He seemed unconcerned and emotionless at their attempts, wounding their egos. Guy got results and was our best runner without exception, often finishing the five-thousand-meter races nearly a minute in front of our next runner.

Scott, Paul, and I were hanging tightly together. Soon we were speaking in short bursts to one another, coaxing an advance.

"That's enough of this," Scott finally said. "Let's get moving."

We had settled somewhere in the middle, and opponents were strung out before us. We picked up the pace and "pulled the rope" on the runner immediately ahead. As we sprinted by him, our momentum carried us past another pair of opponents. Suddenly we were picking off runners and feeling exultant. We had discovered a technique we would learn to exploit consistently. The three of us ran as a pack and hunted our quarry together. To our surprise, we realized that few cross country teams had runners closely matched in speed. They were usually dispersed on the course, battling opponents on their own.

The three of us loped in unison over the course. Our footfalls converged into a rhythmic cadence as if we were running to the beat of a drum while we pursued our prey. With a softly uttered cue, we crept up on each opponent and sprinted past him all at once, with such a burst that by the time the runner realized what was happening, there was a five-yard gap. Each was usually running alone—the first, second, or third runner from a team—and not used to being quickly overtaken. We found that the technique saved energy.

Increased resilience and intimidation were other benefits of running as a pack. It became an addictive frenzy, like sharks with blood in the water. We were kind kids when not competing, but we savored the anguish of our opponents. We learned to become ferocious on the course that day. It was addicting, and we kept doing it, reeling in runner after runner, more uplifted as we went along. The technique was harder to apply on the hills, but the effect was greater. Other runners would never mount a challenge when passed on a slope. Occasionally we'd hear an audible sigh of disgust or cursing from behind after passing them. It was too much to ask from their egos. It took too much to mentally recover and then counterattack three runners from the same team, holding together in strength of numbers near the front of a race. In time, we knew each other's tendencies so well that we did not need words to coordinate our attacks, and pack hunting became our signature tactic.

Pack hunting during a race. From left to right: Scott, Paul, and Jeff. Photo courtesy of Betty Rich.

A long uphill slope of one hundred meters at the finish of the Black River Falls course served as a winnowing fork. It sifted competitors within sight of the finish while they yearned for an end to their misery. Runners who had spent their last ounce of energy prior to the hill fell prey on the final stretch. That uphill sieve would take its toll, differentiating the field before runners could cross the line. It was a punishing summit with arms pumping and spit flying as runners willed themselves to the chute. Even with a good time, you felt like you had a bad race on that course because it ended so slowly and with such difficulty.

Four of us placed in the top twelve at that first invitational. Gary added up our scores for a sum of seventy-five points.

"How'd we do, Coach?" Guy asked. "Is that a good score?"

Gary wasn't sure how to respond to the question.

"I don't know. We'll have to wait and see how the other teams scored."

It was strange. In every other sport, we knew whether we won or lost as soon as the contest finished. In cross country, emotions remained unresolved until the officials tallied the scores and announced the results at the awards ceremony.

The officials finished their math and then stood in front of the crowd with an electronic bullhorn. The top individuals were announced first, and ribbons were handed out. Then the officials moved on to the team results and the presentation of the trophy. The officials shared placement in ascending order, announcing the last-place team first and then working up to the first-place team. As we sat listening, we grew anxious when our school's name had not been called. The bullhorn crackled.

"In third place is Altoona ... *applause*. The runner-up is Mondovi ..."

No one clapped after the announcement of the second-place team. It was another oddity in this new sport we found ourselves in. We looked around at one another for a moment, puzzled.

I turned to Gary with a look of disgust and blurted, "They forgot us, Coach!"

The race official sensed the confusion and, in another moment, announced that we had won. We were unable to cheer from sheer embarrassment. Usually, the announcement of the second-place team leaves no doubt in the minds of the victors as to the outcome, and they erupt in cheers. We were so new on the scene that we thought the officials had overlooked our team. Our school had developed a culture of losing, which had penetrated well enough that we could not imagine we might win a big invitational on our first attempt. The folly was immediately apparent to the dozens of competitors huddled closely around us, and some chuckles followed. It had been a narrow contest, settled by just three points. We stood up and sheepishly approached the podium to receive the trophy.

Everything changed on the bus ride home. There had been a validation. The measuring stick of athletic prowess suggested that we were worthy of something. At some level, it was foreign to think of ourselves as winners. It was a new feeling to no longer be the underdog—no longer unnoticed and insignificant. After all, we were the traitors and misfits the Jackals wanted to hold in contempt and harass. We began looking at one another differently. We had always enjoyed each other's company, but suddenly our eyes perceived new value. The curtain had lifted, partially revealing the importance of each teammate's role. It was not just an individual effort, and we were not competing against each other. Each member was someone who was needed in a joint effort.

The boom box played cassette tapes at full volume on the bus ride home. We were strumming air guitars, slapping the drumbeat on seats, and shouting the lyrics to Ozzy Osbourne's "Crazy Train," not wanting our euphoria to end.

Judee sat at the kitchen table above the hardware store that night and asked Gary, "What do you think of your team?"

"You know, Judee," Gary replied with a surprised expression, "I think we could be really good. Our kids may have more talent than I realized."

"Really? You think so after winning one invitational?"

"The other coaches kept coming up to me after the meet and asking how long our program had been around," Gary said. "They couldn't believe that this was our first invitational, and we'd won it against those bigger schools."

Judee could see in Gary's face that their comments had shaken his confidence.

"I've never done this before," he said. "I'm not sure I know enough to coach these kids yet."

During the last week of September, Arnie opened the pages of the *Wisconsin State Journal* and turned to the sports section. He scanned down the print with his index finger, searching the small font. There it was! Darlington was listed as the ninth-ranked team in Class C. The Redbirds had competed well enough against larger schools in their early meets to gain recognition from the coaches in the state who ranked the teams. It was the affirmation he was looking for, and it would serve as a reward for his kids. He wanted something to help lift their spirits and continue the work necessary to improve themselves. A state ranking was something Darlington High School had not achieved in a very long time, if ever. It was big news in the community, and Arnie clipped the article out of the paper to bring to practice that night. When he shared it with his runners, their eyes lit up. Someone had noticed them; perhaps they could be winners after all.

CHAPTER ELEVEN
THE YOGI

Judee Brone was directing her first play, *Alice in Blunderland*, during the autumn of 1983. Directing plays would become one of Judee's legacies in the community, starting with the first—a musical. The Brone family attended the United Church of Christ on Hill Street with the Stettler family, and the church had sponsored the effort. Judee had a passion for the arts and had become familiar with theater during her time in New York. Karen Stettler was in the cast, as were several other community members, and the troupe traveled to perform at various local sites that fall.

Before one performance, Karen had lost her voice and was in a panic.

"I'm not going to be able to sing my lines, Judee!"

"Then just speak them, dear," Judee said without missing a beat. "It will be okay, and the rest of the cast will take their cues from your words."

It put Karen at ease, even though her performance was not up to the standard she had come to expect from herself. Judee would find a way to pick a kid up when one of us needed some support. Her motto was: "Always do your best!"

Judee treated us, particularly those on the margins, as special. She engaged each kid, wanting to share in each one's joys and sorrows. Judee was the team's matron, our team mom, the glue. It wasn't just a sport to Gary and Judee; the Brones created a family for all the kids on the team.

After a race, Judee would plant a kiss on our cheeks as we came out of the chute, branding us as one of her own with her lingering lipstick mark. But she would admonish a runner if she witnessed a sub-par effort. She expected each of us to do our best. There was more than one occasion when she saw a kid hold back during a race just to sprint to the finish line, smiling. Leaving too much in the tank at the end of a race was not a desirable trait in a teammate. When that happened, Judee pulled the runner aside and let the kid know she never wanted to see that again. She always expected each runner to give their best for the whole race, no matter the consequences.

Judee Brone. Photo courtesy of Mark Brone.

Gary was a novice coach, but he paid attention to details and had insights that others often overlooked. He was not afraid to embrace new techniques, either. He understood that despite his team's youth, months of intense training would take a toll. Before and after each practice, he led his squad through a nearly twenty-minute stretching routine.

But Gary introduced another post-workout process to our team: yoga. During his time in New York, Gary had received training at the Integral Yoga Institute. After practice, he would have the group lie down on the carpeted floor of the library, where it was dark and free from commotion. He instructed the team members to close their eyes. In a slow, calm voice, Gary gave instructions for rhythmic breathing and drew the individuals' attention inward. With a soothing cadence, he would pull the group into a form of a trance and then focus on each muscle group of the body. He softly gave instructions to flex, hold, and finally release each of those fibers upon his orders. This increased blood flow to those portions of the body after the workout, healing the trauma from training. The mind's focus was on purging daily distractions through deep breaths. In this restful state, Gary then guided the team through a series of positive visualizations. He painted images of running successfully in a race, conquering a hill, or setting personal records. It provided affirmation in the mind prior to the events taking place. He ended the session with a period of silence, absent thoughts. Everything melted away except the rhythmic heaving of chests. After a short time, Gary's voice brought the group back into the moment. It was refreshing and healing to undergo this routine, particularly after a tough hill workout or interval training.

We felt a little embarrassed at first—our fragile, teenage egos concerned about what other kids might think if they saw us all lying on a floor in the dark. We could not bear the thought of the football team witnessing that display. But soon we looked forward to this portion of the practice and understood its benefits. I had not heard of any other team going through such a routine in the early eighties. It was a unique advantage, and with a lack of depth, avoiding injuries was important for the team's success. Today, it is common to see elite college and professional athletes use meditation and visualization techniques as part of their training. Gary was ahead of his time and was not afraid to use unconventional new methods to train his team. He was our first yogi.

Highway 88 intersected with the Great River Road within yards of our high school. It was a winding road that snaked along a valley between the bluffs. The highway followed Waumandee Creek, which melted into the Mississippi through a large marsh near the school. The 88 was a common route for our team. At times, Gary had us log miles using "run-aheads" along that route. We ran in a single file instead of our customary cluster. Each person took turns in the lead, allowing those behind him to draft and save energy. After a brief interval, the last person in line sprinted to the front to take his next turn. The rotation was repeated, providing the entire group with alternating anaerobic sprints followed by longer periods of aerobic exercise. Gary also used Highway 88 for our easy runs the day before a race. The girls ran with us, and the mood was relaxed, the pace modest.

While running on 88, we witnessed the changes underway with each new week. The sultry, insect-laden summer air had become light and clear by October. We saw the seasons transition on the landscape. The corn and beans in the valley turned from green to tan as the crops ripened and dried. In a twinkling, the brilliant leaves departed. Ash and aspen lost their golden manes first, showering over us like confetti. Their multitudes, recently supple, cascaded to the floor to crumble against their will, providing a mosaic beneath our feet. Winter pressed them into submission, leaving their hosts bare to face the bitter wind. New legions erupted into a green cloak on the bluffs each spring, unaware of the generation lying as detritus beneath them, nourishing their own moment of glory. The melancholy onset of winter illustrated the fleeting cycles of life. Our moment together as athletes would follow the same pattern. It was a reminder that nothing lasts, yet some things never change.

By the fall of 1983, Mark Brone was the tallest runner on our team at six feet, two inches tall. He had grown eight inches from the prior year when the Jackals chased him around the football field. He had short blond hair and a fair complexion. He was rail thin as a sophomore, with legs too long for his torso, and he ran with a hunched posture. From a distance, during a run, he gave the gangly impression of an older man, and the image deceptively cloaked the speed he was carrying. Mark was maturing in that first season, both physically and as a young man. He was our team clown, with a big, toothy grin and always looking for a shortcut or a joke. Mark and I shared many attributes, but his personality was my opposite in some ways. I was driven and disciplined, and Mark was an artist—fun-loving and carefree. He was always screwing around, creating laughter, and sometimes going too far. Mark was our source of entertainment when we needed to lighten the mood. He would break dance anywhere he might get a reaction. He had perfected the moonwalk Michael Jackson made famous, among other moves. It was hard to take him seriously at times, but we were beginning to see the signs of his potential in that first season. He established himself in our key fifth spot, which ultimately determines a team's success in cross country.

In fact, Mark's performance mattered more than Guy's performance, or the rest of us for that matter. The fifth runner scores the most points in the team's total, so keeping that number to a minimum was critical to the squad's success. On a cross country team, the least among you

Mark Brone. Photo courtesy of Mark Brone.

becomes the greatest, even if the headlines in the papers neglect that fact. It is another attribute that uniquely defines cross country as a team sport. For better or for worse, the top five finishers all count in the team's final score. We needed Mark to perform well, consistently, and to keep improving. In time, Mark grew into his body and became an exceptional athlete in many sports, not only an accomplished endurance athlete but also a sprinter. He eventually played college basketball and competed in cycling competitions at a high level in adulthood.

Homecoming week for Darlington High School was at the end of September 1983. The male members of the court were selected by the student body from a ballot, exclusively listing football players, using a long-established custom at the school. Members of the football team elected their female escorts. It had always been that way, and other schools had similar traditions. Arnie saw that rule as narrow-minded and wanted to see a change that would allow athletes from any fall sport a chance to be on the homecoming court. But first, he looked for a way to involve his runners in the festivities and came up with a plan for an annual "torch run." Early in the semester, he used

The Darlington cross country team torch relay leads the 1983 homecoming parade down Main Street. Photo courtesy of the *Republican Journal*.

the school's metals shop to craft a torch for that purpose. Arnie's concept was much like the Olympic torch relay. His squad would go to the opponent's hometown, light the torch, and pass it from runner to runner in a relay back to Darlington. The relay was timed with the homecoming parade, which was always held on the Thursday night before the game. The cross country team would arrive in time to lead the parade through the town with the torch. The homecoming game was scheduled against Lancaster, forty miles away. The cross country squad completed the relay and took their place at the front of the parade. When the torch arrived at the high school, it was used to light the bonfire and became a new tradition. The Redbirds' cross country team was suddenly front and center for their community to view.

Arnie's squad finished their season with a 2-2 record in dual meets, both losses coming from larger, Class B schools. They had been competitive in each of their invitationals but had not finished higher than second place in any of those meets. There was no doubt they were stronger than they had been a year earlier, but their record did not reflect that improvement. Nonetheless, they were still ranked ninth in Class C.

The real surprise in their 1983 campaign was the junior varsity performance. The Redbirds JV had finished their season undefeated in dual meets and all of their invitationals. Tom Evenstad had run with his brother and the other skinny freshmen to a notable accomplishment.

By the second week of October, our C-FC boys' team had finished first in three out of four invitationals. All three of our dual meets had been victories, including one sweep. A sweep in cross country is rare and occurs when a team's top five runners have beaten all the runners from the other schools. It results in a perfect score of fifteen points, the cumulative sum of the first five runners. By that time in the season, we were starting to see ourselves as contenders in our races. Confidence was high, and the team had established itself locally as a formidable opponent. Prospects were good as the tournament competition approached.

In Wisconsin, during the early eighties, the tournament was organized through a series of three successive tiers of races to sift out the best teams. The first stage was regionals, the second stage was sectionals, and the third and final stage was the state championship or "state." The A, B, and C school districts were separated from one another and had exclusive tournament competitions. The first three Class C teams in the regional competition advanced to the sectional. In the sectional, the first two teams advanced to the state championship.

The night before the regional, Judee made pasta and set a heaping dish in front of Mark. He ate huge volumes of food but never put on any weight. The utensils clinked against the ceramic bowl as Mark twirled spaghetti in red sauce and slurped a forkful into his mouth. On the eve of a race, Gary directed our team to carbo-load. It was a common practice with marathoners, and Gary came from an Italian lineage.

CHAPTER TWELVE
TRIBULATION

October 18, 1983

The transmission's whining was irritating me on the bus ride. It was a gray day, and although it was dry, the barometer was dropping, with another front moving into the area as we made our way south of Interstate 90 toward Brookwood. The combined effect had given me a headache, and I reached into my duffel bag for a bottle of Tylenol.

It was Amish country, and we passed through clusters of farms along the way, creating a visual contradiction in culture and time. The Amish were excellent horsemen, and through my window, I spied a team of four draft horses working the soil, turning a field that had just been harvested. The Amish in the area commonly used Belgians for their fieldwork. This particular team had their heads adorned with blinders, and I could see their breath collide with the air while they toiled. The horses were straining against the earth's mass, bound to their load through leather harnesses and lines. Their struggle reminded me of Gary's hill workouts for our team, fighting against the same opponent.

Brookwood was a small, consolidated district nestled between the region's bluffs. Their school was similar in many ways to C-FC. The district was hosting the Class C Regional race in our area, and we had to leave school early to complete the two-hour bus ride before the start of the meet. The school's campus was located away from the river, east of La Crosse, between Norwalk and Ontario, Wisconsin. Their teams had a reputation for being well-prepared and were considered among the top programs in Class C. The district was one of those shining examples of small-school success with its cross country program. Brookwood's boys' teams had captured three consecutive runner-up finishes at the state meets in the late 1970s. Their coach, John Smith, was seasoned and intensely competitive. We had not raced them before and were eager for the test. It was a six-team regional, and Arkansaw was also in the field, seeking retribution from our first meeting in September.

After stepping off the bus, our survey of the course immediately raised our eyebrows. It was laid out on their school grounds, but unlike our course, it was within a tighter space. To achieve the five thousand meters needed, it had been set up with several loops over the same ground, including a hill that we would ascend twice. The course was complex, with dozens of right-angle turns. Courses with many sharp turns were often slower than running over modest hills. You had to slow down coming into the turns and then accelerate out of them. It disrupted your cadence and the speed you could maintain. Turns also presented an increased risk of falls in bad weather. Brookwood's course had lanes that tapered into rutted dirt paths where they snaked through the woods. The surfaces varied between dirt, pavement, sand, gravel, and grass. Theirs was a tactical course that would give an advantage to the runner who was familiar with its subtleties. Small things like knowing the spots where you could plant your foot firmly to accelerate out of a corner or the location of a narrowing lane where you could cut off another runner were meaningful benefits. Brookwood's course harkened back to the English roots of the sport, one where hares were chased by the hounds over hedges, woods, and streams. It enhanced the impacts of deception and acrobatics.

As we walked, I looked at Scott and asked, "How'd they get the regional on this course?"

He raised his eyebrows and sighed. "Someone's gonna roll an ankle in this mess!"

The starter's pistol sent us on a chase through a narrow path in the woods. I could not get into a rhythm before again taking a tight turn, ascending a hill, or leaping over a rut. It was a course that took focus. As I went along, I felt hollow. The normal burst of speed from my thighs and my tolerance for the rigors of a race were absent. Paul had paired up with me in the beginning, but he finally had to move ahead on his own. I kept getting passed by opponents and had no strength to counter their attacks. My focus was sharp, but I watched the race proceed around me with no sway over events. It was puzzling, even while I was in the midst of the competition.

Eventually, Scott and Mark pulled up beside me.

"How ya doin', Smiley?"

"Not myself, Space."

"Hang with us!" Scott murmured.

I joined them for a time, but I could not keep up. Over the final sprint to the line, I was engulfed by adversaries. I finished well back of where I should have been, and compared with Paul's time, I lost over a minute.

Arkansaw squeaked out a three-point victory, and we tied with Brookwood for second place. At that time, the top three teams advanced, or it would have been the end of our season.

We had fully expected to win our regional meet, given the success we experienced during the regular schedule. My run had been inexplicable. My performance alone was responsible for the team's disappointing result. To their credit, my coach and teammates said nothing to me. Aggravated, I grimly stood at the school's entrance and watched Arkansaw accept their trophy during the ceremony. You cannot conceal a bad performance in the sport of cross country. Time and position are firmly measurable. It is a team sport that squarely places responsibility on each runner and leaves no place to hide when accountability is assigned. The bus ride back was a slow cooker of frustration and shame.

After arriving home that evening, an answer emerged. Fatigue started pounding on my joints, and chills took hold. My throat became sore within a couple of hours, and a fever developed. Before long, I was bedridden and soaking my sheets with sweat. The next morning, the medication I took to help with my symptoms triggered an allergic reaction. I began vomiting, and hives developed on my neck and back, wrinkling my skin with large, itching welts. My upper lip swelled to twice its normal size. I had not encountered anaphylaxis before, and it was an alien experience for me. Some Benadryl subdued the reaction, but I was a mess as the sectional meet loomed on Saturday. It was tough to get out of bed, much less run. After several calls to the doctor, my mom called Gary on Wednesday afternoon to let him know I would not be at practice. That same evening, Scott rolled an ankle during the team's workout. To make matters worse, after he limped home, he also became sick. In most years, viruses swept through the schools after Thanksgiving, but in 1983 they started early. On Friday morning, I forced myself out of bed and went to school in order to remain eligible for Saturday's meet. Scott did the same. Between classes, I stumbled through the hallways to the bathroom.

I could not stomach the thought of a cafeteria lunch on Friday and spent the hour in the library instead. Alone in the sanctuary, I rifled through the papers and looked at the latest coaches' poll in the *Wisconsin State Journal*. It quickly revealed the level of competition we were about to face. In addition to Arkansaw and Brookwood, to my dismay, four of the top ten teams were in our sectional—Boscobel, Fennimore, Albany, and Darlington. Although we had not set team goals at the start of our season, Gary had been telling us that a trip to the state meet was a possibility if we ran to our potential. I wanted to believe we could reach state, but my mind suddenly struggled with that vision. The competition seemed daunting, and the illness had sapped me. Adversity had finally crashed our party.

OCTOBER 22, 1983

The sweet, pungent scent of mink oil from the driver's leather jacket clung in my nostrils. The aroma was normally pleasing, but with the windows closed and in my stricken condition, the strong odor had a nauseating effect. Saturday had arrived with a dismal sky, and we piled into the bus for a three-hour ride to the sectional meet in Prairie du Sac. The hives on my waist and hips were burning, and while seated, I applied some calamine lotion to suppress the irritation.

I focused on the passing scenery outside my window to keep my mind off my stomach. Peering through the glass, I spotted apple orchards randomly scattered between the dairy farms on the route.

Their leaves had dropped, and their branches were polka-dotted with the red orbs. The hanging fruit gave the illusion of the trees bending to the load carried upon their limbs, burdened until the harvest could provide them relief. In October, the apple orchards were frantic with activity. The harvest was in full swing.

Our bus pulled into the Lake Wisconsin Country Club, where the meet was being held. We stepped off the bus steps into a cold, light mist. The maples had lost their leaves and stood unadorned, adding to the bleakness of the day. The golf course was near the Driftless Area's eastern edge, along the Wisconsin River. The ancient glaciers had not covered the place, but the river had carried their meltwater. Over time, huge deposits of sand and gravel from the glacial outwash formed a broad plain between the bluffs.[3] By the eighteenth century, the Sac Indian tribe had settled in the area to farm its rich soil and trade at the site. Subsequently, the first French traders named the village after them.[4]

Nine teams and a handful of individuals from the southwest part of the state had qualified for the sectional. Our team began warming up with some light jogging, and my mind protested immediately. Scott did his best to conceal the pain while running on his sore foot.

The girls' race was first. We positioned ourselves along their course to cheer them on. Karen ran to a fifth-place finish, which was good enough to qualify her for the state meet. She was the first Pirate runner to accomplish that feat. However, the weather and the competition hampered the rest of the team, and the girls did not advance. With only five runners, they had done well to reach the sectional in their first season.

The Albany boys had sent their team to the state meet the prior fall. Several of those runners were back, and their star, Rich Dallman, had been putting in some notable times over the previous month. Standing confidently in their light blue shirts, they held good prospects to advance.

Coach Russell Beck had brought his Boscobel Bulldogs to the sectional again. Boscobel had been the Class C state runner-up the prior year. Their senior, Mark Reynolds, placed tenth at the state championship and was expected to challenge for the sectional title

---

3. https://dnr.wisconsin.gov/topic/lands/lowerwisconsin/geology.

4. https://www.encyclopedia.com/history/dictionaries-thesauruses-pictures-and-press-releases/sauk-prairie.

in 1983. They also had sophomore Kevin Clark, a new threat in their arsenal, who looked like he could start as a tailback for the football team. He was an accomplished, densely muscled wrestler with extraordinary aerobic capacity.

Coach Vince Lease and his Fennimore Golden Eagles had qualified for the meet. Despite their losses to Darlington and Boscobel, Fennimore had a string of five state championships between 1977 and 1981. Their program was a small-school powerhouse in cross country.

I'd seen Darlington in the poll, but we had not encountered them before. Despite their ninth-place ranking, they had soundly beaten Albany, Brookwood, and Fennimore several weeks earlier at the River Valley Invitational. Darlington had also beaten Fennimore in the regional, where the Redbirds' top runner, Troy Cullen, had finished first. They were a potential threat, and I noted the color of their jerseys.

Arnie's Redbirds had improved dramatically from the prior year. In addition to Troy, he was getting solid performances from his seniors, Jeff Schuetz and John Lange. The underclassmen on the team were also improving, with junior Jay Stauffacher and sophomores James Schuetz and Bob Cullen placing competitively in meets. Arnie's squad showed up on that soggy day with the solitary goal of qualifying for the state meet and becoming the first team in their school's history to stake that claim.

Watching our competition warm up did not help my mood. When it was time for the boys' race, we lined up on the chalk, and I looked at Scott's queasy face next to me.

"How ya doin'?" I asked.

He looked back with a grin. "Shitty. How 'bout you?"

We lurched forward at the crack of the starter's pistol. The course was well-groomed and gentle. It did not matter. Scott and I were like zombies floundering through a fog, begging for a quick end to our misery. The muscle weakness from the illness created an immediate onset of fatigue. I lagged my usual tempo, falling behind runners I normally beat and having little ability to respond. It was like being handcuffed in a fistfight, and it battered my ego. Scott's struggle was worse, enduring the stabbing impact of his swollen foot the entire time. We both finished nearly a minute off our usual pace.

The C-FC boys' team, on the left, at the Prairie du Sac Sectional starting line. October 22, 1983. Photo courtesy of Betty Rich.

When the team results were announced, to no one's surprise, Boscobel had won. Arkansaw was the runner-up, and both advanced to the state competition. Darlington placed third, a mere three points behind Arkansaw. A trivial, two-second shift in performance would have advanced the Redbirds to state. Troy had placed second behind the winner, Rich Dallman of Albany.

Troy's success was not enough to patch the wound for Arnie's team. Jeff Schuetz ran remarkably well. But it was his swan song run, and as seniors, he and John Lange would not be returning. The team felt as if the soul of the program had been ripped out of its center. It was a cruel loss, having been tantalizingly close to reaching their goal in what could have been a distinguishing moment. They could have been the first team to qualify for a state competition from their high school. The team was sullen on their trip south to Darlington under a bleak sky. In Arnie's mind, that gloomy cloud of doubt was hitching a ride with them.

Arnie looked at his kids' faces and addressed them.

"I know how you are feeling right now. We are all feeling it. Sometimes life is not fair. We are a good enough team to have qualified for state, and you have worked hard enough to deserve that reward. But it did not happen, and you should still be proud of the progress you have made. You don't run cross country for the glory. In life, you are rarely going to get a medal for doing a good job. They don't hand out trophies for being a good spouse or a good parent. You will not get a ribbon for paying your mortgage on time or for caring for your elderly parent. Sometimes your best work goes unnoticed. But you don't need that crap! Your satisfaction should come from within—from knowing that you did your best and that you made a difference. Seniors, you have led us to a new level of performance; you have laid the foundation so that others can build on that in the future. For the underclassmen, you need to honor that sacrifice and let this bitter pill drive you to greater achievement. Do not forget this feeling. Let it motivate you, and commit yourselves to being better."

Arnie's heart sank when he considered the forecast for the next season. He could do the math. The drop-off in performance, without Jeff on the team, spelled calamity for their chances to advance to the state meet in 1984. The Redbirds' sixth and seventh runners were a full two minutes behind Jeff in the race, and without those seniors in the mix, the team score would increase by roughly thirty points. It was the dilemma all small schools encountered, finding

The 1983 Darlington varsity boys' cross country team. From left to right: Bob Cullen, Doug Dunham, Jay Stauffacher, Jeff Schuetz, Troy Cullen, John Lange, and James Schuetz. Photo courtesy of Arnie Miehe.

at least five kids who could run near the front of a sectional race. It was exceedingly rare while competing with football for athletes. They had a strong squad with four of their best runners returning for the next season, but they lacked a runner who could replace Jeff. Arnie needed another runner who could push seventeen minutes and propel them toward a championship.

Our squad had fallen short again, placing fourth as a team, twenty points behind Darlington. Guy ran well enough to qualify for the state meet. My feelings were conflicted. The voice in my head wanted nothing more than to be done with that race. At the same time, it was our second poor performance in the same week. Maddeningly, there were no races left to reconcile my frustration. But unlike Darlington, we had not lost any seniors. That fact provided no salve for the wound. Watching Arkansaw advance to state after beating them so soundly in September seared our self-esteem. We felt cheated.

Mark was sitting near the back of the bus on the ride home. He was not his customarily animated self. He was tired of running and was hiding his feelings from the rest of the group. During the season, Mark had developed Osgood-Schlatter disease because of his abrupt growth spurt. It is a common condition, especially for athletes at that age who are running. It causes a tender bony bump at the top of the shin, just below the knee. The knee still functions properly, and there is little risk of damaging the joint. For most athletes, the condition recedes after the growth spurt is over. The usual treatment for the soreness is ibuprofen, but the symptoms can be worse for some kids. Mark had been competitive in our races, but he was not having fun and began to realize he did not like running. With his condition, each practice and each race had been a trial of pain. After the team's poor result in the sectional race, he began to ponder a change.

Gary was not on the bus after the sectional meet, and it felt colder and more dismal without him. He drove separately and was heading to the airport to catch a flight. Gary had set plans in place months before the cross country team had formed. It was his turn to race. He had entered the New York City Marathon and planned to join thousands of other contestants the next morning. The same weather system that had hampered our sectional moved into the mid-Atlantic. It rained on him the entire time. Rod Dixon of New Zealand ran five-minute miles the whole way and won the race in 2:8:59. Gary finished, soaked, in 3:22:23.

OCTOBER 29, 1983

The state meet was held at Christmas Mountain Village, a ski and golf resort near Wisconsin Dells.

Troy Cullen (in center with dark sweatpants) listens to instructions at the starting line of the 1983 boys' Class C championship race. On the right are C-FC's Guy Todd and coach Gary Brone. Photo courtesy of Arnie Miehe.

In the boys' race, Chetek won the Class C championship with their star senior, Al Severude, far outpacing the pack and finishing a few seconds under sixteen minutes. It was their second team title in two years. Boscobel placed fourth as a team, and Arkansaw came in fifth. Individually, Troy finished ninth, twenty seconds and three places in front of Guy.

Karen made the medal podium with a remarkable sixth-place finish in the girls' race. During the regional and sectional meets, Karen had been defeated by Jenny Tormoen, a fine runner from Port Edwards. On the Christmas Mountain course, there was a steep hill about a quarter mile from the finish. Gary's hill workouts gave Karen an edge that day. She passed Jenny on that slope and ascended it with strength. When she reached the top, no one was around her, and she sprinted down the last stretch to the chute. She surprised herself and all of us with her success. After high school, Karen would attend St. Olaf College in Northfield, Minnesota, to run track and cross country. In 1987 she was a varsity runner on St. Olaf's women's cross country team that finished sixth at the NCAA Division III National Championships. Karen only ran with us for one season before graduation, and she made the most of her opportunity.

Darlington's Troy Cullen attacks a vicious hill near the finish on the Christmas Mountain course. Cullen placed ninth at the 1983 state meet. Photo courtesy of the *Republican Journal*.

The unexpected potential revealed by the early victories and state qualifications had surprised the school district. Still, I was disheartened after the sectional run. The ride had been a roller coaster, lifting expectations above those of a losing culture to one where we had anticipated the possibility of running at the state meet. The opportunity had evaporated in an instant. I could not seem to escape mediocrity, and my feelings of bitterness returned. There had been a change inside me during the preceding months. We started our journey not knowing what to expect or where our running might lead. But over the season, I had come to expect excellence and victory. Hence, I felt the sting of disappointment. Had we not had success and new expectations, I might not have been as upset. Failure can spur determination, or it can cause withdrawal and despair. There is a conscious choice made when confronting it.

Karen Stettler. Photo courtesy of Karen (Stettler) Wilson.

Upon Guy and Karen's return from the state meet at Christmas Mountain, the rest of us celebrated with them above the hardware store. After supper, Gary had the group move into the living room and take their seats. The room was not big enough for a crowd, so a few sat on the hardwood floor. Gary sat in his chair with his back to the window overlooking North Main Street as he addressed our team. He wanted to set goals together for the next fall. That was something different: a coach pushing us to think about the future a year in advance. He did not want an easy goal either, but something that would challenge us to be better than we were. Gary knew we needed a purpose for our running in order to sacrifice and rise to our potential. He wanted something that would require his team to stay committed to a vision and accept some risk of failure. Our coach would not let us remain driftless as we had been in our first season.

We did not understand that when you reach for ambitious goals, the benefits are clutched by risk. Great accomplishments are surrounded by adversity. We did not grasp the value that comes from the struggle. We wanted the possibility of glory but with easy success and without risk of failure. Failure was all too real for us; why would we want to tempt more? Gary worked on us by probing with questions and appealing to our sense of possibility.

"Guys, think about it. You were undefeated in your dual meets this year, and you placed first as a team in three out of the five invitationals you raced in—against bigger schools! You've already beaten Altoona and Arkansaw. And both of those squads placed in the top five at the state meet today. We've only just begun our training. You've gotta believe that we'll be improved next year, so why couldn't we do better?"

Gary never questioned our potential, and he maintained his constancy of purpose. He worked to convince those around us that anything was possible for our team. Gary had to believe for us when we could not believe for ourselves. This was especially true when we faced adversity.

After some discussion, we decided to reach for an undefeated regular season and qualify for the state meet in 1984. We had failed to reach both new aspirations in 1983, so there was some risk. No team from our school had ever reached a state competition before; if we could get there, it would be a first. The goals were a natural progression, and they would drive us to make sacrifices. We still had something to prove to ourselves, but it needed to simmer for a time.

The Jackals ended their senior football season with a 5–4 record. Father Time usurped their power, and they withdrew to the den of anonymity.

A yearbook photo shows the Cochrane-Fountain City High School entrance during an early 1980s winter.

Shortly after our team meeting above the hardware store, winter gripped the landscape. Walks outdoors came with a stark reminder of nature's authority. The chatter of birds and squirrels had ceased. In a single night, the bluffs were blanketed with white fleece. Trees perforated the new coat, sheathing the bare razorbacks with quills. Ice seized the countryside, and stillness reigned, rarely broken by a milk room pump or a shrieking coyote. As the sun yielded to a taciturn moon, nightfall's chill descended through the coulees, carrying the faint scent of wood smoke with each stinging draw. Warm thoughts of a distant stove struggled to pierce the desolation.

CHAPTER THIRTEEN

RENEWAL

On schoolday mornings, it was common for kids to assemble in the gym prior to the bell and shoot baskets in their street clothes and sneakers. One winter morning, Mark and several other sophomore players were running at the baskets and leaping to see if they could grab the rim. It was a test of prowess. The WIAA had just allowed dunking in games, and nearly every kid wanted to hear the crowd thunder when he slammed the ball through the net. Most were in awe of Michael Jordan, the great basketball star. Dunking had been prohibited until the early eighties, and most kids of reasonable talent and average size could not dunk a basketball—and never would. Working on shooting proficiency, free throws, or ball handling was far more productive. But the lure of the crowd's adulation tempted the young athletes to strive toward a dunk in a game. Mark was a couple of inches over six feet and had good leaping ability. As a sophomore, he had not conquered the dunk, but he was getting better. As his friends watched, Mark trotted toward the hoop and reached for the rim, grabbing the edge with one hand and pulling the breakaway hinge down. It was a major step, and after dropping to the floor, he looked back at his peers with his toothy smile.

At that moment, Guy walked along the bleachers, heading toward his locker before class.

Mark called to him, "Hey, Guy! D'ya think you can touch the rim?"

Guy had not played organized basketball, and he stood five feet, eight inches tall. He was a wrestler in the winter months. When Mark called him out in front of the other kids, Guy approached the hoop. Then, in one swift motion, he exploded off the hardwood and grabbed the rim with both hands, plunging the hinge downward. After swinging on the hoop, he floated to the floor. Mark stammered in surprise, and the other sophomores stood speechless. Guy glanced over his shoulder with a sly grin and walked out of the gym, never saying a word.

Our basketball season ended with a handful of wins and three times more losses. Mark gained some valuable floor time on the varsity squad as a sophomore, and the team's record was slightly improved from the prior year when we had only won a single game. But the victories had not come easily, and our team's record was another bitter pill to swallow. Mediocrity persisted. I could accept losing as a normal part of life, but the relentless losses dampened my mood after another dismal season. My knee throbbed ceaselessly, and the swelling took several weeks to recede after the last game.

During the winter season, the Darlington Redbirds' basketball team produced another losing record. The bitter taste of losing did not fade quickly for Troy. He now had another challenge before him: passing his college entrance exams. Troy wanted to go to college, but he wasn't sure he could if he didn't do better on his tests at school. Math had always been a struggle, and his algebra assignments were maddening. His teammates, Tom and Jay, excelled at science and math. He needed someone he could trust alongside him as he tackled his assignments. That person was Tom. Troy started visiting the Evenstads' home in the evenings so Tom could help him with his algebra.

Teamwork is an intricate web and often goes unseen. Troy helped Tom become a better runner, and Tom helped Troy become a better student. We all have unique strengths and unique challenges. We are not perfect creatures, and frequently our strengths and challenges are not obvious. The strongest bonds formed between us develop under shared hardship in life. We're better off combining our strengths to cover our individual limitations. The benefits are revealed when facing adversity together rather than alone. Troy Cullen went on to graduate from the University of Wisconsin–La Crosse and became a successful high school basketball coach—and a remarkable math teacher.

Tom Evenstad poses with the children and staff of the Darlington Day Care Center after receiving a certificate of appreciation for his Eagle Scout community service project that created a playground for the center. Photo courtesy of the *Republican Journal*.

As winter transitioned to spring, I was applying to universities. Scott and I spent a Saturday morning together at Winona State, taking our ACT exams. It was another reminder that our time together was slipping away. Springtime was track season, starting with cold workouts on gray afternoons in snow, rain, and mud. I began logging miles in mid-March and ran along the shoreline of Buffalo City to build my endurance. Those workouts provided a chance to shrug off the ghosts of the basketball season. Among them were the ten pounds I had gained after we finished running cross country in the fall. The city's streets stretched along the river's edge for miles. It was a bedroom community, so the traffic was always light, and it made for a nice training run as I prepared for track and field. Large shards of ice were still clinging to the banks of the Mississippi, their counterparts floating away in the current. I could hear the ice bellow from the warmth, pleading audibly for winter to hold its bonds. But signs of life were also emerging along the shoreline. The eagles were back, sometimes perched on a limb over the pewter surface of the water. Other times I'd spy them standing directly on the ice, feeding on thawing fish claimed by winter. The hardiest species of waterfowl were returning ahead of the throngs of songbirds. Canada geese were flying sorties and staking new claims as the retreat of winter ceded more marsh. Mallards, mergansers, and scaup were there, braving the frigid waters in their brilliant plumage. The waterfowl bugled the advance of spring. They were the last to leave and the first to return, a colorful squadron probing against the southernmost front of winter. They skirmished with the ice for months. Some battled all winter if they found a sliver of open water. Each year, an overnight freeze took casualties that could not escape winter's clutch.

Woodpeckers and nuthatches were still amongst the trees, easily identified by their sawing jabber, even if they were hard to spy. They were seemingly unaware of the company they'd shortly receive. The squirrels were emerging from their leaf nests on more frequent forays to the ground, searching for nuts they'd cached in the fall. The air was very cool, not unlike the temperature in the early winter. Yet, it seemed easier to draw into my lungs with the returning daylight.

Track and field had something for everyone and nearly all body types or abilities. Distance runners, jumpers, sprinters, throwers, and acrobats all had something that fit their skills. Coaches of other sports encouraged their players to join the track team to hone their speed and agility. It was not difficult to fill the roster for track and field; hormones were compelling recruiters. The sport offered a co-ed experience with girls' and boys' teams using the same practice facilities and riding the buses together to track meets. It was also a chance to form new friendships with kids from other schools. By May, the sunshine was warm, and the songs of life were in the air.

While I enjoyed both track and cross country, there were differences in the two running sports. Track had many individual races with specialists for each race. It lacked team tactics other than the coach distributing the runners into events where they could maximize points. There were times when even that objective could be compromised so an individual could qualify to advance to a state meet. Team championships and team trophies were awarded in track, but it was essentially an individual sport where the individuals reaped the accolades.

Cross country, on the other hand, was a team sport that depended upon individual contribution. All the competitors were on the same course, at the same time, running the same race. In cross country, runners had to deal with uneven terrain, multiple surfaces, sharp corners, and hills. We were immersed in nature's amphitheater rather than running laps on a paved oval. A runner's speed was always better on the track, but the tactics in cross country were more intriguing. Maneuvers used on hills, turns, and pack hunting were opportunities for teams to affect an outcome beyond their raw talent. The team result was the focus; the individual results were secondary. The fifth runner was even more important than the first. We wanted to perform well as individuals, but the fulfillment came through the team's success. We celebrated team victories in cross country and were somber in team losses despite our individual performances. In cross country we ran for each other, not for ourselves.

The junior prom came as spring merged with the end of the school year. Most of us were involved in hanging streamers, setting up tables, and filling balloons with helium for the big event. In the early eighties, the girls' gowns were generally short-sleeved pastels. Wrist corsages were popular. Most of the guys rented tuxedos with cummerbunds and bow ties to match the girls' dresses. Boutonnieres were pinned to the lapels of their jackets. The teenagers packed themselves into their parents' cars and drove to restaurants for a meal prior to the dance. Guy was on the court, and Scott was crowned prom king in the spring of 1984. I was asked to emcee the ceremony, and Karen accompanied me to the dance that evening. As was customary, there was live music on the stage. But Mark's breakdancing performance was what captivated the crowd, including his freezes, backspins, moonwalking, and the worm.

Darlington High School had limited homecoming court to only boys who played football. No such traditions existed for the junior prom, and Tom Evenstad was voted prom king in the spring of 1984.

It was a late night, but Tom and the others still got up for ten-

Holy Rosary Catholic Church, Darlington, Wisconsin. Photo by Jeff Rich.

thirty Mass at Holy Rosary down the street. Groggy from a lack of sleep, Troy sat in the pew and fought to keep his eyelids up as the priest droned on with the service.

Afterward, he and the Evenstad brothers wandered down to the 76 station. Kent Ruppert was already there. As the only son in a farm family with five girls, he looked for opportunities to hang out with the guys. A few of the football players had also shown up to drink soda and hear the gossip after the prom. Brian Whalen was among them. He had attended Mass with Tom and Troy after milking cows that morning. Brian had sandy hair, strong legs, and a six-foot frame. His broad shoulders tapered to a narrow waist. He was another farm kid accustomed to hard work, and he was going to be Darlington's starting quarterback in the fall. His buddies nicknamed him "Helmer."

After Tom stepped inside, Brian looked at him and smiled.

"Hey, Evie, are those bags under your eyes? Did you have a little too much fun last night?"

Tom set down his soda, removed his sunglasses, and leveled his gaze at Whalen.

"Helmer, do you think you could make it through a 5K without puking?"

Troy chimed in, "Nah, he'd be heaving halfway through. Besides, look at him. He'd rather get pummeled for sixty minutes in front of the cheerleaders!"

"You better stock up on detergent," Tom retorted. "You're going to have a lot of grass stains on the back of your jersey!"

Brian was good-humored with his friends and smiled at their jeers. But they had touched a nerve that he had been keeping buried. The boys were close enough that Troy and Tom sensed an unspoken opportunity. They'd all gone to grade school at Holy Rosary together, and each could read the other like a book. Their teasing was intended to induce their friend to spend more time with them in the fall. Brian was tired of taking hits at quarterback, and more than anything, he was sick of losing. The football team had been winless his junior year with an offensive line that averaged a paltry 160 pounds per man. Brian had been chased around the field in each game. He went through most of the season with a bruised tailbone from getting crushed by opposing defenses. Brian wanted to taste winning like his buddies had. But he did not disclose what he was wrestling with inside. His dad had played football on Darlington's conference championship teams during the 1950s, and Brian did not want to disappoint him. He already felt guilty for playing sports when he knew his folks were struggling on the farm.

Tom and Marilyn Whalen raised three daughters and three boys. Brian and his brother, Kevin, were the two youngest and were needed to help milk their 150 cows in a 53-stall barn twice each day. The seven-hundred-acre property took a huge effort to manage most of the year. On a typical summer day, they'd put up fifteen wagonloads of hay in addition to their milking chores, fencing, and other needs around the farm. The anemic milk prices and debt of the operation were stacking financial pressure on his parents. Brian could see the worry in their faces. He felt torn between his desire to play sports and his sense of duty to his family. There was time left to deliberate. Football was still king in Darlington, and walking away from the starting quarterback position would carry consequences.

The track-and-field season was in full swing by May. Arnie was coaching Darlington's team and discovered some new talent. One surprise was Todd Johnson, who had been on the golf team his freshman year, but as a sophomore, he abruptly quit golfing to join the track squad mid-season. When the lanky kid showed up for practices, he was clearing six feet in the high jump and posted a four-hundred-meter time under fifty-four seconds in his first meet. That performance showed overlooked potential, and Arnie took notice. Some sprinters can will themselves into becoming good cross country runners, but it exacts a price. That level of endurance demands hundreds of miles during the offseason to transform oneself into a formidable distance runner. Arnie could see the possibility, but Todd would need to commit if he was going to contribute on the varsity cross country squad in the fall.

One day, shortly after classes ended, I drove to Fountain City and parked in front of the auditorium on North Main. I trotted across the street and stepped into the hardware store. The bell above the door jingled as I entered, and the scent of past decades rose from the hardwood floor to greet me. Gary was behind the counter helping another customer, so I looked around for a minute. The building had been used for its merchandising for a long time. There was an old wood-fired stove in the center of the store with its pipe rising through the tin ceiling. The wooden counter and cash register were in front of the brick on the north wall. Displayed prominently behind the counter was a glass case holding stone field points gathered by a former owner. It was a remarkable collection of local artifacts from the Paleolithic and Woodland tribes that had inhabited the hills of the region for centuries. The relics were mostly knapped from chert found within the limestone of the surrounding bluffs, but there were also a few items made from silicified sandstone or other materials that had traveled many miles through trade. The case included corner and side-notched tips, spear points, scrapers, ax heads, fishhooks, awls, and stone knives. Most customers stared at the collection and pondered the original purpose of the hardware before purchasing their own made of steel.

By June, Gary was selling bikes for supplemental income, and he had a variety of foreign racing bikes displayed. He was passionate about endurance sports, and biking was a way to cross-train and stay fit. For me, a workout on a bike was preferable to pounding my knee on the pavement during a long run. The speed was exhilarating, and I covered more ground. Bike racing had a natural allure for endurance athletes, and my teammates and I were fascinated.

"Hi, Jeff! What can I help you with?"

"Hi, Coach. I was thinking I might buy one of those road bikes you're displaying, but I'm not sure which one. I've saved a couple of hundred bucks, but I want to hear what you think about each of them."

Gary launched into his sales pitch, extolling the features of each bike to help me with the decision.

Several of us purchased our first road bikes from Gary in the summer of 1984 to mix up our training regimen. I started climbing the bluffs on long rides and became addicted to the speed on the descents. I convinced my brother Kevin to drive the car in front of me so I could draft behind it. He clocked the speed on the declines at between fifty and sixty miles per hour. At times, I was able to ride with Scott and Mark. None of us wore helmets back then, and the behavior carried risks, which, being sixteen, I ignored. I got lucky that summer and avoided a serious accident.

After chatting with Gary about the bikes, I drove to the south end of town, stopped at the ball diamond, and pulled a load of heavy bags out of my trunk. On most weekday mornings, I held practice for the Fountain City Little League team. The high school had restarted its baseball program the previous summer. I had once been a shortstop but chose not to play, deciding that the abuse to my knee was not worth it. Instead, I coached the Little League team before my senior year and made the drive to Fountain City regularly. Gasoline prices had risen above a dollar per gallon, keeping my wallet thin, but I enjoyed working with the younger kids. I was able to share some of my knowledge of the sport despite having to give it up. The ritual included batting and fielding, during which I was frequently the pitcher and the hitter running the crew through their drills. By the time I arrived, the kids were waiting for me on their bikes and helped me carry the bags inside the fence. In a few minutes, the tinny chime of the aluminum bat rang out as I pulled my shoulders through and vaulted a ball to the center fielder. The fifth-grader took a drop step and twisted his torso for a sprint toward the fence. He made the catch before the ball hit the ground and gathered himself. Dust was kicking off the cleats of the base runner rounding for home as the ball sailed to the plate. I stood back and watched the catcher, Jesse Brone, step up and retrieve the ball before sweeping it against the sliding runner's leg. Even at that early age, he had potential as an athlete, much like his older brother.

Many of my classmates lived on farms just a few miles to the east and worked from dawn until dusk, all summer long, milking cows and doing chores. Some of them never got the chance to learn to swim or spend a day fishing on the river. There were no "lazy days of summer" on the farm.

Paul and Dan were two of those kids. They spent their summers under an oppressive sun, itchy from hay and choking on its dust. Although Paul lived with his parents during the school year, he spent summers on his cousin's dairy farm in Irish Valley, east of Waumandee. Paul's cousin Roger was his senior by fifteen years, and Paul worked for him as a hired hand. Paul did not have a car and had to borrow Roger's truck to go to town. He lived there all summer, and we did not see him much during that time. Once school started, Paul spent his weekends working on the same farm. Dan was hired as a hand on another farm along Highway 95 between Fountain City and Arcadia. After the summer toil ended, he got the chance to further his punishment on that same road with Gary's hill workouts.

The farm kids in Darlington were accustomed to sharing the burden during haying season. Many would make the rounds to each other's farms and assist one another with the weather-dependent labor. Once cut and dried, it was imperative to get the hay baled before the next rain came and spoiled the crop. They became familiar with each haymow. The Kelly family's mow was exceptional in one respect. They had a full basketball court inside with hoops on each end, surrounded by bales. The kids would use it to play "barn ball." There were few rules in barn ball. Dribbling wasn't required, and tackling was permitted. If you could reach the end of the court, you could launch yourself off a bale and dunk on the nine-foot rims. One day, Shawn Hauser and several other classmates showed up at the Kelly farm to play barn ball together. Soon afterward, Dale was running toward the rim when he took a severe hit in the jaw.

He stood up with a bloody mouth and said, "I think my lip is bleeding. Shawn, take a look at my mouth."

Hauser went over for the inspection, and his own mouth dropped open.

"Dude! I can see the inside of your tongue!"

Thinking that Shawn was joking with him, Dale scoffed at the comment.

"Give me the ball and let's keep playing."

Shawn pulled the ball back from his hands and said, "No, man. I'm serious! You just bit through your tongue!"

Later that day, Dale had emergency surgery to repair the barn ball damage.

JUNE 7, 1984

It was early in the morning, and Arnie found himself sitting on a hard plastic chair in the middle of a high school cafeteria in St. Louis, Missouri. Dozens of other fit individuals were assembled in the room with him, including Cardinals' shortstop Ozzie Smith and former Olympic gold-medalist sprinter Wilma Rudolph. They were each among the 3,636 torchbearers in the Olympic torch relay through the United States that summer. On that day in early June, the torch was passing through St. Louis. In the spring, Arnie had seen an advertisement in *Runner's World* magazine seeking nominations for torchbearers in the relay. The relay was used as a fundraiser for the Youth Legacy Kilometre Programme, and each nominating organization was required to raise $2,000 in donations for an entrance fee. The Darlington community, high school, and cross country parents raised the funds, and Arnie was designated as a torchbearer. On that day in St. Louis, he carried the Olympic flame toward Los Angeles for his one-thousand-meter segment. After finishing, each torchbearer was allowed to keep their torch. To this day, Arnie keeps the 1984 Olympic souvenir at his home.

The next evening Arnie made the long trip from St. Louis to Darlington. Upon returning, he heard some harrowing news. A series of strong storms had passed through Iowa into Wisconsin the night before, spawning devastating tornadoes in their path. The worst was an F5 twister that directly hit the small town of Barneveld, forty miles north of Darlington. The village of six hundred residents was leveled, and the tornado killed nine people. Tornadoes were not uncommon in the southwest corner of the state, but they rarely carried such scale and cruelty. The damage reached tens of millions of dollars. Word traveled quickly, and residents in the surrounding communities responded to the immediate need for help.

I occasionally ran in a road race at one of the local events to stay sharp during the summer. In early July, Mark decided to run with me in a five-mile race in Nelson, north of Alma. It was a hot day, and the course was set up on a gentle road near the river bottoms. We had both been putting in some miles over the summer, and we set out on an aggressive pace. A couple of experienced runners finished ahead of us, but Mark crossed the line with me in twenty-nine minutes. We were pleased. It was a respectable time, considering our cross country season was still a month away.

The following weekend I traveled through Nelson once again toward the shores of Lake Pepin for the Pepin tournament. The small community on the Mississippi's big lake held a two-day baseball tournament for dozens of Little League teams from the region each summer. It was the eagerly anticipated crowning event for the small-town kids. My teams from Fountain City were entered, and two advanced to the final. The fourteen-and-under team captured the championship in their division. It had been a long time since that had happened for a Fountain City Little League team, and it was the capstone to a winning season. The ten-and-under game took place afterward on the lower field with a dusty diamond and no outfield fence. It was a hot day, and a crowd had gathered to watch the final contest.

The Brone family had shown up to watch Jesse play. With roles reversed, Mark sat in the bleachers eating hot dogs and swallowing Mello Yello. The game did not start well, and the opponent jumped out to an early lead. By the bottom of the final inning, I was standing on the third base line clutching my clipboard and pencil. We still trailed by one run, and our first two batters had struck out. The next batter connected with the ball and got to first base safely. Hope was still alive as Jesse approached the plate with a look of determination. His first swing was a clean miss, and he stepped out of the box and took a couple of practice swings. On the second pitch, he connected but sliced the ball foul near the first base line. Jesse grimaced skyward and stepped back to adjust his helmet. I called over to him, and he glanced my way.

"Keep your swing level and watch the ball meet the bat. Come on now; you can do this!"

When the next pitch made it to the plate, the bat chimed, and the crowd erupted. The ball leapt beyond the infield like a missile. The center and right fielders raced toward each other, and the ball squeezed past them before they could close, bounding into the brown grass beyond. The right fielder planted his foot to change direction, but the dry turf failed to hold his cleats, and his legs went out from underneath him. The center fielder nearly tripped over his teammate and rounded toward the ball as it raced away. Seizing the moment of chaos, I shouted to our first runner and frantically carved circles in the air with my arm to motion him toward home plate. As Jesse rounded second base, his eyes locked with mine, and I sent him ahead, chasing his teammate. By that time, the center fielder had picked up the ball but was more than two hundred feet from the plate. The kid's arm and Jesse's feet would decide the issue. As Jesse rounded third base, the ball was bounding past the cutoff man toward the catcher. Judee's voice rose above the din and beckoned her son forward. Jesse accelerated out of the turn and, with a few more strides, stretched his legs into a slide, sending his helmet bouncing in the dirt. The catcher swept his arm through the cloud of dust and slapped Jesse's shin. But the ball broke free and rolled into the cage, sending the umpire's arms outward. "Safe!" The dugout emptied and mayhem ensued. Mark's little brother was in the spotlight.

After Little League ended in late summer, I started to prepare for the upcoming archery season. Like most boys in the area, I loved to deer hunt, and I'd purchased a used bow from Scott the previous fall. I was instantly hooked and never missed a chance to escape to the woods. The season opened in mid-September, so one day I made a trip to Adler's Gun Shop in Cochrane to purchase new broadheads for my arrows. Scott's parents owned the business, which was attached to their home on Main Street. They sold hunting equipment, guns, fishing tackle, and archery gear. Scott's family struggled financially, and he frequently helped his dad tend the shop. Arden Adler had come from hardscrabble beginnings, often without enough food to eat. He did not graduate from high school and worked two jobs to make sure his kids had food on the table. In addition to working in the shop, Scott bused tables, cleaned dishes, and cooked at a restaurant in Buffalo City. He had an impeccable work ethic. Scott was quick to offer his help to others and never complained about his troubles. When he competed, I could see the fire in him that wanted a better life than his parents had.

As I stepped inside their shop, Scott was behind the counter with his mom, Carol. She looked up as I closed the door.

"Hi, Jeff! How are you today?"

"I'm fine, Mrs. Adler. I just thought I'd get some things for the archery season."

She smiled at me and addressed her son.

"Scott, I have some laundry to fold inside, so if you need me, just ring the buzzer."

Despite raising three kids, Carol had a gentle and quiet demeanor. Her voice provided a calming presence in a room, which she had used effectively as a den mother for our group of eight-year-old Cub Scouts years earlier. She had always been thin, but I noticed she was even thinner now. Though my mother tried to hide it, her face wore a look of concern when we would see Carol at church. Carol had been diagnosed with multiple sclerosis (MS), and bouts from the disease had been pillaging her nervous system by the time she was in her forties. It was not a secret, and most of the community knew what she was facing, but we did not talk about it. There wasn't much anybody could do to change the progression of the disease, so we all tried to carry on as normally as possible. But inside, everyone was worried, and her plight was visible to us.

After his mother stepped out of the room, Scott faced the shelving on the wall and continued stocking ammunition.

"Did you hear about Mark?"

"No. What?"

"He is planning on going out for football in the fall."

Scott's head dropped as he said it. "I heard from Paul," he went on. "He said Mark mentioned it to him."

I could feel the heat build in my cheeks.

"Well, that won't work!" I said. "He's the one that started this thing and asked us to go out for the team a year ago! If Mark goes, then Dan will probably go with him. We won't have five runners for a team."

"And we need a good fifth runner," Scott said. "Not just anybody."

There was a short pause as we both considered the situation.

"Do you know if Gary has spoken with him?" I asked. "I mean, really, was that goal to reach state together just a bunch of crap? Doesn't Mark see that he is a key to making that happen? Do you think Gary will quit coaching cross country if Mark plays football?"

"I don't know," Scott replied, "Do you think there is someone else we could recruit?"

I thought about it for a few seconds. "How about Dan Walker?"

Scott looked at me and raised his eyebrows. Dan Walker was one of our classmates. He was on the wrestling team with Scott and did not play football. He did not run high school track either, but he had consistently beaten Scott and me in grade school. Dan had the genes to be a good distance runner and kept himself in excellent physical shape.

"Possibly. But remember, we talked to him last year, and he didn't want to come out when we started the team. I'll talk to him again, but he seems more interested in running after girls right now."

"Okay," I said. "I'd forgotten that. Ask him anyway. Beg if you have to."

We both thought for a moment, and then Scott offered, "What about Steve Phillips?"

Steve Phillips was the best natural distance runner in our class. He had beaten Guy Todd in our elementary and junior high track meets. He was nearly six feet tall, with long legs and a respectable stride. But his best gift was his indifference to pain. Steve seemed to enjoy starting a race with an insane pace and running people into the ground. He wasn't a great sprinter, but we had never seen him wear down in a race before all of the other runners fell apart. There was only one problem: Steve was a farm kid from a poor family.

"Do you know why he quit track our freshman year?" I asked Scott.

"His old man made him quit so he could help with the chores on the farm. Steve loves to run; he would have rejoined the track team if he could have this past spring. Paul spoke with him last fall when Mark was recruiting us, and Steve had to say no. We can ask him to talk to Steve again, but I bet that door has closed."

We both thought through our classmates and those underclassmen who might have potential. After a few minutes of scratching our heads, we could not come up with another candidate.

The conversation with Scott boiled up the frustration within me. I kept wondering what Gary knew and why he wasn't letting us know about our predicament—if it were true. When I got home, I gave him a call at the hardware store.

"I'm hearing rumors that Mark is going to quit our team and go out for football this fall."

"Jeff, I can't believe it," Gary said, "but that is what he has been saying. I don't know what has gotten into him."

I almost dropped the phone and could not contain my frustration any longer.

"What! How can that be? If Mark leaves, then Dan will leave too. We won't have enough runners to race as a team. It won't matter if we have four guys who can run a course under seventeen minutes. Without Mark, we have no chance of reaching our goal!"

"I know, Jeff," Gary said calmly. "I've tried talking with him several times, but I'm not getting through. He keeps complaining about how his knee is hurting him. I don't know what to do."

There was no doubt Mark was feeling pain from Osgood-Schlatter's. Then again, we were all feeling some pain from various ailments, and I was in no mood to let someone lecture me about running with knee pain. Mark had a high pain threshold and could push through more suffering than most teenagers if he wanted to. I had seen him run well in some grueling races.

"Gary, I'm not buying it. Mark just ran that race with me in Nelson, and he wasn't complaining to me then. I think he is looking past this year in his head."

There was a pause, so I asked Gary, "Do you mind if I talk with Mark about it?"

"I think that would be a good idea, Jeff. I don't see how it could hurt. I can't seem to get through to him, but maybe he will listen to you."

Gary got Mark and handed him the phone.

"Mark," I began, "I can't believe what I'm hearing. Why would you leave us? What is the issue?"

"Smiley, my knee is hurting me every time I run."

I took a breath before replying.

"How do you think my knee feels each time we run? You didn't seem to have any trouble the other day when we ran in Nelson. If you're worried about your knees, why would you ever consider playing football? Can't you see what happened to me?"

I then appealed to him to reconsider.

"Mark, don't you see the opportunity we have together? That's not gonna happen for the football team or for any other team sport you're likely to play at our high school."

"You don't know that!" Mark shot back.

I changed my negotiating tactics and threw some guilt at him.

"How could you abandon us at this point after the sacrifices the other guys have made? Scott gave up his starting position in football last year. Do you think that was easy for him? For Pete's sake, you were the one who pulled us together in the library and asked us to join this team!"

I paused for a moment, and Mark was silent, suddenly considering the impact on others.

I went on.

"What about the effort your parents have put into this, Mark?"

"This isn't about my parents!" he snapped. "They'll support me no matter what I do!"

The lack of consideration for those close to him made me furious. I changed tactics again and became very sharp with him.

I knew that Mark loved basketball. He had played on varsity the prior season, and his prospects were rising. He had noticeable talent. Despite my knee troubles, I was the captain of the basketball team.

"Listen here, you skinny shit! I'll see to it that you ride the bench in basketball."

For good measure I threw in, "Oh, and don't think you're going to play football either. Adler and I will beat the piss out of you once school starts. You better grow some eyes in the back of your head!"

I hung up the phone, partly for effect and partly out of fear of what his answer might be.

The threat was an ugly tactic, perhaps even worse than Mark's fickle commitment to our team. It was a bluff, although Mark did not know it. I knew he was not yet confident in himself, and I was banking on Mark caving to the pressure in that moment, or we would both lose. The tactic was one the Jackals used to force compliance, and I detested the fact that I'd copied their example. It was in direct conflict with the person I wanted to be. I was not the kind of kid who would have followed through with violence to solve a problem, and I was ashamed afterward.

Mark's indifference had stung as I had laid my heart bare on the phone. The cross country season had become more important to me than the basketball season. It was no longer something I did to fill time and stay in shape for other sports. It had replaced something in me that had been lost after my injury. I had begun to cherish our opportunity together and understood its fragility. Mark could not yet see the gem in his hands amid the stones.

I did not discuss the threats I gave to Mark that day with anyone else. The gamble could have ruined a number of relationships.

One hundred and sixty miles to the south, Arnie Miehe was preparing supper when the phone rang. He picked up the receiver, and Brian Whalen's voice was on the other end of the line.

"Coach, I'd like to run cross country this fall if it is okay with you."

Arnie nearly dropped the phone. It was more than okay with him; he had the sense that Brian could be quickly developed into a contributor for his squad.

Brian had become frustrated with the football team's losing seasons and wanted a change for his senior year. There was another factor in his decision to switch sports. He had taken Arnie's health class in the fall semester, and Arnie had provided Brian with a new experience. In December, he'd invited Brian to join a group of runners for a Saturday trip to Madison to run the Frigid Five fun run. Brian finished the five-mile race and found that he enjoyed the experience. Miehe had made him feel welcome despite his novice status as a runner. It convinced Brian that he could run even if he really didn't know much about the sport.

Arnie told Brian to begin logging miles and what to expect when practice started in mid-August. He hung up the phone and sat down at the table to eat. The phone call was a potential solution to the problem Arnie had been wrestling with since his team lost their number two runner, Jeff Schuetz, to graduation. Darlington's first four runners were solid, but there was a big drop-off after that. The younger runners could not yet step up and fill the gap. Whalen was an all-around athlete with quick feet. It remained to be seen if he could race well for five thousand meters, but suddenly there was a ray of hope for the Redbirds' 1984 campaign.

The late afternoon sun was beating down on me, and I was awash with sweat on our concrete driveway. It was a daily routine that lasted for an hour or more. I repeated post moves, jump shots, ball handling, and free throws during the ritual to keep my skills sharp. My palms were slick, and my eyes were stinging as I focused on my free throws. My self-imposed requirement was ten in a row before I could finish. As I released the ball on my tenth shot, the phone rang in the house. The ball hit the front of the rim, bounced off the backboard, and fell through the net, sparing me another round. My mom answered the phone and called out the kitchen window to let me know it was for me. When I stepped inside the door, she was cupping the receiver with her hand and whispered that it was Gary Brone.

"Hi, Gary! What's up?"

"Hey there, Jeff, I just wanted to let you know that Mark decided to go out for cross country this fall. So, everything seems to be back on track."

I paused for a moment to absorb what he had said. We had nearly lost our team, but to Mark's credit, he had considered the consequences for others with his decision.

"Wow, is that ever a relief!"

Gary went on, "No kidding, I didn't know what I was going to do. What did you say to him?"

"Oh, I just asked him to reconsider and think about the other guys."

Mark and I never spoke of our phone conversation again and went on as we had before as teammates. No harm, no foul. The rest of the team knew that we had spoken but did not know the details, only that Mark had changed his mind.

CHAPTER FOURTEEN
A COHESIVE TEAM

The next week I was shooting baskets again in the driveway when the ball slipped out of my wet hands and bounced across the street. Before I could cross, the postman pulled up and reached through the window to give me our mail. One of the envelopes in the bundle was addressed to me. It was a letter Gary had sent to each team member prior to the start of the season. In it, he gave some details about the first practice that was approaching on August 13. He also reinforced that those who had not been running should start immediately. He stated that he was expecting a great season and that we would be working hard to achieve our goals.

The letter created a problem for Paul. His cousin, Roger, needed him on the farm. The workers were putting in incredible hours to get everything done, and he could not afford to lose a hand.

Paul felt an obligation to help Roger during the difficulty. He also needed the income to buy necessities for himself. Gary needed each of us to start some strenuous workouts by August if we were going to be prepared for the fall season. If one of us failed to do that, the whole team would fail.

Despite our efforts, there were no new recruits on the boys' team. The success of the previous season had not yet sparked enough interest. We still lacked the depth to withstand injuries if they developed. In other sports, advancing to a state competition with a few exceptional players and a solid supporting cast is possible. However, in cross country, a team with fewer than five outstanding runners cannot get there. A squad can have the four fastest runners in the sectional and still not qualify if the fifth runner is slow. With just six runners, we were one shy of a full squad, but we still met the scoring minimum of five and believed we had a cohesive team. There was just one problem: Paul was working on the farm in Irish Valley full-time.

That first week in August of 1984 was stifling in the Upper Mississippi watershed. In the evenings, I retreated to the air-conditioning and watched the broadcast of the Olympics in Los Angeles. The Cold War was still being waged, and the Soviet Union had boycotted the games. As a result, the U.S. dominated the medal count. Mary Lou Retton was winning the country's heart in gymnastics. Carl Lewis was adding to his treasure chest in the long jump and sprints. I watched with humility and disbelief as Joaquim Cruz of Brazil set an Olympic record in the men's eight hundred meters, twenty seconds faster than I'd run it during the spring. No matter how fast you think you are, someone is always faster.

The running events were among my favorites, but one stood out dramatically. On August 5, the women's marathon took place under a hot sun. Joan Benoit of the U.S. crossed the line first and captured the gold. But the runner who shocked the audience was Gabriela Andersen-Schiess. Schiess was from Switzerland and had won two marathons in the U.S. the prior year. When she entered the Los Angeles Coliseum for the final four hundred meters of the race, she was not herself. The heat had brought her to the point of collapse, and she had lost full command of her limbs. She swayed and lurched on the track, stopping several times to hold her head. Race officials approached, and she refused to let them touch her, fearing disqualification. She had hit the wall so hard that she was in peril. It took her nearly six minutes to make that final lap on the track when it should have taken her one. The medical staff swarmed to her side when she crossed the line and rendered care. Schiess recovered, but the troubling sight of her last lap caused me to pause and consider the human condition. What could possess someone to do that to herself? What medal could possibly be worth that level of suffering and risk? I had not yet experienced a race so consequential, one in which I'd been pushed to the precipice and could not turn back.

The first practice of the new season started the next week. I pulled into the school parking lot and stepped out of the car. Scott, Mark, and Dan were already there jabbering under the morning sun. As I walked up to meet them, the jabber ceased, and their heads turned abruptly, staring past my shoulder. Mark's jaw dropped open, and Scott's grin widened.

Dan shouted, "What in the hell—did he tell you guys about this?"

I turned to see what the fuss was about and nearly fell over. An orange 1971 Mustang spun into the lot with a throaty growl. It gleamed under the sunlight as Loverboy's "Turn Me Loose" blared from the aftermarket speakers. The vehicle terrorized the pavement like a tiger before screeching to a halt at my feet. I was speechless for a moment while I watched Guy exit the car. His shades concealed the gleam in his eye.

"Hello, boys. How ya doin'?"

We smothered him in an instant, and the jabber resumed. Guy had cashed in his savings on the muscle car. We all coveted it, and none of us turned down the opportunity to join him for a ride when he offered. After the semester started, we rode that beast through the Winona State campus, seeking attention from co-eds.

Some new recruits had joined the girls' squad. They had lost Karen to graduation but had added Dana Duellman, Vicki Blank, Janet Brommer, and Teresa Jumbeck to the roster. It was a vote of credibility. The girls' squad was attracting a broader group of kids.

Heidi was starting to fill her sister's shoes as the girls' captain. She had distinguished herself as a runner the previous fall and was unmatched for speed on the team. Not only was she an excellent runner, but she was also an honor student like her sister had been. Heidi was quiet and diminutive with an easy smile. We both played trumpet in the band and sat next to each other. Even though she was a year younger, Heidi was the better musician and occupied the first chair. Her smile and soft brown eyes belied her intensity as a

Heidi Stettler. Photo courtesy of Heidi (Stettler) Frey.

competitor. She was carrying the mantle Karen had passed on to her, and she led by example.

Mary, Becky, and Tracy had returned for another season. I admired their commitment to the team and as pioneers for the program. They had all improved from the prior year. The girls were competitive, but unlike our boys' squad, they were not yet challenging for team titles at invitationals. While Karen and Heidi had distinguished themselves individually as runners, the rest of our girls' team carried the same burdens without prospects for tributes. They had to endure the hill repeats, interval training, and long runs in the sun. They suffered the same nagging injuries and put themselves willingly into oxygen debt to do their best for their teammates during a race. It would have been easier for them not to join the team and just jog on their own for self-improvement. But that was not their nature. They enthusiastically embraced their roles and supported the entire team as fully vested members of our program. Their joy did not come from athletic achievement. Their fulfillment came from being a part of something bigger than themselves, and that example was a lesson to me.

Our training regimen began with more familiarity than the previous fall, but there were a couple of noticeable changes. After Guy's entrance, Gary rolled into the school parking lot with a maroon Volvo station wagon. Gone was our yellow nemesis, replaced by the new model, which we would learn to despise equally.

The other change was welcome. Over the summer, due to our success in the program's first year, the school district picked up the tab and offered cross country within its athletic budget. The booster club, encouraged by the first season's result, provided some modest funding for gear. Gary went to an athletic store in Winona and ordered a set of warm-ups for each member of the team. The outfits were black windbreaker tops and bottoms with blue trim. They were sharp and suitable for the purpose, but the school colors were black, white, and red. The warm-ups had been on sale at a bargain discount. It was all he could afford to outfit the team and remain within the budget. Nonetheless, the outfits gave us a new sense of team pride, and we no longer looked like a bunch of ragamuffins when we stepped off the bus on race day.

As the new season started, I had an odd feeling about events involving the team. There had been traces of it the year before, and the feeling was back with the new season. The word *fate* is often used to describe a world in which events are predetermined by a greater power. People and factors overlap in a way that our actions cannot direct. It is "destined." We are all driftlessly running toward some unknown, preordained finish. That philosophy seemed too simplistic and could not explain the real pain we were experiencing on our new journey. It did not explain those anxiety-stricken moments while striving toward an outcome that was still in doubt. Nonetheless, it seemed as if there were crumbs on a trail, and we could choose to follow where they led—or not.

Those crumbs were not as obvious on the other journeys I had experienced. The ability to recognize opportunity is a gift. That vision is a tremendous advantage, so when opportunity is unfurled in plain sight, not obscured, it causes one to pause. For me, with my damaged leg, it felt as if a divine hand had lifted a veil to reveal new possibilities. The choice to commit to the hardship of the path was our own.

To turn opportunity into something transformative takes more than vision. It takes the faith, courage, and perseverance of a pioneer. It takes an unwavering commitment to the mission, no matter the cost or suffering, even at great loss. Blazing an uncharted course always brings hardship, isolation, and vulnerability. A pioneer must believe in the opportunity in order to endure the hardship. There are many historical examples and all of them started with visionaries, who saw an opportunity, held hostage by hardship. Their achievements were still in doubt when they acted, the transformation not yet realized or accepted. It is no coincidence then that many opportunities are left fallow in the fields of time, either unrecognized for lack of vision—or, more often, for lack of willingness to endure hardship. But like steel hammered in a forge, our personal growth in life comes through the self-reflection borne under adversity.

The events that propelled us toward our goal could be called fate, but they seemed more than that. The opportunities lay in front of us; we had to commit to the hardship necessary to create a new reality. Even if divine intervention laid the crumbs before us, we had to fight through adversity to reach the trail's end.

I felt that way about our team. I had blindly stumbled into a group that had talent in uncommon numbers for a small school. Our coach had unique gifts and the right temperament to cultivate that talent. We had runners who would sacrifice for one another. Each member was willing to play his role and fill any gap when it occurred. All of that had been obscured from my view only a year earlier, but by the autumn of 1984, I could clearly see a trail of crumbs. Nonetheless, to move from vision to incarnation requires a price to be paid.

The culture of losing was still lurking in the shadows. It whispered inner doubts seeded in past failures. Deep down were fears that some unforeseen twist of fate would rudely steal our joy, negating the sacrifice. The world of low expectations seemed familiar and secure in its predictability. After all, losing could be predictable, and that offered some security as a consolation. It did not require sacrifice and heartache, it did not result in embarrassment, and most importantly, it did not demand that we change. Self-doubt and a lack of self-worth creep easily into the teenage mind. Courage can be hard to muster when doubt persists. To help us overcome this tendency, Gary constantly sowed the seeds of success in our minds, helping us see what might be possible.

Arnie Miehe and the Darlington Redbirds had not stumbled into anything. Arnie had been intentionally sowing the seeds of Darlington's program for two years. The cookouts, the alumni meets, the grade school races, the torch runs, and the yearbooks took energy to manage. Along the way, Arnie had made sure to celebrate the program's successes, both big and small, in the local papers. The kids and the community had responded to those efforts. His dedication was beginning to yield fruit. The Darlington cross country program no longer had a numbers problem when practice began. The Redbirds' 1984 squad consisted of twenty-eight boys and nine girls. And some of the younger kids who were showing up were promising athletes. Arnie's recruitment efforts and the team's success had convinced more than 10 percent of the student body to join the team. Troy and Tom had been essential to building those numbers.

Tom was back for his final season and hoping to finally break into the varsity seven as a senior. He had been there with his buddy Troy the whole time, running the same hills and enduring the same punishing workouts. It had been hard for him, yet he had stayed with it. Tom's leadership set the proper tone for the squad, and the younger kids followed his example. But as the 1984 season got underway, Kirk was finishing in front of his older brother in practice. With the increased numbers, the competition to make varsity was intensifying. It was humbling for Tom. He had a strong work ethic; he was an excellent student; he had been prom king; he was one of the most popular kids in the school; and he was improving. Yet he could not seem to break through, and his little brother was running in the top seven. Tom enjoyed being part of something bigger than himself. He enjoyed being part of a winning team and feeling needed. He would not have traded his role in cross country to go back to football, but his confidence was fading. He started to question whether he had the right stuff. Although the other kids didn't say it, Tom wondered if maybe he wasn't as cool as he thought. He found himself wearing the JV uniforms and warm-ups at the meets, which were not as snappy as those Troy, Kirk, and Tom's classmates were wearing on the varsity. He had to run separately from them on the JV squad with the underclassmen. Tom wanted to shed his JV uniform and suit up with his buddy Troy in the starting seven. He longed for that chance.

AUGUST 25, 1984

The stifling heat of August persisted as the month neared its end. On the first Saturday of the new school year, a crowd of runners and spectators gathered for the annual Redbirds alumni run. The temperature was well into the nineties, and the air carried a tropical dew point. Given the conditions, some questioned the sanity of the event. Nonetheless, a large group of alumni showed up to race, and they all bolted from the line when the starter's pistol cracked.

Under the oppressive heat, runners flirted with collapse on the course. When it ended, the strong alumni team won convincingly, 20–35. But the big surprise that day was Brian Whalen. In his first race, he placed sixth overall and established himself clearly in the Redbirds varsity's second spot. Kirk also showed his potential, finishing in the Redbirds' seventh spot and propelling himself into the varsity lineup as a sophomore. The squad guzzled water in the parking lot afterward, and Kirk walked up to Brian.

"Hey, Helmer. Way to go out there! Man, I still can't believe you're actually running with us this year. This is going to be great!"

Brian smiled back and gave Kirk a high-five. The compliments helped reinforce his contentious decision to walk away from football. He instantly attained status in his new sport and lifted the team's prospects for the new season.

SEPTEMBER 8, 1984

The second Saturday of September arrived with a bright blue sky and a beaming sun overhead. The heat of the summer had finally broken, and the air carried the promise of another approaching autumn. The River Valley Invitational was held each year at the Spring Green, Wisconsin Golf Club, and the scene was glorious. The annual invitational was a premier event and fielded many of the top Class A, B, and C teams in the southwestern part of the state. Several of the largest papers covered the race, including the *Wisconsin State Journal*, and it was viewed as a who's who for the state meet later in the fall. The results carried significant weight in the coaches' poll rankings, and a good showing catapulted teams into the spotlight. The course was flat and beautifully draped on the valley floor of the Wisconsin River, not far from Taliesin, the home of architect Frank Lloyd Wright.

Arnie's team, including Class B and C teams, warmed up for the small school race. Seven of the preseason top ten Class C teams, including Albany and Brookwood, were on the course. The Redbirds had already defeated Albany at the Darlington Invitational two weeks earlier. In that contest, Troy finished more than twenty seconds ahead of Albany's star, Rich Dallman, avenging his losses to Dallman in the 1983 sectional and state meets. The victory had given the Redbirds a boost of confidence, and the level of competition at the River Valley Invitational was another chance to validate how far they had come.

Darlington ran well again and finished as the runner-up, falling short of Class B Lake Mills by just one point. Brookwood was a close third. The result was a big boost to the Darlington program. But the Redbirds would have run away from the entire field had it not been for Brian's off day. Early in the race, Brian developed a cramp and struggled over the course, finishing nearly two minutes behind his normal pace. The sport was new to him, but his impact, positive or negative, was already obvious to the Redbirds.

On Monday morning, Arnie was sitting in his classroom preparing for the first hour when there was a knock on the door. He turned to see Tom and Kirk standing at the entrance and summoned them closer.

"What's up, guys? Nice job on Saturday. You both ran great!"

"Coach, we need to talk," Tom said.

Arnie's brow furrowed with concern. "What's happened?"

"Well," Tom said, "you've probably heard that our sister Mary is engaged to be married."

"Yes, that is great news," Arnie said. "So what's the trouble?"

Tom swallowed and explained, "Well, she's set the wedding date for Saturday, October 27."

Arnie sat back and immediately recognized why Tom and Kirk looked concerned. The state meet was scheduled for October 27, and the Redbirds had an excellent chance to finally qualify this season. Kirk was solidly running in the top five for his squad, and Tom was recently running well enough to make the starting seven. Without two of his top seven runners, Darlington's chances to place well at the biggest meet in school history could be jeopardized.

Arnie thought for a moment and responded, "What is your sister thinking? Honestly, who in their right mind gets married during the middle of the harvest? Your dad must be beside himself!"

The tension released, and they all laughed for a moment.

"Well, guys," Arnie continued, "I'm not touching that one with a ten-foot pole. That will be up to your family to decide."

With a look of bewilderment, the Evenstad boys turned around to go to class. It was not a problem—yet. They still had time to figure out a plan within the family. The team had a long way to go before making the state meet, and it was never prudent to assume success. But it weighed heavily on their minds. Their commitment to their teammates mattered, and the thought of letting them down in such a big event was tormenting.

That afternoon, the staccato pounding of leather on a hardwood floor echoed throughout the Darlington gym during volleyball practice. The Redbirds cross country team had assembled on the stage with the broad curtains pulled shut to minimize the distraction. The stage was a haven of sorts for the squad. It was a place to gather and bond before each practice. It was a place to discuss the happenings of the day and of the previous race. It was a place to set shared goals and shared dreams. It was a place for becoming a team and then a family. The kids had gathered on stage before their coach arrived, and there was only one topic of discussion: how poorly Brian had run on Saturday.

"Did you see that Shirz kid from Fennimore pass Helmer at the end?"

"Yes! Isn't he a freshman?"

"I heard him complaining about his eyesight after he got out of the chute. Sounded like he got arc flash from Helmer's white legs in front of him!"

"He had to pass him just to keep from going blind!"

The group seized with laughter.

After each one-liner, Brian attempted to offer an excuse for his placement. His teammates were having none of it and shot him down each time.

It was futile, despite the cramp. His peers ridiculed Brian mercilessly and would not let him forget it. His performance had lagged so much that the top five runners on the Redbirds JV squad posted faster finishes. Brian was a hard worker and as competitive as anyone on the team. Yet, he was good-natured enough to accept the verbal beating with a smile. He set his sights on the next opportunity.

Arnie heard the laughter from his squad as he approached the stairs to the stage. He paused for a moment to eavesdrop and quickly picked up the mood. It was a good omen. He knew his kids were friends, and the banter was a means of endearment. They were growing closer and had reflected on how well they had run over the weekend. They knew they would have won the first-place trophy if Brian had run his normal race. They were among the best Class C teams in the state, and they were starting to believe it.

Arnie trotted up the stairs as if he had heard none of it. The chatter ceased instantly, and all eyes fixed on the coach.

Arnie cleared his throat and snapped, "Coach Smith! Start the warm-up."

With that, Ann began leading the group through their normal practice calisthenics: push-ups, crunches, toe raises, core work, and stretching. Ann's voice commanded, and the bodies followed habitually. With Ann leading the routine, Arnie could focus on his motivational speech. The minds were more pliable when the bodies were occupied.

JEFF RICH

"Two points, two lousy points. What could each of you have done to get us two measly points? What would it take to run two seconds faster? Every interval of every practice could make that difference. How well you eat, how much rest you are getting, whether you are properly hydrated ... there is an endless list of factors that could take two points off our score, and you have total control over that! So, take control, do the extras, and then be ready to make it happen. You beat number two Brookwood, number six Albany, number seven Boscobel, and number nine Fennimore—and all of them are in our sectional!"

"Now, if we can just get Helmer to run a little faster, we could win the whole thing!"

The stage erupted with laughter. Even Ann stopped her drill cadence to laugh. Brian smiled and gave his coach the "thanks a lot" look. Regardless of the jesting, the underlying message had been loud and clear. Darlington's squad was on the rise, and they realized the opportunity before them.

There was another story developing for the Redbirds that day. Their JV squad had run exceptionally well at River Valley and was showing a level of depth that Darlington had not enjoyed before. In the JV race, the Redbirds placed second. Tom had led the effort by placing third overall, with Kent Ruppert right behind him. Both of their times would have put them in the top five for the Redbirds had they run on the varsity squad that day. Arnie had a good problem. He now had a pool of kids capable of making the starting seven any time they were needed.

After the warm-ups, Arnie sent his JV squad with the varsity to run Larson's Loop. He wanted to see if the JV guys had a fire in their bellies big enough to hang with the varsity runners. He wanted to see if they could do it as a team. And they did. At practice that night, the Redbirds found a renewed sense of purpose.

Afterward, Tom and Troy sauntered out the front doors into the parking lot. Brian was waiting for them.

"Hey! Climb in, and let's take a few laps."

The pair did not hesitate and piled into Brian's new ride, a Rally Sport Chevy Camaro. Their first stop was about a mile east of town, where they picked up a couple of pizzas from Vinger's. Then they headed past the county fairgrounds and back into Darlington to begin their laps. "Taking laps" was a common pastime for teenage boys in Darlington. Main Street was divided by a median, creating a venue for exhibition. Brian's Camaro was light blue with a black hood, and it prowled through the downtown. He'd committed most of his savings to purchase the car. It was his pride and joy, the perfect magnet for the boys to turn heads. They cranked the speakers as they cruised up Main Street from the Pecatonica River to Veteran's Memorial Park at the top of the hill. Brian turned the car around, descended to their origin, and repeated the route for additional laps. They finished only after they'd absorbed their fill of attention. Brian parked next to the median, and the boys sat on the hood of the car with their pizzas. They stuffed slices into their mouths and listened to REO Speedwagon's "Take it on the Run" flow from the speakers.

Looking south along Darlington's Main Street toward the Pecatonica River.
Photo by Jeff Rich.

SEPTEMBER 11, 1984

The brakes yelped as our bus pulled into the Neillsville High School parking lot for their twelve-team invitational. The weather was sunny and calm. We stepped onto the pavement, fresh off a convincing victory a week earlier at the Tiger Invitational in Black River Falls. The boys' race had been more successful than the previous season, yielding a forty-point rout over the runner-up in the thirteen-team meet. The entire team had improved dramatically, and several of our runners matched Guy's time from the prior year on the same course. Our offseason workouts had done their job. It was a good omen.

By the time we arrived in Neillsville my mood had soured. While boarding the bus at our high school, Paul was not wearing his jersey under his warm-ups, and he had his street shoes on. I turned around to face Scott in the seat behind me and asked, "Why isn't Cud wearing his uniform?"

Scott's smile evaporated, and he looked back at me with a furrowed brow, which he usually reserved for the agony of a hill climb. He sighed and then uttered, "Cud had an unexcused absence at school today. He attended an offsite workshop in Winona but didn't get his permission slip signed. They nailed him on it when he got back to school."

I sat back and turned my face to look out the window. The athletic code forbade athletes from competition on any day with an unexcused absence.

I fumed silently for most of the ride after learning the news. I'd always liked Paul, and I bit my tongue to keep from saying something to him I'd regret. At times, I felt sorry for him. None of us had much money, but his wardrobe often reflected his financial difficulty. Even more obvious to us, his parents were never at our meets. He seemed to be on his own, and Paul lived in a world of low expectations. He was much younger than his siblings, and he was small. He was a follower and had not distinguished himself as a student. As a result, Paul was often overlooked for his abilities, and from time to time, those low expectations yielded poor performance. But as part of

150   DRIFTLESS RUN

our scant team, Paul had differentiated himself as a talented runner, carrying precious worth. With that unfamiliar spotlight came new expectations for Paul and new responsibilities to others. Once off the bus in Neillsville, I walked over to Gary to vent my frustration.

"Coach, we can't have Cud messing up like this at school! We don't have the depth. Does he understand how hard this is on the rest of us?"

True to his nature, Gary calmly listened to my rant.

"I think it is already weighing on him, Jeff."

"Did you set him straight?"

He paused, looking me in the eye for a moment, and then responded. "I'll sit down with him after the meet. But what I need you to do right now is to focus on this race. We're going to need the best from all of you if we're going to have a chance."

The goal of an unblemished record was already in jeopardy, and the season had barely started. Most of the teams in the race were Class B schools and larger than C-FC. Making matters worse, one of the teams at the invitational was Class C Altoona, who was ranked ninth in the state coaches' poll. They had placed third at the state meet the prior season, ahead of Boscobel and Arkansaw. Even if the rest of the squad set personal records, the chance to emerge with a win was remote without Paul.

Not long afterward, my mood improved. We started to walk the course for our pre-race scouting tour, and I saw Mark's head turn abruptly. It didn't take long to identify the distraction. The Auburndale girls were stretching about fifty yards away on the grass, and Mark was instantly sidetracked. Auburndale was a school we had not raced against previously, and their ladies were lithe, tan, and lovely. It was a benefit of the sport, mingling with shapely members of the opposite sex. Mark promptly set a plan in motion.

"Hey, Guy! Let's begin our strides over by the starting line. Lead us out."

Guy nodded back at him and surged forward. The rest of us followed in his wake. He steadied his cobalt eyes on the turf ahead, oblivious to anything other than stretching his legs in good form. He served as the figurehead on our ship. Mark steered the rudder. When Guy passed in front of the Auburndale girls, they snapped their heads in unison. Mark coasted through their stares and made eye contact.

With a wink he snickered, "Hell-ooo ladies!"

The golden-haired sirens laughed. He had been noticed. Mission accomplished.

Paul had to watch from the sidelines as the remaining five of us stepped to the line for the race. Once the starter's pistol cracked, Guy sprinted to the lead, and I decided to go with him. A quick glance suggested that he was surprised to see me at his side for the first few hundred yards. The impulsive decision was a risk but also a good test in a race where we all needed to lay it on the line. There was some logic to it. I had improved as a middle-distance runner the prior spring during track season. Having trained with Guy for those events, I knew we were well-matched up to a mile. But after a mile I also knew Guy's lighter build and superior form would eventually bury me. But if I stayed with him, I'd learn where my limit might truly be. I thought perhaps I'd been restricting my potential by holding back for fear of hitting the wall. The decision was sudden, and after the first half mile, I was committed to the strategy.

The course was well-groomed and had a single climb on the route. At the one-mile mark, the two of us were about two hundred meters in front of the next runner, and our lead was stretching. We were deserting the rest of the field, negating the need for a scorching pace, yet Guy was trying to shed me. Still, my longer legs and sprinting speed kept me at his side. Soon after, we began to climb the hill in the middle of the course. I focused my mind on the techniques we used for hill running, pumping my arms and breathing deep, steady breaths. Guy was his placid self, his lighter frame gracefully ascending the slope by my side. He showed no emotion, silently and calmly breathing, his sandy hair flowing. By contrast, I was fighting Newton with every stride up that incline, mentally conquering the dissent within my mind, ignoring the agony. I succeeded in keeping pace and climbing the hill with him. When we crested and made a right turn, I was convinced I had made it through the worst. I felt a hint of elation, and for a moment, I thought I could stick with Guy for the rest of the race. We had a short, straight stretch in front of us before turning right again to descend the same hill we had just scaled, then onward another mile to the finish.

As soon as we started our long strides down the hill, I felt a crash of heaviness in my limbs. My lungs could not get enough air, and the sky dimmed around me. Sounds faded, overwhelmed by the drone in my ears. It was then I grasped that I might collapse. We trained to push up and over the crest of hills, only releasing our stride on the descent and allowing our respiration to recover at that point. And it usually would recover. But this time, my body's response panicked me. The oxygen debt would not release me from its grip. I had rejected my mind's dissent so strongly on the climb that I was hitting the wall on the downhill stretch, and it would not abate. I cursed myself for not letting Guy ascend in front of me and then using my longer stride on the descent to close the gap. I realized I had jeopardized the outcome for our team, and I was overwhelmed with dread. I immediately yielded the pace, coasting downhill, hoping I would not black out. Guy stretched ahead of me, pitiless, with his sandy mane waving good-bye to my face. There was no change of expression or acknowledgment that I had been with him up until that point. The attempt had been lunacy; I could not be his wingman.

By the time I reached the bottom of the hill, I felt like I was running in slow motion with another mile to go before the finish. Although lucidity had returned, my body was gripped by lactic acid. I glanced over my shoulder and noticed the next runners were 150 meters behind me. It was a significant gap, but I was plodding along and wondering if I could hold on. Each yard was a struggle, as if trying to stride through quicksand. There were two more turns, a long straight stretch, and a loop around a softball field before the finish. On the first turn I tossed a glance to the side, and the gap had closed to about seventy-five meters. My pace was lagging, and the mob was closing. At the next turn, the gap had narrowed to twenty-five meters, and the horde was still closing with each stride. It was a fight to keep panic from overwhelming me as that lead evaporated. Even if Guy was well in front of me, a second-place finish would still be a great help to my team. But stride by agonizing stride, they were reeling me in, like a bad dream, as if I could not escape my pursuers. I was running alone and had become the quarry of the beast behind me. Often, when a pack reaches a lone runner, his ego deflates, and he is swallowed by the competition. My foolish strategy had failed, and I was going to ruin our chances for an undefeated season. The thought of letting the other guys down flooded me with shame. The bellows in my chest were pulsing as hard as they could, and panic crept into my mind—*RUN!*

With a quarter mile left on the course, I entered the loop around the softball field before the final straightaway to the tape. As I started around the loop, two opponents surged to my side and then passed. I attempted a feeble counter but failed. My mind protested with disgust at yielding the second spot. Moments later, there were audible footsteps behind me from another runner. Strength was returning to my arms, and my cadence increased above the lumbering slog of the previous mile. After completing the loop, one hundred meters remained in my race, and I could hear the opponent breathing off my shoulder. My contempt for losing reared up. In that moment I found an extra gear, at last rejuvenated with enough oxygen to command performance from my limbs. I held on and crossed the line. Relief crashed over me as my diaphragm impatiently heaved. I had failed in my strategy but had salvaged my self-esteem.

Scott came in sixth place. He had been near the front of the throng pursuing me. As he pulled into the tapering chute, his left leg seized with pain. The patellar tendon running over his kneecap had been injured. He struggled to walk through the chute, and a runner from Colby pushed past him, even though they had already crossed the finish line.

Pointing at the offender, Scott exclaimed, "Hey, Ref! That guy passed me in the chute after we finished!"

His plea fell on deaf ears; the officials had not seen the intrusion and would not reverse the order. It was the only time when a runner would steal a place from one of us in the chute. Scott had been vulnerable as he limped through, and the kid had taken advantage of it. The officials recorded Scott in seventh place.

Moments after Scott finished, Mark came across. We did not know it then, bent over at the waist searching for air, but each of us had set personal records in our attempt to remain unbeaten. Guy had set a new record for Neillsville's course, running the race in 15:32. The team result was left in Dan's hands—or rather, his feet.

Dan Lettner was a good runner. For anyone who has run a five-thousand-meter race over uneven terrain, clocking a time under twenty minutes is no small feat. Dan consistently finished in the top half of the field. He was strong-willed, but he liked to laugh and was dependable. Dan was of average height with a muscular, sturdy frame and was not prone to injury. After high school he joined the

Marines, which in hindsight was a good fit for him. But none of us could have predicted he would become a grade school teacher and dedicate his life's work to helping kids discover the joy of learning. Underneath, Dan had a big heart.

He was a hard worker and in excellent shape. Yet, unlike Guy or Paul, Dan did not have the advantage of a graceful stride. He had to perform his role under a greater burden, separated from us and alone during a race. His gift was a stubborn resilience we could not see when he was clowning around. At the time, I misunderstood how good of a runner Dan was since he was usually a couple of minutes behind me during a race. I knew he was competing back there somewhere, but I never saw him during the competition. Rationally, I understood his importance to the team, but we had never "needed" him before. My measuring stick of athletic prowess hatched subconscious segregation in my teenage mind, even if it was not intended maliciously. Under examination, Dan was a formidable opponent for the other teams on the course. He would beat many of their fourth and fifth runners, piling points on them and hampering their team scores. In a sense, Dan was playing defense for our squad during a race.

On that day in Neillsville, we needed Dan more than ever, and we all knew it. During the race, Dan had been pressing himself, determined to perform his duty as our fifth runner. With about one hundred meters remaining, a struggling opponent came into view ahead of him. During a race, Dan's creed was to focus on the next runner and then pass him. As the line approached, he stubbornly committed to one last attack. Our whole team gathered along the final stretch to cheer him on. Dan violently pumped his arms during his charge and passed the opponent. He stumbled across the line in thirty-fifth place, nearly collapsing in the chute. Dan set a new personal record, running the course in 18:09. We anxiously awaited the official score, unsure if the effort had been enough.

When the race official announced the second-place team, our clan erupted. We had captured a thin, one-point victory over the host, Neillsville. Altoona placed third. Dan's final assault on that runner in front of him had made the difference. Dan walked up alone to receive our team trophy, hoisting it triumphantly over his head.

The Auburndale maidens giggled nearby and clapped, holding their own trophy.

It had become customary for our girls' and boys' teams to take a group photo with the trophy after a victory. In the photo at Neillsville, Dan was kneeling front and center, beaming with the prize prominently displayed on his knee. He was our Neillsville hero. Dan had recognized the opportunity and seized it, accepting the hardship to fill the gap. It confirmed his value to our team. It validated that our squad could win a big invitational with one of its six runners out of action. Numbers were lacking, but we were a cohesive team.

Dan Lettner accepting the team trophy at the Neillsville Invitational. September 11, 1984. Photo courtesy of Betty Rich.

CHAPTER FIFTEEN
ADVERSITY'S RAIN

The tough thing about adversity is that it does not usually end with one distinct event. Adversity seems to revel in coming in waves. It is like a rainstorm that increases in intensity hours after the first drops, leading to a downpour and eventually a flood. It slowly wears one down, weakening the will over time, until the dam breaks and it overwhelms entirely.

The dishes shook in the cupboards, and the train's horn announced its arrival as Gary sat at the kitchen table the day after the Neillsville race. The residents of Cochrane and Fountain City lived within a few blocks of the tracks where the busy Burlington Northern Line hauled taconite, coal, and oil. A train passed by every hour, and the inhabitants learned to sleep through the disturbance as they did with their own heartbeats. But the rattle seemed to have a frequency above the rumble of the train, and when Gary heard it again, he realized the second source was from the door on North Main. Gary stepped down the staircase to see who was knocking, and his jaw dropped as he opened the door. Scott was leaning on crutches before him.

"You're not going to like this, Coach," he muttered.

His leg was in a large brace, stretching from his calf to his hip, holding his knee in a fixed position.

JEFF RICH

Scott had developed a serious case of runner's knee. It had been simmering below the surface from the training and was aggravated from the stress he incurred during the Neillsville race. Runner's knee is a term for irritation and swelling of the tissues surrounding the kneecap. The pain can become so excruciating an athlete cannot run on the leg. It is usually caused by overuse and aggressive exercise of the knee joint. Most of us encountered a twinge of runner's knee at some point during our training. Typically, when it occurred, we backed off for a few days, iced the knee, and maybe invested in new shoes. But Scott's case had suddenly flared up. He had gone from setting a personal record at Neillsville to limping immediately after crossing the finish line. The next morning, a physician looked at Scott's left foot and determined that he needed customized orthotics that might resolve his knee trouble. He began wearing them in his shoes immediately, but it was unclear whether it would be a season-ending injury for him. Scott was our captain, and we needed him back.

During lunch on Friday I walked into the school library looking for the *Wisconsin State Journal.* The state rankings had been published in the papers, and I was sizing up our competition. The C-FC boys were projected as the fourth-best team in Class C, right behind Brookwood and Darlington. It marked the first time we had been ranked. Our squad was from a small, obscure school on the western border of the state, but a few members of the Wisconsin Cross Country Coaches Association (WCCCA) had noticed us. They did not know that the team's injuries were starting to pile up and that our depth was lacking. Chetek was ranked first in the poll, which was no surprise. Chetek, in northern Wisconsin, had just won two consecutive Class C titles. But what concerned me was that Darlington, Brookwood, Boscobel, Albany, and Fennimore were all ranked in the top ten with our team. In another month, we would need to face all of those squads in our sectional meet. It was a foreboding thought. Of all years, we had drawn what was likely the toughest sectional assignment in the state. We could not achieve our goal of advancing to the state meet unless we successfully passed through that gauntlet. I began my daily ritual of poring over the papers, researching the runners and times from those squads.

SEPTEMBER 15, 1984

For the second Saturday in a row, the Darlington Redbirds were on a bus traveling to a large invitational. This time it was near the Madison media market in Mount Horeb. The mild weather continued, and the ranked teams of Albany, Boscobel, Fennimore, and Monticello were part of the ten-team field, as well as a number of bigger schools.

On their way to the meet, not far from Mount Horeb, the Redbirds passed by what remained of the community of Barneveld. The tornado had left an apocalyptic scene. The buzzsaw had traveled right down Main Street as if it were following traffic. The water tower was left as a lonely witness to the carnage. Trees that had not been uprooted were sheared off at their trunks. Few houses remained untouched, and the ones along Main Street had been swept clean off their foundations. But only three months after the disaster, signs of renewal were emerging. Crews of volunteers had removed much of the debris from the site, and residents were patching up the salvageable structures. The green of summer had covered some of the scars, and new construction was beginning. Despite the adversity, the community was rising from the ground.

After their warm-ups, the team huddled at the starting line, and Arnie searched their eyes for that renewed sense of purpose he had seen in practice on Monday. He didn't have to look long; the kids were hungry to prove they were the best Class C team in the state. Arnie then glanced at his captain.

"Troy, get out with those guys and take it to them. The rest of you, be smart at the start, and then get up where you belong and get it done."

This time, Rich Dallman of Albany crossed the line first, with Sean Currie of Cambridge on his heels. Troy finished fourth behind Boscobel's lead runner, Kevin Clark. But Brian rose to the occasion and regained his identity, leading a charge from his teammates to dominate the meet. Both Evenstad boys ran in the Redbirds' starting lineup, and Tom placed twenty-fifth out of seventy runners. The Redbirds won convincingly by thirty-four points over runner-up

Albany.

The race's outcome was so obvious that the Darlington clan did not have to wait for the official results. The entire Redbirds squad knew instantly they had won the meet, and the kids high-fived each other with gleaming smiles. A celebration ensued at the finish line and spilled over to the bus ride home.

The Darlington Redbirds walk off the course after winning the Mount Horeb Invitational. Photo courtesy of Arnie Miehe.

A big win on a big stage was something sports teams from Darlington had not experienced in many years. It was a special day for the Redbirds. Even the underclassmen on the JV had placed well, finishing third behind two Class A schools. The ride home was filled with gratification and security. They were the "hicks from the sticks," running against wealthier kids from larger towns. But the farm boys abruptly realized they were now the real deal. The unfamiliar label of "winner" had been stamped boldly on their identities. They were affirmed, doubts melted away, and they marveled at the moment. Suddenly, they weren't just another group of kids. They mattered.

"Troy! Fire up that boom box!"

Troy scowled at Tom and fumbled through his duffel bag.

Troy had a new boom box he had purchased with some of his

earnings from the gas station. It was a Sony, nearly three feet long, with massive speakers on the ends and dual cassette players. He proudly brandished it during bus rides. But when the power cord could not be used, the beast gobbled up eight D-cell batteries on one trip to and from a meet. He brought extras in his duffel for every ride.

"Found 'em!"

He opened the tab, turned the boom box over, and changed the batteries.

"Where are the tapes? Did you bring Bon Jovi?"

"Give me a minute, Evie! They're in here somewhere."

Troy slid in the cassette, slammed the door shut, and punched "play." Roy Bittan hammered staccato notes from the keyboard on cue, and "Runaway" satiated their exuberance. Troy sat back in his seat, slid on his sunglasses, and smiled back at Tom. The Redbirds had hopped aboard a runaway train. They had been validated, and the future looked bright.

SEPTEMBER 17, 1984

Duran Duran's "Hungry Like the Wolf" blared from the boom box in the warm afternoon sunshine as our bus pulled into the parking lot. The driver opened the creaking door, and we stepped onto the pavement in Galesville for their thirteen-team invitational. There was good karma with the course, and we had set personal records each time we raced there. We looked forward to the opportunity to repeat the performance, but we expected a battle. Without Scott, we knew we'd be in the same predicament we were in at Neillsville, and we were anxious.

Dan ran another gutsy race, only nine seconds off his personal record in Neillsville. But it wasn't enough. Mondovi, a larger Class B school, soundly defeated our team that day, 48 to 61. They were a formidable squad and would go on to win their Class B Regional meet in October. We had beaten them several times before, and the loss was tough to take. The goal of achieving an undefeated regular season had slipped through our fingers. It had become another failure to add to our list. The result in Galesville drove home how critical depth was in the sport. We were walking a tightrope between achievement and anonymity.

Even though we had run well, the mood was sullen on the ride back to our high school, and Mark did not provide his usual amusement. His throat was hoarse from the exertion, and it did not clear. When he arrived home, his eyes began to ache, and he became feverish. By the next morning he was bedridden. The virus had found a new host. Our team was scheduled to race at another invitational in Winona that afternoon, but Gary could not field a boys' team and pulled us out of the competition. Instead, he opted to form a co-ed relay team at the event from the healthy kids who remained.

The C-FC team poses with the first-place trophy at the Winona Cotter co-ed relay in Winona, Minnesota. Scott Adler can be seen on the right side of the photo wearing a brace for the injury he had suffered a week earlier at the Neillsville Invitational. His knee never fully recovered during the 1984 season. Photo courtesy of Betty Rich.

Arnie's squad was about to face some hardship of its own in the form of the Platteville Hillmen. Platteville was ranked first in the coaches' poll for Class B schools, and their coach, Dick McKichan, had built a bulldozer of a program. The Hillmen had won the Class B title in 1979 and 1980, and they simply reloaded their depth chart with fantastic talent each year. In 1984, their star runner, Kurt Udelhofen, was considered by many college recruiters as the top high school runner in the state. He and Troy had gone head-to-head in track meets since they were in junior high. Udelhofen had edged Troy in the eight-hundred-meter run each time, and he only got better with more distance. The new state rankings had come out a couple of days after Darlington's big win at the Mount Horeb Invitational. The Redbirds had ascended to the top ranking in Class C. What was once viewed as their usual conference dual meet instantly became the number one ranked Class B school versus the number one ranked Class C school. Expectations went through the roof, and the buzz in the community was palpable. Darlington had finally produced a winner, and the district worked itself into a lather for the upcoming home meet.

On Monday afternoon, Arnie trotted up the stairs to the gymnasium stage. This time, there was no laughter when he got there. The exuberance that had dominated his group a few days earlier had been replaced by apprehension. The Redbirds had just won the biggest victory in program history, and they had been rewarded with a number one ranking. But on that stage, Arnie could feel the tension as he looked at his kids. They were on edge at a moment when they should have been brimming with confidence—when they *needed* to be brimming with confidence.

"Let's face it. They're tough, really tough, or they wouldn't be ranked number one. In order to beat them, we have to match them guy-for-guy, and our pack has to beat their pack."

"We can beat those guys!" Troy chimed in.

He didn't have to say anything else. His teammates knew how much Troy hated to lose, and they would do anything to help him break Platteville's spell over Darlington. Arnie knew that he needed his team to believe in themselves to have any chance of getting a victory over the Hillmen. He didn't waver while speaking to his team and exuded confidence in his demeanor. He had a strategy, and he began sharing it with the kids to get them to focus on what victory would take and to stop worrying about "not losing."

"Troy, you're going to win this race! It is your home course, and you know it better than anyone else. You can use that edge to make the difference and surprise Udelhofen. Be crisp on the corners; accelerate out of the turns. He will need to be more cautious because he is unfamiliar with the terrain."

He went on. "Brian, Kirk, and James, you are all capable of running under eighteen minutes and beating Platteville's second runner, Scott Weldon. Don't let him out of your sight. Work together to demoralize him and lift each other up. Target him during the race, and get it done! Do that and the numbers will work for us. We will beat them!"

The math was simple on the chalkboard. But to move from vision to incarnation demanded a price.

Minutes before the race, Arnie glanced over to the parking lot where a throng of people was filtering in to watch the highly anticipated contest. He glimpsed Walter "Wadzy" Martens pull up in his car, causing Arnie's heart to skip a beat. The tall, lean eighty-year-old stepped out and walked toward the course. Wadzy had come to view the race and see what all of the fuss was about. Martens was a legend in Darlington. He coached the football program between 1926 and 1960 and served as a school board member after retiring from teaching in 1968. Wadzy held a distinguished reputation within the Wisconsin football scene. He had been president of the Wisconsin Football Coaches Association, was a charter inductee in the organization's Hall of Fame, coached the Wisconsin High School All-Star Team, and had been a scout for the University of Wisconsin football program. Wadzy was not just a legend in Darlington but a legend in the state. The Redbirds' football field had been named after Martens in 1982 while Arnie was on the staff. Dignitaries from all over the state had attended to speak to the enormous crowd assembled for the dedication. In Darlington, the two most important men were Jesus and Wadzy Martens. To see him attend a cross country meet spoke to the event's significance.

The starter's pistol cracked through the air, and the Redbirds charged from the starting line to establish themselves in the lead. For the first mile, Arnie's plan held firm and anticipation grew. The swarm of spectators lining the edges of the course shouted earnestly as the runners struggled past. Betty Cullen was tending to the 76 station at the bottom of Galena Street at the time of the race. It was nearly a half mile away from the high school, but she could hear Arnie's voice roll through the valley, pleading with his squad to attack the course. Platteville's depth of talent started eroding Darlington's strategy by the second mile, and the Hillmen nailed the coffin shut over the final stretch of the race. In the end, Platteville won 18–45 in a blowout.

Troy placed third, a full minute behind Udelhofen. He was also soundly beaten by the Hillmen's second runner, Scott Weldon, and had only narrowly edged Platteville's third runner. The rest of the top eight contestants to cross the line were from Platteville.

Worst of all for Arnie, he glimpsed Wadzy's sedan exit the parking lot after the runners passed the second-mile marker. Martens had seen enough. It was a humbling rout, one that Arnie hoped would not block his team's upward ascent. The Redbirds had let a rare opportunity slip through their fingers. They could have shown others how good they were and, more importantly, validated it for themselves. The confidence and enthusiasm that had been building during the past two weeks had come to a screeching halt. In fact, their confidence had taken several steps backward within twenty minutes of the starter's pistol going off. Arnie watched his squad walk from the finish line with their heads down to get their sweats and change shoes.

Like a punch-drunk boxer, Arnie's mind was in a fog. Woody Hayes, the long-time Ohio State University football coach once said, "Few things clear the mind better than a good ass-kicking."

Arnie realized that his team had just received an ass-kicking, but it seemed to cloud his mind more than clear it. Disoriented, he wandered over the course after the race, picking up flags. Tom was also on the course, having just led the JV squad to a victory over their Platteville opponents. Despite that triumph, Tom had to watch helplessly while his brother and classmates got trounced by the Hillmen. He saw the state his coach was in afterward and beseeched the underclassmen to help pick up flags and stow the equipment.

Arnie was at a loss for what he could say to his varsity squad to salvage their egos. On his walk back into the school, he finally concluded that they had work to do. The only way that was going to happen was to lick their wounds, learn what they could from the experience, and move on with more determination than before. Arnie plodded up the stairs to the stage where his team had assembled. He could see the dejection on Troy's face, his eyes swimming in despair. Getting blown out was more than he wanted to deal with. Troy had had his fill of getting beat by Udelhofen and his team.

"I ran like crap. This sucks!" Troy kept muttering.

Arnie didn't make a big speech that evening. He simply checked on each of his runners to make sure they were okay and reminded them that Platteville was the best team in Class B—perhaps the best team in the entire state.

"Guys, I know it hurts, but we have to accept the fact that we simply got beat by a bigger school. We need to keep working to get better."

That night, Arnie's sleep was restless. The vision of Wadzy Martens's car leaving the parking lot kept replaying in his mind. The big breakthrough and affirmation he sought as a young coach would have to wait.

The day after we withdrew from the invitational in Winona, we logged some miles on Highway 88 with Gary. Mark and Scott could not participate, but the rest of us continued to build on our base, trying to find a way out of the funk we found ourselves in. After showering, I stepped into my parents' 1978 Buick LeSabre and drove north on Highway 35 toward home. Looking through my windshield, I noticed the sky was turning green. It was the Northern Lights, the aurora borealis. After I parked the Buick in our driveway, I stepped out and sat on the trunk to watch the display above the bluffs. We were far enough north to occasionally see the aurora. It was not as frequent at our latitude as it was near Lake Superior, but it was sometimes there for us to view.

That night, the waning crescent moon was not yet up, the sky was clear, and the aurora had a star-speckled black canvas for its performance. The aurora was lime-green, which was predominantly the color we would see at our latitude. Sometimes it was just a green glow peeking above the skyline of the bluffs' ridges. But that night, vertical columns of light streaked high in the sky. They were like radiant curtains, increasing and decreasing in intensity, rising and falling from their peaks, and shuffling position from back to front. I stared at the waltz in the sky as the dancers altered their gowns throughout the performance. The movement of color was captivating. It seemed alive, and when I saw it, I could not help but be hypnotized by the beauty of nature. The aurora was as miraculous and as fleeting as youth.

That brief moment of witnessing the aurora was therapeutic for me. The prior month's schedule had been harsh, running frequent races between intense training sessions. The cumulative trauma was starting to take a toll, and there were a lot of races waiting on the schedule. Gary kept a pulse on his squad's health and adjusted the training regimen to aid in healing.

Ann was leading the Darlington Redbirds through their warm-up calisthenics the next afternoon while Arnie fashioned the team's mental fitness.

"I hope all of you got some rest last night and that you're ready to start working again. I've heard a lot of whining out there from people who have control over their situation in life. I hear it from students all the time. In most cases, they have control over their outcome. Generally speaking, they'd rather whine about their predicament than commit to the work to change the result. If you don't like your grade, then study more. If you want a good-paying job, do the extras it will take to get that job. If you don't like getting second, then commit to the sacrifices it will take to win! It's a mindset choice. Either you decide to do what it takes, or you must tolerate the results. I don't know about you, but I don't like the taste in my mouth right now, and I don't want to swallow defeat again. Remember that taste. Let it motivate you to do the work to change the outcome. We're starting today's practice with a new theme: Beat it or eat it."

CHAPTER SIXTEEN
SKIN IN THE GAME

Most of us ran better on sunny, pleasant days. In nice weather our spirits were lifted, helping us manage the mental battle during the contest. But a cumulative negative effect was associated with bad weather on our pain thresholds, and the elements got worse as the season progressed toward winter. Headwinds aggravated our cadence. Precipitation created slick surfaces, causing us to slow down to avoid falls. If one of us fell, it disrupted his rhythm in a race, even if he was not injured. We had to be wary not to trip over other runners falling in front of us. Rain caused vision problems, magnifying the chilling effect of the cold. Any skin directly exposed to frigid air would turn bright pink and sting until it finally numbed later in the race. Our minds were processing all these irritants subconsciously as we struggled to parse the truth from the brain's internal battle during a race. It lowered our tolerance, and we would wear down more easily. Our resiliency ebbed.

Everyone was subjected to the onslaught from the elements, negating the advantage of speed and efficiency of stride that the best runners possessed. Less skilled, robust runners would leverage their attributes of strength and stability in bad weather.

By the fourth week of September, the jet stream was switching its flow in the upper atmosphere, and the dome of high pressure we had enjoyed earlier in the month had been pushed to the east. It was a hint that winter's breath would soon drift over the landscape. Some years the jet stream shift might take place in November; other years it could be late September or somewhere in between. In 1984, the shift began in late September.

I'd discovered in the papers that the state coaches' poll was also shifting by the fourth week of September. The runner-up finish in Galesville had caused us to slip to a sixth-place ranking. Darlington had risen to a tie for first with Chetek on the heels of their success in the River Valley and Mount Horeb Invitationals. In the coaches' view, their loss to Platteville had not affected the Redbirds' status in the Class C field.

SEPTEMBER 25, 1984

The frustration clicked audibly from the Rubik's Cube as Dan tried to force his will during the bus ride. He tossed the puzzle over his seat in my direction, but the vexing diversion did not appeal to me before a race, and I tossed it back. I glanced over at Paul, sitting in a seat adjacent to me, absorbed in a textbook for his homework assignment. He looked up at Scott and asked a question. Scott offered an insight, and Paul jotted a note on his tablet. I smiled; he was making his grades. We were on our way to Mondovi for their home invitational. Mark was still recovering from his illness, and Scott had not run for two weeks. They were both dressed and felt compelled to race in their weakened conditions to avoid another team withdrawal. A tempest was moving through as our bus pulled into the Mondovi golf course. We were treated to temperatures in the upper forties, with twenty-mile-per-hour winds and sleet in our faces. It fit our stormy mood, coming off the defeat to Mondovi in Galesville.

Bad weather should have been an advantage for me during a race. I was more robust than the gazelles at the very front, and nasty weather should have provided me with an edge. But I hated running in bad weather. My knee would ache even before the race began. It was a pattern I had started to notice the previous spring. When a low-pressure system moved in, pangs would radiate from within the knee's core, even if I was off my feet. Thankfully, it just ached and never seemed to swell from the change. Growing up, I had heard the old-timers complain about their arthritic joints and heard them say they could predict when bad weather was coming. I had always thought they were spinning tall tales to impress the kids, but I was beginning to experience the same odd pain. As we walked onto the pavement that day in Mondovi, my knee was throbbing, and my mood was sour.

The course was equally miserable with climbs and descents throughout its length. It was a brutal race, but we persevered. We avenged the loss at Galesville, burying the field and edging Mondovi by three points. Twisted Sister's "We're Not Going to Take It" bellowed in our ears and launched our celebration on the ride home.

In Darlington, Arnie was starting to exploit his new advantage. He had the luxury of depth. Troy was a standout talent, with Brian, James, Kirk, Jay, and Bob consistently placing in their squad's top six. But behind them was a handful of runners that, on any given day, could trade places for the seventh spot. Tom Evenstad, Doug Dunham, Kent Ruppert, Dale Kelly, and Tony Robichaud were all pressing to break into the starting lineup. The competition was complementary and offered Darlington new opportunities. Arnie began entering his JV runners in dual meets as part of the varsity seven. He kept one or two of his best runners in those lineups and filled the remaining roster with members of the JV squad. This allowed those runners to improve through varsity competition and to differentiate themselves if they performed well enough to be in the top seven. They also got to letter in the sport and help the team win. Perhaps most importantly, it gave Arnie the chance to rest his best runners and keep injuries to a minimum. He was saving his talent for the big invitationals and tournament later in October. The combined effect created leverage that other small schools, with less depth, could not match, and it built camaraderie within the ranks.

Cross country coaches attempt to balance victory in the next meet by "peaking" the team's performance late in the season in order to make a deep tournament run. It is a delicate balance and particularly difficult for small schools that do not enjoy depth in numbers. If the training is too intense early in the season, a team might have initial success, but injuries will likely emerge and diminish their ability to excel later when it counts most. It is less of a concern if a team has great depth, with runners who can step up when injuries occur. Conversely, if a coach does not push a team hard enough early in the season, conditioning will suffer, and the team might not peak in time for the October tournament runs. Arnie's numbers gave the Redbirds the opportunity to do both. The season was only about two months long, so the training regimen was tight and had little room for error.

The strategy worked. Over the next two weeks, Darlington swept Lancaster and soundly defeated Southwestern in duals. The varsity runners rested their legs and went on to dominate the small-school division of the Platteville Invitational.

The first couple of weeks in October were productive for our team. We swept a quad meet on our home course and captured a forty-two-point victory in a fourteen-team invitational in Lewiston, Minnesota. We ran our last race of the regular season against Lake City, Minnesota, on October 9. The dual meet took place on our home course, and the weather was beautiful. During the race, the football team stopped their practice to line up along the route and cheer us on. It had only been fourteen months since we started the cross country program, but the culture was already changing. It was becoming one of mutual respect and support. We easily won our last home meet that day, but it was a bittersweet moment for us seniors.

The regular season was in the books, and our team had fallen short of our first goal. The second-place finish in Galesville was the only blemish on an otherwise undefeated season. The WIAA coaches' poll ranked our team eighth prior to the regionals. Our runner-up finish in Galesville and the limited press from the meets we ran in Minnesota had kept our profile low. The major media markets in the state rarely covered our rural district. We were completely unknown in the Madison, Milwaukee, and Green Bay markets. The *Winona Daily News*, from the small city across the river, was the only regional newspaper that regularly featured our team. In a way, the lack of attention was comforting. It was an honor to be noticed, but we did not want the pressure of expectations that can come with such polls.

JEFF RICH

We did not want targets on our backs.

It had been a season riddled with more injuries than we had dealt with the year before. Adversity had been steadily raining on our squad, and the dam was close to breaching. We could not afford another casualty, and the pestilence of 1983 was never far from our minds.

Gary was focusing on the state championship meet a couple of weeks away. He had been at the Christmas Mountain course the previous fall coaching Guy and Karen through their individual races. One thing that stood out to Gary was the hill near the end of the course. It was not that intimidating at an initial glance, perhaps a 150-foot climb, and not as big as some of the slopes we tackled in the bluffs, but it was steep, it was grass, and it was about a quarter mile from the finish. Gary had witnessed its effect at the 1983 championships. Runners ran into the hill underestimating the toll it would take on them after battling premier competitors up to that point. The slope was a cruel test that overwhelmed many while they were in oxygen debt late in the race. If the grass was wet, runners would slip and fall, spoiling their chances without enough distance left to recover. The few who were able to attack the hill and conquer it swiftly were greeted by a downhill slope with the finish in view two hundred meters below. But for many, defeat occurred on that hill. Runners trudged to its crest, and before they could recover from the climb, they found themselves in a blurry-eyed, suffocating flounder to the line.

Our coach began sending the team into the hilly streets of Fountain City during practice. Gary knew that his squad had a good aerobic base and that given the short time left in the season, it would not erode. He was banking on the hill work to help his kids place well at state, preparing for the possibility of the team reaching that meet. In Gary's mind, the hill repeats would differentiate his team at a key point in that race. It was a gamble. During the regular season, the squad had barely threaded the needle with health issues. Scott was struggling to keep up with Paul and me during our meets. His sore knee tendon simmered under the surface. Even with a tender leg, Scott was still a formidable runner but had lost a step. He said nothing to us, and we pretended not to notice. Our coach surmised that the risk was worth it in order to reach for the opportunity.

We grumbled through it all. Our team was perched on a tenuous balance. We had been logging too many miles on paved surfaces. Guy had run the course the year before and didn't mention a scary hill. But then again, he was a man of few words. We suspected that our coach was building up the hill at Christmas Mountain to be more sinister than it really was. He wouldn't stop talking about it. Every now and then, Gary would profess that we were the best hill runners in the state: "Just look at where we live and train." He would even describe it to us and have us imagine conquering the hill in our visualization sessions after our workouts. It was a marketing campaign, and we weren't even at the state meet yet. We still had regionals and sectionals to get through. We had been taught that prudence required us not to count our chickens before they were hatched. "Don't get ahead of yourselves" was a common mantra for coaches. "One game at a time" was another customary phrase to help teams keep focused on the next hurdle. What on earth was Gary thinking? Why was this guy having us visualize the state meet course?

Gary had already moved beyond our goal of getting to the state meet to a new goal of winning the whole thing. We weren't there with him yet. But that didn't hinder Gary's pursuit or subdue his enthusiasm. It was a mind game. His role was to make us believe in what was possible and then get us to reach for it.

We met in Fountain City on Friday afternoon for another round of hills when a metallic noise approached us from behind. The clicking of a chain sliding against its rear stay was audible as the pursuers pulled up alongside us. Jesse Brone and his friends were on their bikes, attempting to keep pace with our pack as we loped over the street. They furiously cranked revolutions on their single speeds and became our escorts for several blocks, finally succumbing to the effort as we attacked another slope. We became a common sight for the residents of Fountain City. Our team swarmed up and down the streets in the evening while many were returning home from their work in Winona. Through the windshields, there were nods from those familiar with our campaign. Our pack cruised in front of homes and businesses as we followed our serpentine routes of torture. Kids stopped their play to wave when we passed. For a moment, we became a recognizable presence in that town. Like the fountain itself, we poured ourselves onto those streets.

CHAPTER SEVENTEEN
FALLEN

October 16, 1984

Arnie's squad was shooting baskets in the Darlington gymnasium after class. Tom was not with them. In his senior season, he was ready to take his place on the varsity seven for the tournament competition. He had given up football and worked hard for the last three years to achieve that goal.

Senior Doug Dunham, junior Bob Cullen, and sophomore Kent Ruppert were in the mix with Tom for the sixth and seventh varsity spots. The four were evenly matched, and the runners in those positions were expected to step up if one of the first five had a rough day. Bob had been on the team since the first season in 1982. He and Dunham had run in the sectional the previous year, and both had been consistent varsity performers. Kent was pushing the upperclassmen in practice and had been trading places at the front of the JV with Tom all season.

All things being equal, Arnie leaned toward awarding the two spots to his seniors. But at the last minute, the rug had been pulled from under Tom's feet, and there was nothing Arnie could do to fix it. Tom could not shake the virus and had been unable to practice with the squad over the previous week. The Redbirds were the top-ranked team in the state, and they had a legitimate chance at winning the school's first state championship. Having each kid at his peak performance for the tournament was critical, and Arnie had to make a tough choice. Doug and Bob stayed on the varsity to complete the tournament roster. Kent would serve as the alternate in the eighth spot. Tom made one more sacrifice for his team.

Tom Evenstad (left) prepares to pass an opponent in a JV race. Photo courtesy of Tom Evenstad.

It was the kind of choice that gnaws at a coach's heart, and it was particularly hard on Arnie. He knew from his high school days what it was like to lead the pack and receive the accolades. But his college years had also taught him what it was like to be in the back of the pack, where sacrifices for the team largely went unnoticed. Tom's leadership had meant a lot to the program, yet his reward eluded him.

Darlington was hosting its regional meet. Since the Redbirds did not need to spend time on a bus, they used the extra time to stay loose, shooting hoops instead. The tactic worked too well, and the team had troubles after the race began. The soaked course acted as an equalizer, and the Redbirds' focus slipped when they needed it most. Rich Dallman of Albany and Sean Currie of Cambridge finished in front of Troy. The Albany Comets had all shown up with intensity. Brian Whalen, who had consistently performed as the Redbirds' second runner for most of the season, had another off day. In the end, Darlington narrowly defeated runner-up Albany, a team they had beaten soundly several times during the prior two months.

Pulling out a victory despite a poor showing is a sign of a strong team. But Arnie was unhappy with his squad's performance. The Redbirds suddenly faced the reality of their number one ranking. A great team can be beaten if that team has one or more runners fall short of their standard in a critical race. It was a lesson they needed to grasp quickly if they were to advance past the sectional on Saturday. Arnie did not want a repeat of the 1983 sectional loss, and he reminded his team of that gut punch.

"If you're in a close race, you'd better win, or you'll never forgive yourself! Do you remember how you felt when the season ended last year? Do you remember how you felt after the Platteville dual? Beat it or eat it!"

It was an ugly win, but a win nonetheless, and the Redbirds were advancing to the sectional with their number one ranking intact. After Arnie dismissed his squad, Troy picked up the boom box, and the crew "banged their heads" to Quiet Riot as they walked off the stage.

Mark was groaning as his thumbs hammered the buttons on the Coleco electronic football game. He and Dan were in a battle over the dim red dashes on the display of the handheld device. It was a common distraction, and the winner maintained control until a challenger vanquished his reign. The wet road glistened under a gray sky, and the windows were fogged from our breath touching the cold. It was not an uplifting view, and memories of the discomfort at the Mondovi race were needling my thoughts. I pulled up the collar on my letter jacket and did not relish trading its warmth for the elements we were about to encounter. For the second year in a row, we found ourselves bouncing on the long bus ride to the regional meet at Brookwood. Our contempt for the humiliating defeat on their course the prior year was still simmering. Brookwood was ranked fourth, ahead of us in the Class C coaches' poll, and the anticipation of the rematch had been building all season. We were not happy about racing on their treacherous course, but that was a secondary concern. We had improved and had suppressed our thirst for retribution for an entire year. It was time for payback.

The girls' race was held first. I watched as each squad lined up on the bleeding chalk line facing the wind and rain. The starter pistol fired, and a frenzied sprint ensued before the lane narrowed into the woods, and the contestants disappeared. Heidi finished in third place as an individual and led our girls' squad to a second-place finish, which was good enough to advance them to the sectional meet.

The soaked chalk line was nearly indistinguishable as I took my place for the start of the boys' race. The starter went through his commands, and the pistol's smoke had not cleared before we were in a maze of right-angle turns between the trees of the course, skipping over ruts and dodging runners who were losing their footing. It was an awful day to run, and the course was an equalizer. The fact that the ground was wet only magnified the effect. Runners were packed together more tightly than normal, causing elbowing and falls. Mud was flying everywhere. Form went out the window. Eyes shimmied back and forth intently, searching the ground ahead for hazards. The advantage of swift efficiency had been negated by surefootedness and anticipation.

For most of the race, Paul and I were running near the front, able to avoid some of the melee in the pack behind us. On our second climb up the hill, with about a mile to go, I planted my lead foot and slipped. *Fruumphh!* Suddenly my face bounced against the cold earth, and my teeth cracked together. The fall was completely unexpected and bewildered me for a moment. There had been no contact with competitors, and the tumble had happened at an unremarkable place on the course. Paul and I were simply climbing the hill together on a wide, straight lane. I scrambled back to my feet, unhurt but with a soaked torso. The disruption threw off my cadence and ceded my position in the race. I frantically attempted to catch Paul, whom I could still see ahead of me with three Brookwood runners between us. Disgust flooded my mind for the decision to leave my threaded cleats in my duffel bag. A short distance later, I crept up on the heels of the Brookwood runners and plotted an attack. As we approached a sharp right-hand turn, I burst past, cutting them off at the corner. As I planted my right foot to accelerate out of the turn, my view of the world went sideways. *Fruumphh!* The earth crashed into my side, and an opponent's shoe clipped the back of my head. My legs instinctively clambered to restore my upright position and move my stunned brain forward. But the trio had separated from me, and the finish line was drawing near.

From left to right: Paul Abts and Jeff Rich ascend a hill together at the regional meet in front of a group of Brookwood runners. Photo courtesy of Betty Rich.

At that moment I wanted a timeout—I *needed* a timeout! However, in cross country you don't get timeouts. In other sports, a coach can stop the action to regroup when a team runs into adversity and the momentum swings. It provides a few moments for the team members to collect their wits. But in cross country, runners must deal directly with misfortune. They are forced to confront adversity and carry on—or quit.

The shock of the falls and the short distance remaining in the race were too much for me to overcome. I had lost valuable placement, and despite gutting it out at the end, I finished far below my standard. I was not alone. Scott, Mark, and Dan had each fallen once and lost position. The condition of the course was so poor that all our times lagged our usual performance by a couple of minutes.

The assembly gathered in Brookwood's gym to hear the results. Muddy socks and rank jerseys dripped onto the floor. The smell of sweat permeated the place while we sat through the ceremony. Brookwood's runners had navigated their home course well and stayed upright throughout the race. They beat us 36–44. It was a bitter loss, made even worse since it was the same result for the second year on the same course. Adversity laughed in our faces. We watched Brookwood's team revel in their win over a ranked opponent, and we drank our dose of humility. The course and its condition had been infuriating. We had come expecting victory, but at that moment, we had to stomach our first defeat of the season by another Class C team.

I could not believe we had lost. It was harder to accept than the failure of the prior year when illness had weakened my ability to compete. None of us was sick, yet we had still failed. However distasteful, we cannot change the past. We can only learn from it and apply that knowledge in the future. The more bitter the disappointment, the more intractable the lesson.

Gary got on the bus and stood before us, looking at our team and fuming. He then unleashed his frustration with our performance.

"What was that? Do you think you can make it to state with an effort like that?"

He went on for another minute, venting his fury, and then sat down for the quiet ride home. The boom box remained silent. He had mistakenly perceived the result as a lack of effort on our part. We bore his surprising rebuke. It was uncommon for Gary—with his insight so well-tuned to our psyches—to misjudge us. His reaction was a reminder of the authoritarian methods we had experienced under other coaches. Each one of us hated to lose, and there we were, muddy and soaked from the effort. Any further tongue-lashing wasn't going to motivate us or change the result. That tactic might work to spur a different set of kids, but with us, it was more likely to have the opposite effect. We were already seething.

After the bus dropped us off at the high school, Gary and Mark hopped into the Volvo to return to Fountain City. Mark had recently gotten his license and was behind the wheel. One of Mark's talents was his ability to read a room. He often used that skill to create some comedy in a group when the moment was ripe for a laugh, but his radar could also detect negativity when it wasn't obvious to others.

JEFF RICH

The mood on the bus had not set well with him. The nonverbals from his teammates indicated a caustic response to his dad's rant, and he was concerned about the effect it could have. In Mark's mind, his dad had crossed a line, and he spoke up as soon as he pulled out of the parking lot.

"Dad, what were you thinking? You were wrong to lay into the guys like that! It wasn't like we tried to fall."

Gary turned to Mark, a bit surprised, and Mark continued.

"Don't you think we're hard enough on ourselves? You're the one who has to keep us positive!"

We all had moments of weakness, and there were times when each of us was held accountable by another on that team, even Gary. Mark had come to expect better from him. In the end, excuses don't taste very good, and we had to accept that Brookwood had beaten us fairly on that same cruddy course, running under the same conditions. They had used their knowledge, talent, and grit to beat us. Fortunately for us, the top three teams in the regional advanced to the sectional.

After the loss at Brookwood, the buzz around the state did not include our team, and I checked the papers to get the latest perspective. We had slipped to ninth place in the final poll. The upcoming sectional featured a juggernaut of talent in the Class C rankings. The first-ranked team, Darlington; the fourth-ranked team, Brookwood; and the seventh-ranked team, Boscobel, would all be at the sectional. Albany also qualified and had been ranked before their near-miss in Darlington. We had become a footnote to the headliners that were stacking the field in Reedsburg on Saturday.

It was homecoming week at C-FC with banners and crepe paper streamers throughout the hallways and in the gymnasium. Cutout paper footballs were taped to players' lockers with their numbers and names. As with Darlington, C-FC limited the homecoming court to boys from the football team. However, in the fall of 1984, the senior class did not have enough football players to fill the boys' positions on the court. We had a number of members on our team who were popular within the student body, and the school made the one-time exception to include cross country runners on the ballot. Scott and Paul were both voted onto the homecoming court. One of the traditional activities was "Skit Day" on Wednesday. The student body gathered on the gymnasium bleachers in anticipation of the performance. Each class developed skits for the audience. The skits were humorous, containing action scenes and dialogue to evoke a response from the crowd. Students would dress up in costumes or in drag, often imitating celebrities or school officials. The eagerly-awaited event was amateur fun for the student body.

Paul was in one of the skits about halfway through the production, with the scene taking place on the gymnasium floor. He was behind a curtain on stage, preparing for his entrance, when he took a flight of stairs to the gym floor and missed a step. He landed on the side of his foot and buckled into a heap. Several of us noticed the commotion on the edge of the gym and went over to help Paul off the floor. We took him into the locker room to look at his foot. Paul's eyes were wet from the pain. We helped him to a bench, where he lay back and extended his leg. Someone retrieved a cold pack from the medical kit. We punched the pouch to start the reaction and put the pack on Paul's foot.

It did not seem to help. Within minutes, the ankle was as swollen as a grapefruit, and blue streaks stretched up the side of his ankle and across the top of his foot. He could not put his weight on the joint or flex it. When Gary showed up for practice, he abruptly told the rest of us to run up County YY and then took Paul to the emergency room in Winona. The X-ray films dismissed a fracture, but the attending physician confirmed a bad sprain and advised Paul to stay off the ankle.

Per our coach's instructions, the rest of us gathered for practice in Fountain City and strode south to our old foe, YY. The collision of the warm earth with the cool air and soaking rains had spread a dense cover over the great valley. The ceiling of visibility reached just above the ridgeline before fading into an opaque charcoal blanket. Thermals rising from the coulees cast vapor plumes above the bluff. The image gave form to the beast waiting in its lair, eager to snuff out our dream with its breath. We welcomed the battle. Our anger was simmering under the surface, and our running was deliberate and

The Beast, County Highway YY, near Fountain City. Photo by Jeff Rich.

JEFF RICH

punishing. The defeat in Brookwood and Paul's injury brought back memories of the prior year when a golden opportunity was snatched from us. We had a lot of emotion to release, and that damned road could absorb our rage. We didn't talk during our toil, preferring to seethe in silence while we attacked the beast. The exertion was cleansing. In a way, our masochistic addiction helped us to cope better with our frustration.

After Gary arrived home, he entered the kitchen without a greeting and sat down at the table. His face was drawn. Judee sat down next to him.

"Gary, what's wrong?"

Gary glanced at her and said, "The team will not be going to the state meet this season."

Judee chuckled. "What are you talking about?"

"Paul has a severe ankle sprain. He fell down some stairs during a skit today at school. The doctor said he needs to stay off his foot, and he should definitely not be running. There isn't enough time for him to recover and race on Saturday."

"Don't we still have five runners?"

Gary's eyes dropped to the table again before he spoke.

"There are too many ranked teams in our sectional. It will just be too competitive. For us to have a chance, we're going to need each of our front five runners, and Paul is one of our best."

Judee's smile evaporated, and she put her head into her hands. She had witnessed the sacrifices Gary and the kids had made to reach their goal. She had allowed herself to hope with them. Beholding her husband's state in front of her, it seemed that, too often, the price for hope was despair.

After taking a deep breath, she raised her head again, put her hand on Gary's shoulder, and said emphatically, "Well, we can't let the boys hear that!"

Adversity was sneering at us by Friday morning. Paul was hobbling in the hallway, and we had twenty-four hours before our sectional race. He was sick about it. We were all sick. It had happened innocently enough, and there was no judgment, but Paul felt awful. He believed he had let us all down over something trivial. Paul did not need to ask for forgiveness for the mishap. He was our gutsy little guy with a big heart, and we loved him.

We said nothing, but we knew that racing on a sprain like that was fantasy. The healing powers of youth are tremendous, but there was only so much that could be done in a short amount of time. A high pain threshold was a requirement to race well in cross country, and although Paul was the smallest, he could tolerate more pain than any of us. Even if, by some miracle, he could limp through the race, his time would be poor, and the result for our team would be the same. It had never been more apparent to us that we were utterly dependent upon one another.

The time had come to face the cruel reality that our team's season would be over in a couple of days. We would commit to our best effort, but we knew our opportunity had vanished. After all the work we had put in over the prior fifteen months and having withstood a multitude of health problems, our goal would elude us. None of it had mattered. Adversity had won, and our sacrifice had been in vain. We all felt that gut-punched feeling in our core. The doubts and the sense of inadequacy we had overcome together were, again, front and center in our minds. Our hard work and sacrifices did not matter. Good guys finish last.

CHAPTER EIGHTEEN
RESURRECTION

October 20, 1984

The bus was already idling by the time I hoisted my duffel bag and trotted up the steps. The fumes from the diesel engine left the familiar acrid taste in my mouth. Saturday morning had arrived, and we loaded up for the two-hour ride southeast to Reedsburg, located at the eastern edge of the Driftless Area near the Wisconsin Dells and close to the site at Christmas Mountain, where the state meet would be held. Later that evening, the homecoming dance was planned with Prince's "Purple Rain" as its theme. The sun had risen gloriously on a perfect October morning without a cloud in the sky. The temperatures were forecast to be in the sixties by midday. But despite the sunny weather, there was a pall over the bus as we knew the reality of what awaited us. This was to be our last ride together, and a purple rain was following us down to Reedsburg.

At the top of the stairs, I saw Paul sitting in the front with his leg extended on the seat and his ankle bare. He wore his warm-up suit, and the joint was still a puffy palette of color. The unexpected sight stopped me in my tracks. I could not believe he was entertaining the thought of running, and I looked at him with disapproval. His eyes glared back at me in defiance.

"Dammit! I didn't go through the last two seasons to sit this one out!"

Gary had settled into the seat ahead of me, and I turned to him, seeking a reaction. He looked up with resignation and shrugged his shoulders.

"There isn't much to lose at this point. If he wants to run, then I'll let him run. He won't take 'no' for an answer anyway."

Paul was pigheadedly determined to limp through five thousand meters and finish the season with his pride intact. It brought back memories of Scott's struggle at the sectional a year earlier, only Paul's ankle was worse.

"There's a roll of athletic tape in the medical kit," Gary said. "Can you tape his ankle?"

Mark and I had some experience taping ankles from basketball. It was not a skill Gary possessed. I put my duffel bag in the opposite seat and sat down facing Paul. We went to work, and upon touching his foot, Paul flinched.

"Easy!"

Mark and I exchanged glances, and Paul calmed down to let the process continue. I crisscrossed strips of tape over and around the joint. I wanted to create a tape cast, but Paul would not have been able to fit his foot into the racing flats we all used. I did what I could with a minimal amount of tape. After we had finished, Paul's ankle was mostly immobilized, reducing the chance of further injury. But it would hurt like hell when his weight pounded down on that foot; no amount of tape would prevent that. Paul pulled up his socks to cover his ankles and conceal the wound.

Arnie rolled his car into the empty parking lot at Darlington High School. He arrived long before anyone else on Saturday morning. He had not slept well, and his stomach was in knots. Arnie buried his emotions as his arriving runners stepped out of their cars. He calmly greeted each of his kids with kind words and handed them copies of the course map so they could study it on the bus. He saw the tension in his squad's eyes. It had been 364 days since the bitter disappointment at the sectional in Prairie du Sac, 364 days of waiting for another chance, 364 days of waiting to be legitimate.

As the bus left the parking lot on its journey north, Arnie gazed out his window in deep thought. He had thrown his whole being into the last three seasons. A trip to the state meet would send the community into a frenzy and reward his kids for their commitment. But another gut-wrenching sectional loss could crush all of them. He could see Jeff Schuetz and John Lange in his mind. The bitter memory was as clear as the day. Just two more dedicated seniors who barely missed their chance to be affirmed. Arnie knew that anything could happen, that the sectional would be a dogfight, and that there was no predicting the outcome. He wondered if perhaps he cared too much. Caring makes the highs higher and the lows lower, becoming a sickening emotional roller coaster. Arnie looked at his kids in their seats on the bus. He remembered their sacrifices and dreams. He remembered their commitment to each other, their friendship. He wanted it so much for them. Perhaps caring meant he'd made a difference in someone's life? Perhaps caring was what gave life meaning and fulfillment? Oh, he wanted it so badly for them—and for himself.

As the Darlington bus neared Reedsburg, Arnie's mind began to focus on the task in front of them. He had seven kids with seven different personalities to properly motivate. What could he say to each one to fire him up without making any of them too nervous? Arnie felt the helplessness of a cross country coach during a competition. He cannot call a timeout or make a substitution, and there are no halftime adjustments. He must have everyone ready to go before the start of the race.

The team finished its pre-race survey of the course and gathered by the starting line. Ten minutes before the start, the Redbirds sat down on the grass and replaced their training shoes with spiked racing flats. Arnie beheld his team on the grass before him. Each kid needed to believe it was possible to run faster than ever before. They each had unique personalities, but they had to merge into one force at that moment.

After the two-hour ride, we stepped off the bus in Reedsburg and familiarized ourselves with the course. There would be a couple of laps over the same stretches, but the route was relatively simple. With the exception of one modest hill, the terrain was open, well-groomed, and flat, with a few tight corners.

The day was so beautiful that, if not for our misfortune, we would have had high hopes for the race and the homecoming dance yet to come. Instead, it was hard to escape the realization that this was it, the last time we'd stretch together, the last time we'd warm up together, the last time at the starting line together, and on and on. The start of the season had held such promise that our reality shocked and confounded us.

Our group walked toward the starting line to perform our stretching routine and remove our warm-ups. We began by striding over the initial stretch of the course. We kept Paul in the middle of our bunch in an attempt to conceal his limp from the probing eyes of coaches gathered in the vicinity. He suppressed the pain and did not let it show on his face.

The C-FC boys' team warms up before the Reedsburg sectional race.
Photo courtesy of Betty Rich.

On our first pass, we jogged past the Darlington Redbirds. I looked them over, sizing them up as they worked their routine. They were the only team with their names on the back of their jerseys, so I was able to personify the numbers I'd tracked all season in the papers. Their best runner, Troy Cullen, was easy to pick out. I had seen him at the sectional a year earlier, and his long stride was immediately familiar. While in motion, his knees were elevated higher than anyone else's, and he leaned forward, extending the length of his gait. It was a fluid motion, and he made it look easy. His arms were also more active than those of most of his competitors. But he never looked tired, just determined, with his jaw set in an intense gaze.

Darlington had been occupying the first-place spot in the coaches' poll. That was remarkable because they had been ranked ahead of the reigning champion Chetek, and Darlington had never before raced at a state championship. The two teams had never met in competition either. For Darlington to be listed at the top meant that the coaches felt they had something no one else possessed. The Redbirds had the magical combination of fast runners and depth. Their top five kids were certainly impressive, judging from the times I'd seen in the papers. They didn't seem to notice us as we passed. If we had met a week earlier, I would have inspected their other runners more closely. But at that moment, we were wounded and the contest was not in question. Darlington was the alpha pack on the course.

Albany was warming up nearby in their powder-blue tops. A few veterans from their state qualifying team in 1982 were on the course. Their leader, Rich Dallman, had won the sectional in 1983, and I'd read in the papers that Albany narrowly fell to Darlington in their regional. I'd seen them listed in the rankings for most of the season. The Comets were formidable and could easily walk away with the trophy.

The Boscobel Bulldogs were back again, defending their sectional crown from the previous year. Although they'd lost their best runner, Mark Reynolds, to graduation, they were now led by a pair of brothers, Kevin and Richard Clark, who were exceptional distance athletes. Sophomore Greg Bell was also placing well, and the Bulldogs were ranked ahead of us.

The Brookwood Falcons were warming up at the far end, wearing their jerseys with red long-sleeved T-shirts underneath. Seeing them again after just a few days brought back the sting of the regional loss. The faces of the Brookwood runners carried the self-assurance gained from the recent victory and from watching us lick our wounds. None of them knew of Paul's injury, but their posture still projected dominance in our presence. To them, we were the vanquished, the subordinates with our tails between our legs.

Arkansaw, Cambridge, Fennimore, and Southwestern each had talented runners. But in 1984, none of them had enough depth to challenge for the team championship at the sectional.

I was not the only one inspecting the competition. Darlington's coach was scanning the squads striding on the course in front of him. Arnie was confident but had a bit of concern with Albany, given their close contest earlier in the week. Still, the Redbirds had beaten Albany three times over the prior two months, and "the enemy you know is better than the one you don't." His squad had also beaten Boscobel, Fennimore, and Brookwood at the River Valley Invitational a month earlier. They were all familiar to him, but Brookwood still posed some threat in his mind. The margin of victory during the first meeting had not been that great, and a team can improve over the course of a season. He knew that Brookwood had won their regional, and they were exuding confidence. Arnie had noticed our C-FC squad in the papers during the season, but we had steadily slipped in the polls. Brookwood had emerged victorious in our regional, and we only had six runners warming up in front of Arnie. That combination pointed to depth issues and a diminished threat. Arnie focused on Albany and Brookwood to judge his team's status during the race.

When the countdown passed five minutes, Arnie called his squad into a huddle.

"We've waited 364 days! We've worked hard and we've improved. We're finally here, so let's show everyone what we can do! Get out smart and find your groove. Don't force it; let the race come to you. Then push hard over that last mile!"

Troy burst in, "Let's do it, guys!"

The Redbirds broke the huddle with their customary chant and commenced their final speed strides. Tom had made the trip up to Reedsburg and stood in the sunshine, watching his brother and teammates from behind the ropes. Arnie and Ann walked off the course when the countdown hit two minutes.

The colorful line of runners hopped in place, slapped their legs, and shook out their hands. When the official commanded, we

Coach Arnie Miehe gathers his Darlington squad moments before the start of the Reedsburg Sectional. Photo courtesy of the *Republican Journal*.

stepped up to the line and became still. The gun cracked, and the vibrant swarm hurtled down a long, wide stretch. As usual, Guy was pressing for the lead. Upon rounding the first turn, I found myself alone and without my wingmen, who were further back in the mob. Given Paul's trouble, I had hoped Scott would be with me, but Scott was still struggling with his knee and could not push the pace. The race was already an unfamiliar battle without my pack. The fleeting thought made me think about Paul's technique of creeping into the race from behind, preserving energy for later in the chase. His tactic was not my style, but at that moment I was in a good position to ease into the race. Paul could not run by my side, yet emulating his approach could give an isolated runner some strength late in the struggle. My pace was brisk but not suffocating, and my legs settled into an efficient cadence.

For the Redbirds, Troy also forced himself to hold back. He was prone to surging to the front early in a race, and the habit was hard to break since he was normally faster than the rest of the field. He was fast enough that his competitors rarely caught him, even if he became fatigued late in a contest. But the sectional competition was a step up, and Troy had already met Dallman, Currie, and Clark several times during the season without prevailing. He now forced himself to recall Arnie's words in the huddle before the start.

"Let the race come to you. Let the other guys tire themselves out over the initial mile, then pick them off as you move along."

It was a struggle to hold back, watching lesser runners move past him toward the front.

One benefit the athlete has over the coach is the chance to shed nervous energy during a competition. Arnie had to bear his anxiety, no longer having any control over the outcome. A coach yearns to see each of his top five runners dominate his opponents from the start. But in a sectional meet, the competition is too intense to allow a "relaxed" win. Arnie found himself running from spot to spot along the course as a cheerleader, like the rest of the crowd.

At the first-mile mark, my breathing was rhythmic, and the gap between the runners in front of me gently closed. Gary had warned us to guard against becoming too comfortable while hanging back during a race. Endorphins would kick in, and the mind could drift into the pacification of a steady pace, insulated by the surrounding shield of runners. The mind's muted voice could beguile the runner into letting too much ground pass under the feet before making a move. The opportunity had to be pressed with enough time left in the race to place well.

I was at the point when Paul typically moved to my flank and prompted me to overtake the field with him. One opponent and then two slipped behind me easily, and my spirits picked up. A couple of runners from Boscobel had been clinging to me, and my accelerated pace shed them. After each conquest, my eyes became fixed on the next runner, and the gap would shrink, providing positive feedback as it closed. Another runner wearing Albany's blue jersey came into view, and he yielded when pressed. Each repetition lifted my spirits and strangely did not cause me suffering. My mind was muted, barely noticeable, and my will was flourishing in the sunlight. Familiar voices were calling to me along the course, cheering me on. Each stride forward consumed more ground than the last. I suddenly realized why Paul coined his second mile of a race "momentum." It was becoming a game in my mind, reeling in one runner and then picking off the next one, creating a successive challenge after each triumph. The new tactic was the perfect tonic. It achieved the right balance of reserving energy without yielding too much distance to the leaders.

Darlington's Brian Whalen (second from right) climbs a hill near the end of the first mile of the sectional race. C-FC's Jeff Rich (white jersey) is in close pursuit. C-FC's Paul Abts and Mark Brone can be seen in the background. Photo courtesy of Arnie Miehe.

The Redbirds' Troy Cullen was starting to move up the column as well. He had been hanging back, keeping within view of the leaders and preserving his energy. It had been excruciating for him, but he'd done what Arnie had asked. He had kept his pride in check until this point, and now he could unleash his commanding stride and attack the field. Troy fixed his eyes on Albany's Rich Dallman, who was up ahead and in a battle with Boscobel's Kevin Clark and Sean Currie of Cambridge. Dallman had edged Troy at the 1983 sectional by a mere two seconds. A mere two seconds and three points had been the difference between advancing to state as a team and going home. The memory of the bitter loss kept prodding Troy forward. They'd met three times in the prior two months, and Troy had been victorious twice. He had work to do in order to reclaim his place, and he began passing opponents.

Halfway through the race, the Redbirds' James Schuetz found himself in a duel with Albany's third runner, Bill Karls. The two were running abreast of each other as they passed opponents on the course. James had prevailed on Tuesday, but Karls was suddenly filled with voracity, intent on launching the Comets into the state meet. Karls' constant pressure was withering James with each repeated attack. Neither could gain an advantage, and James knew the consequence if he could not hold his counterpart at bay. Arnie had drilled it into him. Passing the Albany runner was paramount.

When there are dozens of runners in a race, colors blend, and it is easy to miss someone as he runs by. Before computer integration in the sport, the calculator in the coach's head had to compute the jersey, placement, and total sum in real time. Arnie knew his crew had gotten off the line well and seemed to be comfortably leading Boscobel and Brookwood by mid-race. But the light blue of Albany's jerseys mingled with those of Cambridge and Southwestern. Albany's runners were heaped in a close competition with the Redbirds' front five, and Rich Dallman was leading the entire field.

With a quarter mile left in the race, Troy was not where he had hoped. Dallman was out of his sight, and Troy had a large gap to close in order to catch the next runner in front of him, Guy Todd.

Guy Todd rounds a corner five hundred meters from the finish at the Reedsburg Sectional. Darlington's Troy Cullen can be seen in the background, closing the gap. Photo courtesy of Dick Rich.

He wondered whether he had held back too long before making his move. Troy reached into his reserve and locked his focus on that next runner.

I was in a sprint to catch as many rival jerseys as possible. A cascade of runners who had been pressing the lead early in the race succumbed to my surge. The first runners from Brookwood and Fennimore were among them. They were yielding to their minds' tantrum late in the contest, and my spirits lifted after each success.

Darlington's coaches had lined themselves alongside the final leg of the course, calling for their harriers to pass the next opponent. The crowd was in a frenzy, blaring unintelligibly as the runners struggled in agony over the last two hundred meters.

On the final turn, I passed Darlington's second runner, Brian Whalen. He did not give up easily and tried to mount a challenge, but there was more left in my tank at that point. On the closing stretch, with the fingers of oxygen debt grasping for my jersey, Guy came into view ahead of me. My eyes glimpsed Darlington's Troy Cullen overtake him near the finish. I fought to deny their second runner the same success, working to close the gap on the blue jersey ahead of me, Southwestern's leader, Paul Reynolds. Thoughts rushed forward, begging the legs to obey the brain on my swan song dash. The digital clock was in view for the entire desperate sprint. I ran out of turf before I could catch Reynolds, and the finish line passed beneath my feet, ushering a wave of relief.

It was not a personal record, but it had been my best tactical race. Whalen, Darlington's gritty second runner, crossed one second behind me. Guy qualified for the state meet but failed to finish ahead of those adversaries who had beaten him the year before.

My reserve had been spent on the course. Oddly, my feelings of disappointment were reconciled during those first seconds in the chute, drawing the sunshine into my lungs. Despite the misfortune our squad had suffered with Paul's injury, I felt a sense of fulfillment with each breath. I had saved my best race for my last race. I had done what I could for my team.

As I took my placement card from the official and stepped out of the chute, I turned back to view the finish. The sight jolted me. Paul was crossing the line in fifteenth place, on Mark's heels. I looked at the digital clock, and my heart leapt, but I could not believe what

I was seeing. How was it possible that Paul could have run five thousand meters in 17:35 on an ankle most people would not have walked on? Did he miss a turn on the course—or an entire loop? I had held that ankle in my hands a couple of hours earlier on the bus. My mind could not process it. It was miraculous to me and hard to comprehend the misery he had just gone through. Nearly forty years later, I can hardly believe it actually happened.

Before I could regain my composure, Scott charged into the chute in twenty-second place, completing a gutsy run on his sore knee. His mother was waiting for him at the end. Carol's gait was unsteady from the MS devastating her body, but smiling with pride, she was there to receive her son.

Gary had been watching our placement compared with the runners from Darlington. Troy Cullen had beaten Guy by one place, but the rest of our next four runners had finished ahead of their Redbirds counterparts. Suddenly, we dared to hope again.

After Dan came through the chute, our clan murmured a continuous and anxious buzz. While our team worked to restore clarity to our oxygen-starved brains, our fans shared their observations on opponent placement with Gary. Other coaches approached him and offered their preliminary tallies, along with congratulations. Within

The C-FC boys' team is welcomed out of the chute while Paul Abts and Mark Brone fill their lungs on the right. Photo courtesy of Dick Rich.

a matter of minutes, the math vaulted our prospects. I stood there while the commotion swirled around me, stunned from the effects of the race, stunned from Paul's performance, stunned from the realization that we would be advancing to state.

Arnie had seen our first five runners cross the line and realized that a sectional championship would be out of reach for his Redbirds. His mind immediately switched to the goal of advancing to state with a second-place finish. He rushed to his runners as they came out of the chute to see their placement cards, simultaneously filled with excitement and agony. For the second season in a row, he had two runners in the top ten at the sectional. Arnie knew that Brookwood's third through fifth runners had crossed after his top five had finished. They had passed that test, but he was still concerned about Albany and was asking his breathless kids who they saw finish in front of them.

Arnie had seen Rich Dallman of Albany win the race, so the Redbirds were down three points after their respective first-place runners. But in the blur of colors that followed, he could not confirm Albany's score. The third through fifth runners from both teams had been clumped alternately at the finish. He went through each of his crew, testing their oxygen-starved minds to recall whether they'd beaten their Albany counterpart. Through the first four runners on each team, Arnie calculated a tie. He initially surmised that Albany had eclipsed his Redbirds, but it was unclear if his fifth runner, Jay Stauffacher, had beaten Albany's fifth or sixth runner. He was feverish with angst.

"Jay, was Feeney behind you?"

"I'm sure I beat him, Coach. I know there was an Albany runner a couple of places behind me."

"Are you sure? Was it their fifth or sixth guy?"

"I'm not completely sure," Jay said meekly.

Arnie wrestled with his anxiety until the awards ceremony. As with many things in life, he had to rely on hope in the end. Hope is an interesting emotion, one counted upon after completely losing control. Hope has been the driving force behind many impossible dreams achieved by humanity. But it can also be the root of deep despair when the desired outcome does not materialize. Arnie was hoping his seniors had not run their last race.

Coach Arne Miehe gathers his team as they exit the chute at the Reedsburg Sectional on October 20, 1984. Runners James Schuetz, Troy Cullen, Brian Whalen, and Kirk Evenstad can also be seen in the huddle. Photo courtesy of the *Republican Journal*.

The officials began announcing the team results to the large group gathered at the awards ceremony.

"In ninth place, Cambridge. In eighth place, Southwestern ..." On down the line, "Fifth place, Brookwood. Fourth place, Boscobel ..." And then the moment of truth.

"Third place, Albany."

Darlington's crowd erupted at the words. Arnie's heart was in his throat as he watched his seniors celebrate the biggest accomplishment in their school's athletic history. Ann turned and gave Arnie a hug. The Redbirds had qualified for the state meet.

When announced, Arnie approached the WIAA official to receive the runner-up plaque. He then handed it to Troy, the kid who broke the mold and chose cross country over football, the captain and the leader of the first team in school history to qualify for state. The Redbirds lined up outside Reedsburg Middle School and posed for a team photo to mark the accomplishment. Tom stood in the background, delighted at the outcome, cheering his brother and friends.

Darlington's first state qualifying team. The Redbirds' varsity seven line up for a photo after their sectional accomplishment in Reedsburg. From left to right: Doug Dunham, Kirk Evenstad, Brian Whalen, Troy Cullen, James Schuetz, Jay Stauffacher, Bob Cullen, and Coach Arnie Miehe. Photo courtesy of the *Republican Journal*.

When our sectional championship was confirmed, the tension was released, and we all rejoiced. Smiling numbly, not yet believing the revival that had just taken place, my teammates and I walked up to the race officials to receive our plaque. We tallied sixty points, fifteen fewer than Darlington, advancing both of our teams to state. We hoisted the gleaming plaque in the sunlight, too overwhelmed to sense the eyes upon us. We had suddenly become the team to chase, no longer cloaked with underdog anonymity. The glove had been thrown down for a rematch the following week at Christmas Mountain.

After we took our seats on the bus, the result took some time to absorb. A few hours earlier, we had thought our season was dead.

C-FC's first state qualifying team with their 1984 sectional championship plaque. From left to right, kneeling: Mark Brone and Paul Abts. From left to right, standing: Coach Gary Brone, Jeff Rich, Dan Lettner, Scott Adler, and Guy Todd. Photo courtesy of Betty Rich.

Paul sat near the front, and I cut the tape off his ankle. Despite his performance, it looked worse, and he was swelling from the punishment. I elevated his leg on some duffel bags and taped an ice pack around it for the ride home. He needed to take his place on the homecoming court in a few hours.

"How'd you do it, Cud?" I asked him.

"I went out hard, but it was like running with a knife in my foot. After a little bit, Mark came up from behind me. He ran by my side the entire race and wouldn't let me back off. He kept saying, 'Hang in there, Cud. You can make it!'

"He never shut up! It hurt like hell for a while, but eventually it became numb, and I was able to focus on the race. After that, we started picking off runners together."

I sat back in my seat and smiled. Paul had come a long way since joining the team. He had dedicated himself, and it had shown in his schoolwork as well. His grades had improved significantly since his sophomore year. Paul had found where he belonged, committed to his teammates in a struggle for a shared goal.

Over the years I've frequently reflected on that moment. Under what circumstances do human beings decide to sacrifice themselves for the benefit of others? Paul did not need to make the attempt. None of us was pressuring him, and none of us would have blamed him if he had watched the race from the sidelines. On the contrary, we felt it was a bad choice for him, and even if he did not damage his foot, he would be in excruciating pain. At the time, we did not think he could make a difference in the outcome of the race. So why would someone do something like that? After all, each of us is selfish at a base level. It is a necessary trait for survival. Where does that threshold lie when our concern for others surpasses our self-interest? More importantly, what moves that line? Why does that blurred edge vary so greatly among individuals? Some never get past the level of teenage selfishness, yet others can reach great levels of suffering for the sole benefit of others—even absent others' gratitude.

There is an emotional attachment that comes from shared sacrifice for a common goal, particularly if the goal or benefit is uncommon and larger than the individual. A platonic love ensues, perhaps not as high as a parent's love for a child, but still somewhere above the first rung of Plato's ladder. Fellow soldiers form these bonds in battle, as do firefighters, first responders, or any other team of people whose lives and limbs are risked together. The higher the stakes and commitment, the deeper the bonds that develop when each depends upon the other. Our team had not risked our lives for each other, but our relationships had become uncommon, no longer a set of equivalent exchanges. Although not life-threatening, Paul had witnessed his teammates sacrifice for him and for one another. The commitment to something larger than himself had become personal. The team had become his family, and the bonds were strong enough to set aside concern for himself. His pride would not allow him to watch the race from the sidelines. It was better for him to suffer the pain of the race than to suffer the pain of the mirror if he had not tried. Paul believed he could race on that foot, even if the rest of us did not. Above all else, that belief was what mattered, and Mark had believed with him.

Mark was going through his usual antics in the back of the bus. Dan was teasing the girls, competing for their attention. The boom box was blasting Prince's "Let's Go Crazy," and above our heads, Purple Rain had been replaced by a blue sky.

C-FC's Paul Abts struggles up a hill on a swollen ankle at the Reedsburg Sectional. Mark Brone accompanies Paul on his right. Darlington's James Schuetz can be seen trailing closely, next to Bill Karls of Albany. Photo courtesy of James Schuetz.

CHAPTER NINETEEN
CHASING THE WHITE WHALE

Arnie Miehe was exultant as soon as he realized his Redbirds had a lower score than Albany. In his third season, his squad had qualified for the state meet with an excellent chance to compete for the title. It was the first trip to a state competition for Darlington High School in any sport. The bitter sectional loss of 1983 was instantly forgotten, and the world looked bright again. He had been surprised by C-FC, however, after our second-place finish in the regional. When the awards ceremony finished, Arnie approached Gary to congratulate him and chat about the race. Gary told him his kids "ran out of their heads." But that was not the whole truth. What Gary knew and did not share was that he had taken Paul Abts to the emergency room three days earlier, and the young man had "run out of his ankle."

Arnie would not be surprised by C-FC again, and he still had hope for his team's chances at Christmas Mountain. All five of the top runners for both teams were within seconds of their counterparts, so while the difference in score seemed significant, it was close. After the team stepped off the bus in Darlington, Arnie assembled his squad on the stage.

"What happened today did not just happen *today*. It is the result of dedication and hard work. It is the result of your determination and character, even when things aren't going your way. Now look at what you have—the opportunity of a lifetime! This won't be the last time in your life you'll face adversity. There will be plenty of punches that come your way in life. You will get knocked down, and you will feel like throwing in the towel. Don't give in to that crap!"

Arnie paused, and behind the words, his runners could see the joy in his face.

"We're going to be in this thing next week! I spoke with the C-FC coach today, and he said his team ran better than he expected. You were mixed in right with them, and they only have six runners! A fall or a bad day for one runner would finish them. Go home and enjoy what you did. Oh, and don't do anything stupid. We don't need anybody getting injured right now, so lay low and get some rest. Congratulations!"

Arnie watched his kids light up as they walked past him toward their rides. In particular, he noted the contentment on Brian Whalen's face. After three years of football, he had walked away from a starting position at quarterback. It had been a big leap, and it had caused more than a few brows to furrow. But the football team had just finished a winless season, and Brian was heading to the state meet with his buddies. He knew he had made the right choice.

Troy hit the play button on the boom box as the group walked off the stage. The guitar riff ensued, and Def Leppard's "Photograph" escorted them to the parking lot.

On the ride back to C-FC High School, Gary Brone was also gleeful. But he was not stunned by the victory as others had been. Gary knew his team's potential after that first invitational at Black River Falls fourteen months earlier. His kids did not fully believe it, but he did. His stopwatch and his eyes told him the potential that was there, even if the team did not have a lot of depth. He had spoken with other coaches, and they had let him know from the expressions on their faces. But Gary had also perceived something beneath the surface. The Volvo had revealed it to him. He knew his group could show fierce determination and turn a training run into a bruising rivalry, risking injury in order to triumph in a challenge. He had seen how they deflated opponents on the course, running as a pack. He had witnessed their fanatical finishes at the chute. But to harness that spirit, he understood that they needed to have a clear goal, without fear of risk, and that they needed to want it. Gary was not going to let his squad remain driftless. While his team could see the breadcrumbs, they needed a reason to keep following the trail to its conclusion. He did not waste any time setting a new goal. He began his marketing campaign immediately on the bus ride back from Reedsburg. Gary stood up to face the back of the bus and raised his voice.

"Shut off the boom box!"

The chatter on the bus ceased, and the team looked at Gary.

"We're going to go down there next week and win the whole thing!"

Our team's confidence had come a long way in fifteen months. We no longer viewed ourselves as underdogs and expected to win most of the meets we competed in. The goal of qualifying for state had been believable. Obstacles had been conquered, and we had even witnessed a small miracle to get to the state meet. The results from our races had convinced us we had that level of ability, and we had worked hard enough to deserve it. But a state championship? That seemed a bit bold for an obscure, second-year team with only six runners. The team could end up like Brookwood, coming off a tremendous victory only to be soundly defeated at the next level. After all, our season had been on life support just a couple of hours earlier. To us, Gary appeared a bit delusional from the victory. There were still two runners nursing injuries. One more mishap would smother any slim chance of attaining his new goal. Paul was sitting on the bus seat with a bag of ice wrapped around his foot as Gary uttered the words. The visual was not helpful, and his sales pitch seemed contrived.

Sensing disbelief from his team, Gary went on. "We just beat the top-ranked team in the state, so why can't we win it all?"

Gary had a way of making anything seem possible, and he had made an irrefutable point. We smiled and nodded, placating our coach's enthusiasm while still harboring doubts. The goal was adopted on the bus without argument. We were too elated to argue, and the homecoming dance was approaching.

Gary began to hammer his message home by sharing it whenever he got the chance. Though we rolled our eyes at his relentless encouragement, his overture had planted the seeds he had intended. Inside, we were secretly dwelling upon the possibility as soon as he announced that we were heading to state. The adulation appealed to our egos. There was an excited murmur at the homecoming dance that night. For the first time in school history, C-FC had a team competing for a state championship.

Gary gave our squad Sunday off to rest. He had a flurry of interviews from the papers on the west side of the state and across the river in Minnesota. By Monday, photos of our team and articles about the Cinderella squad with the long, hyphenated name were popping up. Gary was telling the press he thought his team could win the whole thing. Our spirits soared with the attention, despite the thought that Gary's comments might put a target on our backs.

Gary was fixated on the new goal. He challenged our pride and shared how other coaches had declared our sectional victory a fluke.

"I won't mention who said it, but a couple of the coaches came up to me the other day and congratulated me on our win. They said it was a real shame that we didn't have seven runners so we could challenge for the title."

It was nearly unheard of for a team to win a state cross country championship without a full squad of seven runners. The last time that feat had been accomplished was a decade earlier, by Fennimore, and nobody could remember another time before that.

He'd make offhand comments about the articles in the papers.

"Well, the *Leader-Telegram* in Eau Claire had a nice article, but the *State Journal* in Madison didn't say much about our win in Reedsburg. The *Milwaukee Sentinel* didn't either."

He talked about the best runners from the other schools that had been featured.

"Yeah, they covered the battle between Dallman and Currie and how one of them would probably win at Christmas Mountain."

He pulled out any fodder he could to fuel our competitiveness. But he would also plug some positivity into the mix.

"We're going to beat them on that final climb. We're the best hill runners in the state!"

In Darlington, Arnie was going through a similar flurry of interviews with the papers from the southern part of the state. The Redbirds were ranked at the top of the poll, but rankings meant nothing going into the state meet. In fact, most of the ranked teams from a week earlier had been eliminated, and the contest was up for grabs. Arnie knew this and that the odds of winning the title were mostly a matter of confidence. Each of the teams that had advanced was physically gifted enough to win. Despite the runner-up finish at the sectional, Arnie wanted to instill in his squad the possibility of a different outcome, that each race was a unique contest with unique circumstances. Perseverance will ultimately yield results, and he needed his squad to believe it was possible for them to stand on the podium. Knowing that his kids would be reading their press coverage, he began talking to his team through his interviews with the papers.

"The number one rating is not even a concern anymore. Now we're just racing."

"I personally believe that the team that runs a solid race is the team that will win."

"You don't have to go in there with the idea of my God, we've all gotta run 50 seconds faster than our best time ..."

"Nor am I overly worried about our team's runner-up finish to C-FC, which was second in its regional and whose runners probably raced over their heads at the sectional."

One other story line was highlighted in the papers. Two-time consecutive champion Chetek would not be running as a team in the state meet, having been defeated on their home course by Stratford and Edgar in the sectional. The previous spring's graduation of their individual champion, Al Severude, had opened the door just enough for their dethroning. The upset shocked the Class C tournament field since Chetek had shared the top ranking with Darlington all season.

Stratford's times had been astonishing, with the top five runners all finishing under seventeen minutes in their win at Chetek. Gary warned us about them.

"If those teams can defeat a program like Chetek's, then they can win the whole thing."

He went on.

"Watch for Edgar's runners wearing yellow or green jerseys and Stratford's wearing orange. Don't let any of those guys pass you late in the race. Reel 'em in on that hill."

On Monday morning, Arnie stopped by the main office at Darlington High School. He bent over to begin writing an announcement to be read over the loudspeaker. It had been a gratifying weekend, and now he could share the news with the entire student body. He glanced up at the students passing by with their books, conducting the normal chatter in the hallway. Then, as his head started to return to his task, his eyes caught a sight that sent him into a panic. His pen fell out of his hand, and he sprinted into the hallway, where he saw Troy moving toward his locker on crutches. Arnie chased after him.

"Troy! What happened?"

Troy glanced over his shoulder and kept moving.

"I twisted my ankle stepping off a curb yesterday, Coach. It will be okay."

"Stop!" Arnie shouted. "Wait a minute! Are you kidding me? How did this happen? Let me look at that foot!"

Troy kept crutching down the hallway, ignoring his coach, and Arnie started to fume.

"I told you guys to be careful this weekend! What were you thinking?"

Arnie looked closely at Troy and noticed a subtle smirk crack on his star athlete's face. Troy then picked up his crutches and walked off to his classroom, laughing.

"See ya at practice tonight, Coach!"

Arnie was hopping mad. However, his relief was so great he could only manage a grunt as he stood there, duped. He started breathing again and turned back to the office to finish writing his announcement. The seniors did not miss the chance to heckle their coach on the stage that evening before practice.

That same afternoon, our coach had Paul sit out of practice but put the rest of our team on the streets of Fountain City for more hill work. The punishment helped our egos stay grounded. Guy was on a mission, and the rest of us were paying for it. He was not satisfied with his fifth-place finish in Reedsburg, and he felt he should have been challenging the leaders to break the tape. He was not accustomed to crossing the line after someone else, and he had finally run into exceptional talent. Dallman and Currie finished about thirty seconds ahead of Guy, and both had outstanding sprinting speeds on top of their endurance. Kevin Clark of Boscobel had outpaced Guy throughout the race, and Troy Cullen had overtaken him near the finish. They had all beaten him at the sectional and state meets in 1983, and Guy wanted some revenge. He did have the solace of defeating their teams in the sectional, but he wanted the individual achievement as well. Guy was our Captain Ahab on the streets of Fountain City. He was at the bow with the harpoon, and we were pulling on the oars. I looked over at Scott as we struggled up the pavement to Hill Street. For once, I was by his side on a climb, and his sore knee had painted a grimace on his face.

As we panted in unison, I uttered, "Shit! He's going to kill us!"

Scott furrowed his brow and mumbled something profane under his breath. We ran for several miles, up and down, up and down, hill repeat after hill repeat. Guy flew up the hills at practice that night, and we struggled mightily to hang with him until, at last, he pulled away, chasing the whale in his head. Guy was more than two hundred yards in front of us by the time we finished at the hardware store. We could not stay with him on those streets, and he put us through hell.

The Redbirds conducted a "normal" week of practice, including several long training runs around Darlington and some interval work. Arnie continued to articulate a "solid" approach to his team for the upcoming meet. He did not want his kids to overthink their preparation, so he surrounded them with normalcy. The mood at the practices was lighthearted, and the team soaked in the moment. As they ran through the streets of Darlington, they took in a multitude of signs displayed downtown. At school, a banner hung over the trophy case, cheerleaders made posters and placed them on the boys' lockers, and signs were taped to the gymnasium walls wishing them luck at state.

Darlington High School did not hold classes on Thursday or Friday due to a teacher convention. Arnie had told his team to meet for their final practice on Thursday at ten thirty in the morning, which was the same start time they would be racing on Saturday. He wanted to simulate the routine they would go through on the day of the meet. The squad stretched on the stage and then left the gymnasium for an easy three-mile run around the school grounds.

After giving his squad their instructions, Arnie pushed through the school's front door to watch his team's workout. At that moment, Wadzy Martens was entering the building to attend to some school board matters. The old coach stopped and smiled at Arnie.

"Young man, you are doing quite a job with your team. You have those kids believing in themselves, and that is what it takes to win. Keep it up!"

Arnie's face glowed.

"Thanks ... I will!"

That small affirmation from the revered coach lifted Arnie's spirit and motivated him at a pivotal moment. Arnie turned toward the parking lot, beaming with gratitude. Like so many others, Martens could have viewed the sport of cross country as a threat to the football program at Darlington. But Wadzy was a visionary, and instead of taking the narrow view, he saw a bigger opportunity. His view echoed the observation of President Kennedy, who once said, "A rising tide lifts all boats."

Martens saw the culture of the school improving with positive results and the pursuit of excellence. He believed those benefits would carry over to all activities at the school and in the community.

After finishing their workout with some quick strides, the Redbirds gathered on the stage, and Arnie walked through the itinerary for Friday afternoon and Saturday. He left no ambiguity, no possibility for anxiety to enter his kids' minds. He covered when they would leave, what they should bring, and where they would stay. He gave each of them a copy of the course map, guided them through the route, and talked about strategy. They were all familiar with the course because they had all gone there the previous year to watch Troy run at the state meet, but Arnie did it anyway. They would approach the meet in a businesslike manner, and he sent them off with a final message.

Darlington High School yearbook photo of Walter "Wadzy" Martens in the 1950s. Photo courtesy of Arnie Miehe.

"Okay, guys. Go home, eat good, get plenty of rest, and don't come here tomorrow on crutches!"

The stage erupted in laughter once again, and Troy smirked as he walked past his coach and out of the gymnasium.

By Thursday afternoon, Paul was back for our final workout. Gary had instructed us to go on an easy two-mile run toward Cochrane and then back to the school along Highway 35. He commonly gave us a lighter practice before a race; he did not want us to injure ourselves before the big meet. We welcomed the change from the hill workouts earlier in the week.

We started jogging at a slow pace toward Cochrane, per Gary's command. Highway 35 carried heavy traffic, so we ran single file to avoid a problem and share the load. As we began, a disturbance above the marsh caught my eye, and I squinted to identify the source.

The sun had not yet sunk behind the bluffs of Minnesota, and a tapestry of color filled the sky. The marsh below mirrored the hues of orange, pink, and blue. The kaleidoscope of color made it difficult to recognize the silhouettes. But the whistling calls left no doubt about their identity. The tundra swans were one of the most breathtaking species we viewed against that sky. They were among the last to flee south and stood over four feet tall with a wingspan of six feet. They were clothed in a plumage of white, with necks as long as their bodies. Thousands of them retreated with winter in pursuit of their food source, which was imprisoned by its icy wake. They gathered to rest on their journey near the confluence of the Buffalo River, a dozen miles north of our school. Tourists also flocked there for an up-close view of the cream puffs floating in the water. On calm, frosty nights I could hear the swans' high-pitched "whistles" overhead as they journeyed south. They maintained a disciplined formation, with each bird taking turns in the lead, each one sacrificing so the others could catch a break in the back. At that moment we were like kin, applying the same technique to our last workout together.

After two miles, we turned around for the return leg, and the pace seemed a little more brisk, comfortable but noticeably faster. It was something we could sense, like a concert band rushing the beat while the metronome tried to hold back the cadence. Then Mark overtook the lead from Guy. It surprised Guy, and he countered with a burst to the front.

"What are ya doin', Space?" he asked Mark.

The rest of us were obliged to keep pace and close the emerging gap. Mark had poked the hive, and the hornets were irritable. Gary had been stoking our competitive juices with the media fodder all week. Guy had been abusing us on the hills of Fountain City. Our egos were simmering with our hatred for losing, and in less than a week, we had come to covet the new opportunity. Then Paul rushed to the front.

Scott squeezed his lane down and murmured, "Knock it off, Cud. You'll get hurt again!"

Once more the rest of us had to close the gap, and it pressed our tolerance. Guy lurched ahead to reclaim his spot at the front, and what had been a comfortable jog turned into a charge. The annoyance had triggered each of us to push to the lead and yield to counterattacks alternately.

"Stop it!" I shouted. "This isn't what Gary wants! We might get hurt! Stop it!"

Logic returned, there was a short pause, and we abated. Gary looked to me in situations like that to act as the disciplinarian for the team. Occasionally I lost control and was unable to overcome my own competitiveness.

Moments later, Guy slid ahead to reestablish himself in the pole position, and I'd had enough. It was one of those times that I lost my composure. The race was on, and I surged to the front. We all heartily committed to the battle. It became a competition with each other, jostling for position, jabbing elbows, and throwing out insults as siblings would in their rivalries. We were crowded together on the uneven shoulder of Highway 35, facing oncoming traffic as we battled south at full speed. It was a scorching pace the rest of the way, as fast as any of the races we had run. It was a senseless act after everything we had gone through up to that point. Our fragile pride had been challenged, and none of us could stand for that. We wanted to beat each other that day and beat our opponents on Saturday. Even Guy was unable to separate himself on the floor of the valley. Determination had set in.

We arrived back at the school and started laughing at one another. The intense exertion had relieved our stress. When Gary walked over and looked at his watch, he became livid. It was rare to see him get angry, but our run had been irresponsible, and this time, we deserved the reprimand. But Gary was also culpable. He understood the nature of his team and had rattled the cage. After a moment of reflection, we each felt guilty that we had let our pride coax us into the fray. The teenage mind does not pause long to weigh risks and benefits before acting. Gary's marketing campaign had succeeded; his team was spoiling for a fight.

Shortly after lunch on Friday, the Redbirds met at the school and loaded up their van. Parents, yearbook staff, and the local newspaper clicked photos to commemorate the school's first state team prior to their departure. The Darlington Fire Department had sent a truck to escort the team out of town, and it blared its siren as the van drove up Main Street. Community members stepped out of their shops and homes to wave at the squad as they passed by. Signs were stapled to power poles and fenceposts for miles on Highway 23 as the Redbirds traveled north of town toward Reedsburg, where they would lodge the night before the meet.

On Friday afternoon, C-FC High School held a pep rally for our team. The entire staff, student body, and some community members were there. Pep rallies were relatively rare and reserved for homecoming or big basketball games if a team went deep into a tournament. This was the first pep rally for a cross country meet at our school. Gary made a few comments to the crowd, and the pep band played the school song. It was another confirmation for our program, and the school gave us a grand sendoff. After the student body was dismissed, we picked up our duffel bags and crawled into a large van to drive to the Wisconsin Dells, where we would lodge on the eve of the race. Stepping out the door, we noticed the van was decorated with posters and had well-wishes scribed on the windows. Becky and Heidi had stayed late after practice the night before to decorate our carriage. It was another way our girls' team could be with us. Traveling south through Fountain City, we received waves from residents and spotted signs on business storefronts wishing us luck.

The Wisconsin Dells was a small town set beside the Wisconsin River near the center of the state. The term *dells* had a French origin and described the sandstone formations that had developed along the river at that point. The community was a natural tourist attraction for its beauty, and by the 1980s, there were many gift shops, restaurants, motels, bars, and water parks. In summer, the attractions drew tourists from Chicago and around the Midwest. For a few months each year, the town swelled in population to many times its usual size. Thousands of high school and college kids were hired seasonally to meet the summertime labor demand. But in September, the tourists left, schools opened, and the community became dormant for the next three seasons.

Gary had booked two rooms in a small roadside motel. It was a dive, with thin walls, musty carpet, and decades-old furnishings. It was also adjacent to the main arterial passing through the community. Most resorts had shuttered for the season, so few options were left in town, with a big meet nearby the next morning. The school athletic budget was minimal, and the accommodations for our team were thrifty. Gary had reserved two rooms that we would share for the night, with two queen-sized beds in each room. Gary got one bed to himself, and Paul and I shared the other bed in the first room. The other four guys crammed into the room next door. It did not bother us. We were hungry, though, and Gary liked to have us carbo-load the night before the race. So we put on our letter jackets and walked through the streets of the Wisconsin Dells until we found an Italian restaurant overlooking the downtown. We gorged ourselves on pasta and filled our glycogen tanks.

At that moment, a few miles away in Reedsburg, the Darlington Redbirds left their rooms at the Voyager Inn to search for pizza. Like C-FC's runners, they were hungry for fuel, but their appetite to avenge the sectional loss was greater. Morale was high, and the squad behaved like a family. Arnie had worked hard during the week to quell their disbelief. The Redbirds were in their rooms early, and Arnie wanted their lights out.

Away from the commotion, in solitude, the mind wanders, and doubt can creep in. Would they measure up when the moment came? James was lying in his bed, staring at the ceiling for some time. The attention and excitement of that day were more than he was used to processing. He was a farm kid and should have been fast asleep, waking in a few hours to help feed and milk cows in the barn. Sleeping in a hotel room, miles away from his home, was not something he was accustomed to, and he missed the sounds of the farm. His roommate, Kirk, was also awake. James rolled onto his side and delivered a little off-color farm humor.

"God, I'm stressed. I could really dig a cow right now!"

Kirk snorted and laughed so hard that he had to hold his hand over his face to keep Arnie from hearing the disturbance.

James was nervous. Kirk was nervous. We were all nervous. Although the competitors did not know each other, each struggled through the same angst. It was more than just pre-game jitters or butterflies in the stomach. I'd experienced that on other occasions before a contest. But the anxiety on the eve of a big cross country meet is different. The mind torments itself under the looming physical expectation, and there is no escape. Your teammates are depending upon you, and your performance will be naked for all to see. You will be measured and judged, and you will certainly suffer in the attempt to avoid failure. Even worse, you will judge yourself. You will know your level of commitment, and you will have to face yourself in the mirror with that memory. Nothing short of your best is acceptable in such a contest. If you perform poorly, your teammates bear the consequences despite their sacrifice on your behalf. There are no second chances to get it right. Excellence requires you to push yourself through agony and flirt with collapse. If one's ego is to be preserved, then torture in the crucible is inevitable. It is a character-building moment.

Everyone handles the stress differently. For me, I tried to think about something else, flush the anxiety from my mind, and focus on nothingness ... drift off to sleep. But I was not successful in finding slumber that evening. The guys in the other room used a different coping mechanism. Mark, Guy, Scott, and Dan told jokes, wrestled, and played cards into the wee hours.

Arnie was restless the whole night, glancing at the clock each time he rolled over. He did not want to oversleep and have a bad start to their planned routine before the meet.

CHAPTER TWENTY
LIVING IN DOUBT

October 27, 1984

The first light of morning trudged in through the curtains of the room as Gary got out of bed. The day had awakened cold and gray. Even worse, the wind was howling outside. It was bad weather for a race. I did not need to look out the window; my knee had given me the forecast during the night. We were slow to get up when Gary roused the team with foggy heads and bloodshot eyes. None of us had gotten enough sleep, but we got up and showered. Then he pulled us into one room and directed us to lie down on the floor. He shut off the lights and started the visualization routine. Within a few minutes, he had created a vivid picture in our minds, sprinting past opponents and conquering the hill triumphantly on our way to the chute. Upon his last command, we opened our eyes, resolute and free of fatigue. Moments later, we were in the van searching for breakfast.

While we were lying on the thin, musty carpet of a roadside dive, Arnie had awakened the Redbirds and driven them to the Christmas

Mountain course. The squad ate a breakfast of peanut butter and jelly sandwiches during their short ride. The course could only be viewed by teams during the morning of the meet, and Arnie made sure his kids were there with plenty of time to familiarize themselves with it. The Redbirds trotted over the route, stopping to discuss each key point along the way—how they would be feeling at that stage and which attributes they could leverage in their quest. Race officials, coaches, and a few other teams had also arrived early to do the same. The enormity of the meet was becoming evident, and the tone shifted from lighthearted joking to serious business. When the Redbirds got to the bottom of the steep hill about a quarter mile from the finish, Arnie stopped and faced his squad.

"When you get here, you will be feeling it, and so will everyone else. It will come down to heart from here to the finish. Don't let this pile of dirt defeat you! Think of your teammates, and run with your heart from here on in."

Arnie had them walk up the hill deliberately to trick their minds and give them the sense that they were flying up the slope when confronted with its brutal reality. They jogged to the finish line and climbed into the van to go back to the hotel and dress.

Gravel popped under the van's tires as we rolled into the Christmas Mountain parking lot. It was mid-morning, and the site was filled with hundreds of vehicles carrying the teams and fans that had made the trip for the big event. Reporters were also there in numbers we had not seen before. Gary opened the door, and his clipboard papers flipped over the top of the clasp and nearly pulled loose in the wind. We sat in the van while our coach walked over to the WIAA's temporary office that had been set up in the chalet clubhouse on the site. The officials had packets of information for the race and bib placards with numbers and safety pins for each runner. Six teams from the state's three sections and an additional dozen individual qualifiers were competing in the Class C boys' race.

While he was at the office, waiting with the other coaches for his packet, Gary bumped into Dan Conway and introduced himself.

Dan was a seasoned coach in his mid-forties who had reached legendary status on the Wisconsin runners' scene. His northern Wisconsin team, Chetek, was a cross country powerhouse. Dan was also a world-renowned, elite runner and had won the World Masters Athletic Championship in France the year before. In the early 1980s, he had consistently averaged five-and-a-half-minute miles over entire marathons. His feats were so well-known that they had landed him on the pages of *Runner's World* magazine. Dan Conway would eventually be installed into the WCCCA Hall of Fame.

Although Chetek had been upset in its sectional the previous week, Dan did have one boy qualify as an individual for the state meet that day. He asked Gary which team he was coaching, and Gary told him Cochrane-Fountain City.

"I've never heard of that school before. Where are you located?"

"We're on the west-central side of the state, along the Mississippi, about an hour north of La Crosse. This is our second year with a cross country team."

"Really? You've brought a team to the state meet in your second season!"

They were both marathoners, so they discussed the distance running scene and exchanged some pre-race small talk for a few minutes. Then Dan wished Gary luck in the race before parting.

Gary walked back to the van and was intercepted by our girls' team. Along with many of the parents, they had risen early to make the two-hour drive to Christmas Mountain. We walked the course together to determine if we could use any of its traits to our advantage.

The tourists were gone by that time of year, and the golfers were off the links. The resort was empty, and it was too early in the season to make snow for the runs on the slopes. On a better day, it would have been a beautiful sight. The course had wide, plush lanes over rolling hills and was immersed in a mature hardwood forest. It was dominated by the red and white oaks that lined the fairways, as well as some towering pines. Most of the oaks had not yet dropped their rust-colored leaves, providing some shelter from the light rain. The course's terrain did not intimidate us, but the weather was a concern. On a slick course, corners would be tricky, and we needed to guard against falls like those that plagued us at Brookwood.

We marched up Gary's infamous hill. Gary had asked some of our fans to concentrate themselves along that sinister slope and asked

The C-FC squad walks up "The Hill" at Christmas Mountain, viewed from halfway up the slope. Photo courtesy of Betty Rich.

others to gather near the final sprint to the chute. He knew the mental anguish we were likely to encounter on the climb. He had seen it in the runners' faces the year before and wanted as much support as we could get during those moments.

"It doesn't look that bad," Paul said.

"The hills back home are steeper, and they're longer too," Scott replied.

I looked over at my teammates.

"Yup," I muttered under my breath. "I think Gary has been blowing it out of proportion so it will seem easy to us."

After the words came out of my mouth, I gave Paul a wink. I feigned confidence, but my heart ached for him. Despite their hushed tones, I had overheard some of the parents talking after we arrived at the course. Paul's parents were not at the meet. The rest of our parents were there for the biggest race of our lives, and it was hard not to notice the absence. Although we never saw them at our races, most of our clan had expected to see Paul's folks attend the state meet on a Saturday.

After the tour, Gary directed us toward the starting line, and we went through our warm-up routine.

Before the start of the race, Ann pulled into the parking lot with a van carrying the Redbirds junior varsity boys' team. Among them were Dale Kelly and Todd Johnson, who had made the trip to support their varsity squad and see the state meet for the first time. Arnie wanted the younger kids to witness the main event to reinforce their aspirations. The crew walked through the crowd looking for their coach and spied him near the starting line.

Arnie was going through his pre-race "chalk talk" with his team.

"C-FC is thin on depth, guys. All it would take is for one of them to go down to open the door. Remember, Brookwood beat them at their regional, so they can be beaten."

Troy bent over and stretched his hamstrings as he listened to Arnie's speech. He had been waiting for this moment, and despite the cruddy weather, he was itching to race. Troy wasn't satisfied yet. Although his career had been remarkable, he yearned to stand on the podium with his teammates. He hated to lose, and this was his moment to realize his vision.

Arnie gathered them in a circle and looked into their eyes.

"We have to be ready to seize the opportunity when it comes. You need to run like every stride matters. Remember, you don't run three miles in a race; you run one mile at a time. Break it down, get out smart, and then run for each other. We have what it takes to get this done. Run like you have all year. This is not hype; this is business. Run your race and attack this course! Seniors, lead us there.

Arnie stepped back, and his runners thrust their hands into the center of the huddle. Troy's resolute voice captured their gaze.

"Redbirds on three! One, two, three, REDBIRDS!"

Nearby, we huddled with our coach for some last-minute instructions.

"Okay, this is it! This is the moment we've been training for. Don't leave anything out there today. The grass is slick, so watch the

The C-FC boys' team conducting pre-race speed strides at Christmas Mountain, October 27, 1984. From left to right: Guy Todd (obscured), Mark Brone, Dan Lettner, Scott Adler, Jeff Rich, and Paul Abts. Photo courtesy of the *Winona Daily News*.

corners and work together if you can. Make sure you attack that hill and pump your arms. Remember, you are the best hill runners in this state, and that is where we're going to win this thing."

Gary paused briefly and his voice cracked.

"I'm so proud of you. It has been such a joy to be your coach. Now go get 'em!"

The unexpected, fifteen-month journey had brought us to a final test. Gary's words were an emotional portent as we knew, without a doubt, that this was the last time we'd be running for each other.

At that moment, the congregation had assembled at Holy Rosary Catholic Church in Darlington for Mary Evenstad's wedding. Tom stood at the back of the church in his tuxedo, having ushered in the final arrivals. The priest entered from the sacristy, flanked by two altar boys, one holding the crucifix and the other swinging a censer of incense. The trio turned to face the altar and bowed their heads. Tom wondered how many weddings, funerals, Christmas Eve midnight Masses, and Sunday mornings he and Troy had stood at the altar with the priest. The organist began as the priest turned to the congregation. Tom watched as his sister and father marched past him and took their places at the altar. Homer lifted the veil from Mary's face and kissed her on the cheek before turning away and shaking the groom's hand. Tom's eyes watched all of it, but his mind was with his brother and teammates. The music stopped, and the priest welcomed the assembly. He then offered a prayer for the Redbirds cross country team at Christmas Mountain.

The officials called out a command for the runners to remove their sweats. The Darlington JV team collected the varsity's garments and stuffed them into a mesh bag to be placed in the van. When the command was given for coaches to leave the starting area, Arnie and Ann began running toward the half-mile point where they could yell words of encouragement and assess their squad's progress.

Runners bolt from the starting line in the Class C boys' state title race. From left to right: Darlington's Jay Stauffacher, James Schuetz, and Doug Dunham (obscured). C-FC's Guy Todd, Paul Abts (obscured), Scott Adler, Mark Brone (obscured), Jeff Rich, and Dan Lettner. Photo courtesy of the *Winona Daily News*.

The officials lined up the teams for the start and gave the runners some final instructions. Darlington was assigned to the lane immediately on our right. We took turns shaking hands and murmured a compulsory "good luck." The Redbirds were seeking retribution for the sectional loss, and underneath, both teams wondered if the C-FC victory had been a fluke.

I set my gaze on the long fairway that would conduct the initial sprint and started a series of rapid breaths. The wind was spitting rain in our faces under an ominous ceiling. Oak leaves scurried across the fairway as if panicked by the looming stampede. The chalk lane felt like a barrel, the powder charge of anticipation rising as the official called out his final command. The starter's pistol cracked, and we shot forward, hellbent for the lead before the first turn.

As Arnie was running, he heard the final countdown on the loudspeaker behind him and then the crack of the gun. Instantly, the crowd erupted with a roar, and a ripple from the din followed the runners on the course, leaving no doubt as to the location of the race.

The fastest runners in the state were packed together, anxiously fleeing from the starting line, footfalls pounding on the wet grass while each fought for an advantage. It was a high-velocity game of inches where one misstep could ruin a race before it started. Shoulders and elbows were rubbing, wet skin sliding off the wet skin of other contestants. Cleats were scraping shins and heels. It was hair-raising for the first four hundred meters. At the end of the initial straightaway, I planted my left foot with force and accelerated out of the right-hand turn, brushing the yellow flag on my shoulder. I kept pressing forward to stay near the front. Guy was in view ahead of me, already in a battle with Albany's Dallman and Cambridge's Currie, the one-two finishers in the previous week's sectional.

The temptation to lead was harder to suppress than in previous contests, and my restraint vanished after that first turn. The stakes were higher, but even more than that, the level of competition hyped my anxiety. I had not been surrounded by so much talent before. Rather than running with a couple of teammates and a handful of competitors near the front, a mob engulfed me. It was tense, and I wanted to avoid a collision within that mass of bodies. They were all pressing to be at the front, and they could all keep pace. Somehow, I had not prepared myself mentally for that change. Angst had committed me to a fanatical sprint, and I had already abandoned one of my few advantages: discipline.

Darlington's Troy Cullen did not get caught in the trap. He hung back and let the lead group punish themselves during the initial sprint. Just as he had done a week earlier, Arnie had preached tactics to him before the race.

"Don't get caught up in the frenzy over the first mile. Let the race come to you, so you'll be stronger near the end."

Troy remembered the course from the previous year and the pain from the wicked hill before the finish. As difficult as it was to pull back the reins, he listened to his coach and kept his composure.

Troy Cullen (#609) during the initial sprint at Christmas Mountain. October 27, 1984. Photo courtesy of the *Republican Journal*.

My legs kept pushing under miserable conditions, not relinquishing ground to the other runners for the first third of the race. The gifts of sprinting speed and a stronger frame helped over that first mile and kept me within striking distance of the front. But my mind's voice of *I can't* began protesting fiercely. I had gone out faster than I should have, concerned that dropping too far behind would forfeit my chance to place well at the finish. The errant logic had ensnared me in the frenzy. My body had been pulled under the grindstone's crushing weight, and the miller would demand a toll.

The scorching pace early in the race had even affected Guy. He was still at the front but could not separate himself from Dallman and Currie.

Paul was a bit behind me, and he was hurting, too. His ankle felt fine, but he had developed a stitch in his side. There was an official calling out splits as we passed the mile marker. I ran past it, already numb to externalities, but Paul heard the callout, and it shocked him. He had just run the first mile in under five minutes, which mocked the definition of his "warm-up" segment. It explained the stitch in his side. One five-minute mile was attainable for each of us. On a cross country course, running two consecutive five-minute miles was a stretch for the very best high school runners in the state. But attempting three, strung together at that speed, meant collapse before the finish line. It was exceedingly rare for any high school runner to break fifteen minutes on a five-thousand-meter cross country course. It spelled doom for Paul's mantra of "attack" over the final mile of the race. He knew he was about to suffer tremendously. Paul struggled to get his breathing under control so he could rid himself of that stitch before the final hill.

Arnie had moved near the first-mile marker and assessed how the Redbirds were faring. The roar of the crowd pushed the runners along the course and into his view. Troy was within striking distance of the leaders, and everyone else seemed to get out okay. But it was too early and still too congested to get a handle on where the Redbirds stood. The pack had started to separate a bit, and Brian was farther back than what Arnie was comfortable with. James Schuetz and Kirk Evenstad were within reach of him and settling into the race.

C-FC's Scott Adler was working the knolls in the midsection of the course to his benefit. Small chunks of sod flew into shins and thighs as the runners accelerated out of those shallow rises. The first and second miles of the Christmas Mountain race were largely run over the same ground on a loop. The course's midsection had numerous undulations that did not intimidate at first glance. We had paid no attention to them in our pre-race scouting tour. Although subtle, the repetition of those small ascents cudgeled the runners by breaking their cadence. The effect of the rolling course left no one unscathed. The sudden shifts in pace required intermittent spurts of anaerobic effort that sapped the body's endurance. But that was an edge for a wrestler accustomed to intense anaerobic intervals. Scott ignored the pain in his knee and buried his emotions.

From left to right: Darlington's James Schuetz, Bob Cullen, and Jay Stauffacher round a corner at the state meet. October 27, 1984. Photos courtesy of Arnie Miehe.

Darlington's Troy Cullen began picking up his pace over the second mile and passed runners along the way. Several of C-FC's white jerseys faded behind him, including mine, as he merged into the lead group. Despite the inclement weather, his confidence was building in the middle of the course. Having raced on that same ground the previous year, he knew how to use the corners and mounds. When other runners momentarily lapsed out of a corner or small ascent, Troy burst past them forcefully. The small victories reinforced his tenacity, but he had not forgotten that murderous hill still looming ahead. The leaders were setting a blistering pace, and Troy's hatred for losing was mocking his ego.

Guy had been rotating the pole position with Currie and Dallman over the first half of the race. They had each been passing one another through the serpentine turns and shallow mounds of the course's midsection. But the course and the pace had become a grindstone pulverizing Guy's stamina. Steve Zoellner, Stratford's lead runner, along with Kevin Kohls of Dodgeland, Kevin Clark, and Troy Cullen, were beginning to press the leading trio from behind. Suddenly, Guy's dream switched from an individual championship to one where he could still finish the race without collapsing. By the last mile, each stride had become a desperate attempt to hold position.

A runner never forgets the anxious struggle to maintain position without succumbing to oxygen debt. For the rest of the race, its fingertips grasped at my jersey, aiming to afflict my stride with its weight and pull me into the sod. By the two-mile mark, I was mentally drained and running without my mates, surrounded by talented opponents and unable to gain an advantage. The veins in my neck throbbed from the cycle of the pump pounding my ears. I tried to focus on my form and breathing, but the elements were harsh. The taste of blood was in my throat, and the wind was buffeting me, hobbling my gait. Adversity was assaulting my psyche. Then Paul pulled alongside me.

"Time to go, Jeff," he said. "Let's get 'em!"

He was calling me to pair up with him, just like we had done many times before. By then, the *I can't* mindset was controlling me, and I could not make myself do it. Paul Abts, the miracle man, was asking for my help but had to go ahead without me because I could not rise to the challenge in that moment of weakness.

Darlington's Kirk Evenstad was in a battle with a couple of Stratford's runners. His teammate, James Schuetz, had pulled ahead of him and Kirk was on his own. Arnie had asked his team to run a solid race, and Kirk focused on the corners to make sure he did not slip. He had passed the tallest Stratford runner several times, only to lose the advantage shortly afterward. With each failed attack, his confidence was slipping. Kirk could not seem to shed the pair of orange jerseys that flanked him. The constant pressure tormented his legs and lungs, but he pressed forward, holding his own.

With a half mile to go, I was tattered from the abuse and disgusted with myself for failing my teammate. Seeing Paul move ahead roused some anger, and I began suppressing my mind's tantrum again.

Scott had moved up to my flank, and his presence gave me a lift. I kept battling to maintain position and stubbornly endured the punishment. I started up the infamous hill with a quarter mile left in the race. As it approached, I could see Paul halfway up his climb.

With a half mile left in the race, the Redbirds' Brian Whalen (center left #614) closes in on C-FC's Scott Adler and Jeff Rich. Photo courtesy of Arnie Miehe.

Darlington's Troy Cullen had already gone over the top and was beginning his frenzied sprint to the tape. Kevin Clark and Guy Todd had been in front of him during their ascent. The sinister incline was now a memory. Despite holding back earlier in the race, the hill had sapped Troy's energy, and he faced another tough test. Just like a week earlier, those same runners were in front of him again. He was running out of real estate. The line was rushing closer with each stride.

Paul was in purgatory. His stitch was gone, yet he drifted into a cloudy stupor as he neared the top of the hill. The rush of endorphins and the agony had combined to numb his consciousness. At that moment, Dan's dad, Tom Lettner, shouted at Paul from the edge of the course a few feet away.

"Come on, Cud! You are almost to the finish!"

Tom's voice had such gusto and was so close to Paul's ear that he was startled back into his sentient mind. He rounded the right-hand corner at the crest of the hill, and the finish line came into view down the slope. It was as if he had been released, and the pearly gates had opened before him. He could see Guy's jersey and flowing mane far below, crossing the line. Paul was off on his mad dash.

On the hill behind Paul, my mind had ceded to instinct. Reason vanished, and my transient thoughts focused on technique, using remnants of consciousness to drive my limbs as we had been trained. They would not obey the brain's commands. Normally, I would have charged up that slope pumping my arms and using my strength to surge over the top. But I was not "normal" and struggled to keep my feet with each upward stride. Gary's voice echoed within my core: "Put one foot in front of the other!" Oxygen debt had hung its weight on my collar, sinking my legs into the earth. The numbing heaviness took root, harnessing me to that slope. Victimized by the punishment, my muscles and pulmonary system mutinied, choosing another master. At that instant, on Gary's Hill, I was in pitiful shape and efforts seemed futile. Time passed in slow motion. In that moment of hell, the only part of me racing was my heart.

On my right I sensed the presence of an opponent surging past me, yet I was powerless to stop it. It was a foreign feeling for me. I was the one who conquered others on hills, not the other way around. The runner was Darlington's Brian Whalen, subjecting me to the same late-race punishment I had delivered to him the previous Saturday. It felt like another week had elapsed before I was able to make the crest, looking less like a runner than a stumbling corpse. Gary had not overstated the effect of the steep climb late in the race. It was as bad as he had built it up to be. In my mind, I can still count the divots on that damned slope.

By the time Brian reached the top of the hill, he had passed a half-dozen runners on the ascent, and his spirits had lifted. Looking down the final stretch, he spotted another white jersey of a Pirate harrier in front of him. Arnie had stressed to him all week about targeting the C-FC runners during the race.

"If there is another runner there to beat, then beat him! Pick them off at the finish!"

Although he was nearly spent, Brian rushed to close the gap.

Upon reaching the peak, a brief surge of blood brought clarity to my brain. The downhill segment to the finish line came into view, displaying the refuge of the chute ahead. The panoramic scene heartened my psyche, and hundreds of fans stretched along the sides of the course, coaxing the afflicted forward with a pulsating roar. At that moment, I was able to pass another runner wearing Stratford's orange jersey. He looked to be in even worse shape than I was, and he could not counter the feeble attack. The triumph gave my mind another boost, and the hip flexors suddenly responded to the brain's commands again, extending the stride and covering more ground with each step. The quadriceps and hamstrings rejoined the fight, finding momentum as the slope pitched forward. The arms then answered the mind's call and were pumping once more. Within seconds I was striding headlong down the last stretch, passing another opponent.

Mark had held back in the race until very late. With a half mile to go, he began a frenetic charge to pass as many runners as possible. By the time I was cresting the hill, Mark had reached Scott on the slope, a short distance behind me. Several of our girls were stationed at that point, screaming at both of them to drive forward. Mark was pumping his arms, surging with the form Gary had drilled into us. As he pulled away from Scott, he passed several other runners near the top. Mark would not be denied. Our team's joker had risen to meet the moment and had morphed into a beast.

During the climb, Darlington's James Schuetz could see two white jerseys in front of him. His lungs were burning, but he was intent on passing the duo from C-FC. Both showed their grit on the slope, and although he ascended smoothly, James could not overtake them on the climb. Once at the crest, the long fairway to the finish came into view, and he realized a trio of Pirate runners was still within his reach. James's breath returned, and he heaved into his final sprint to the line, side by side with Scott Adler.

For me, Gary's torturous hill work in Fountain City had cut the recovery time from the climb. But it was a precarious physiological balance as I careened down that last slope to the chute. As my flight continued, muffled footfalls of another runner were just audible, and pressing. I rushed forward to fend off the pursuit, and the threat subdued.

Fifty meters left. The brain surrendered to involuntary drive.

Thirty meters. Vision darkened and existence narrowed to that merciful line.

Twenty meters. Sounds merged into a high-pitched drone.

Ten meters. The anemic stride withered, and Mark burst past in a blur.

It was over.

Exhaustion crashed down with force. The diaphragm heaved eagerly as it rushed air into the lungs, fending off collapse. Starved legs wobbled from the shock, and hands reached instinctively for a tether to the world. As oxygen infused the blood, self-conscious thoughts awoke in the mind. Fresh air had never carried such bliss. The miller's toll had been paid.

Jeff Rich's and Mark Brone's final strides to the finish on October 27, 1984. Photo courtesy of the *Winona Daily News*.

I coasted into the chute through a blinding fog. As the light returned to my eyes, I saw Paul a few steps ahead in the chute with Brian Whalen right behind him. Scott crossed the line six seconds behind us, on James Schuetz's heels.

We met Gary at the end of the chute. He let us know that Guy had placed sixth, claiming the last spot on the individual podium. Paul had beaten Guy's time on the course from the previous year, confirming a worthy effort from our squad. But Paul did not look good and was bending over repeatedly at the hips, unable to recover. As we stood there gasping, we watched Dan hurtle down the slope to the finish line, holding off a runner from Edgar the entire way. He had covered the tough course, suffering longer than the rest of us in that crucible.

Arnie was nearby and gathered his Redbirds as they came through. He had asked his kids to run a solid race, and they had. Troy improved his time and position from a year earlier. Darlington's runners had clocked times similar to their sectional race but under worse conditions.

After Kirk exited the chute, he grabbed his warm-ups and trotted to the parking lot without delay. Todd Johnson's parents were waiting to drive Kirk to Darlington so he could join his sister's wedding reception.

Despite the poor weather, it had been a strong field. Cambridge's Sean Currie defeated Albany's Rich Dallman for first place by one second, trading spots from the week before.

Darlington's Troy Cullen (left) and Doug Dunham walk away from the rain-soaked chute. Photo courtesy of Arnie Miehe.

Our parents and our girls' team were there to receive us. Judee pasted a wet kiss on each of our cheeks, leaving smears of lipstick. The team results would not be posted until the other classes finished their contests several hours later. We walked over to the van to towel off and get warm. Paul bent over, leaned on the bumper, and started vomiting. He emptied his stomach and dry heaved for several minutes afterward. It was another gutsy performance for Cud.

When I saw Paul throwing up, a wave of guilt came over me. I should have been puking next to him and paying a penance for my mindless sprint at the start of the race. We both might have felt better at the end if I had been his wingman. I gave everything I had in the effort and stubbornly avoided collapse. But I was upset with myself for making the same mental mistake I had made in Neillsville a month earlier. I feared that this time, it had cost our squad a championship. I had no idea if our team was the alpha or omega on that course, and the issue was out of my control after crossing the line. Darlington's runners had finished in a cluster around us, and that alone was cause for concern. Stratford's orange jerseys were also plentiful within the top thirty runners. If it was close, mere seconds might make all the difference. Mark's performance gave me a glimmer of hope.

He had peaked at the right time to run at his potential and fill the gap. I smiled thinking about our phone conversation three months earlier. His physicality had emerged in his junior year, and he had finished in our third spot for the second week in a row.

We huddled in the van, still in a stupor. There was little talk, and the harsh effects of the race did not leave our brains for several minutes. After slowly recovering from the shock, we put our warm-ups back on and went out to watch the boys' Class B and A races from under the oak canopy near the chute.

Kurt Udelhofen and his Platteville teammates dominated the Class B race, taking both the individual and team championships.

When they finished, we walked to the top of "Gary's Hill" to watch the girls' contests take place. Suzy Favor, a future Olympian from Stevens Point, won the Class A race. We stood atop that hill and watched her attack the incline with poise before she sprinted to the line. She had climbed the slope so smoothly and with such ease that it made me question my experience an hour earlier.

Cross country teaches mental toughness. One of the most difficult attributes of the sport was the wait after the last runner finished and before the results were announced. In today's world, tracking tags and computer software can tabulate the team results simultaneously with the finish of a race. But in 1984 these technologies were not widely available, and runners had to wait for the scores to be tabulated and verified. At a big meet, the officials were careful to avoid mistakes. The time passed slowly, filled with doubt and anxiety. It was unlike any other sport in that respect. It was particularly difficult at a sectional or state meet where the competition was packed together tightly and with individual qualifiers merged into the mix. School colors were replicated as runners entered the chute in droves. We understood the placement for our own runners and used that information to estimate our team score, but understanding the scores from the other teams was nearly impossible. Any of the squads at the state meet were capable of beating us. As the girls' races finished, we found ourselves standing under the dripping oaks, still drained from the race and unsure of our fate.

Saturday, October 27, 1984, was a big day for college football. Washington State's Rueben Mayes broke an NCAA record with 357 rushing yards in a victory over Oregon. Closer to home, the Wisconsin

Badgers football team upset the sixth-ranked Ohio State Buckeyes 16–14 at Camp Randall Stadium in Madison. It was a stunning upset celebrated by most of the citizens of Wisconsin. Those stories dominated the major networks and the sports pages of the Sunday papers across the state. The results of the high school cross country championships, sixty miles to the north of Madison, were mostly relegated to the small print.

A race official came out the door and tacked a sheet outside the office where Arnie and Gary had been waiting with the other coaches. We were quite a distance from the clubhouse and did not notice. Several minutes later, Gary walked up to us with a look of trepidation. Heidi, Becky, and Tracy were walking behind him, lending support while he broke the news. We had prepared ourselves mentally for the moment, resigned to accept the update when it came.

As he took his last step, Gary burst forth, "You're state champs!"

The blast from his voice jolted Mark, and he dropped his can of Mello Yello on the ground. The combined effect stunned us for a moment before our brains could process what Gary had said. In another instant, we were locked in a huddle and jumping in unison. Unable to contain themselves, the rest of our jubilant clan engulfed us.

Dan Lettner was not prone to showing his emotions, but after a few seconds he looked at Gary and said, "Coach, I can't believe it. We're

The C-FC crowd celebrates after hearing the official announcement of the Class C boys' results. Photo courtesy of Mark Brone.

state champs!" The future Marine squeezed Gary in an embrace, lifting him off the ground. Our coach had been right all along. A state championship was within our reach.

We defeated Stratford by eight points, and Darlington came in third.

"There is nothing like winning the whole thing!"

Hearing the voice, Gary turned around to see Dan Conway walking over to congratulate him.

As Dan extended his hand with a smile he asked, "Where did you guys come from? You don't even have seven runners. That is just crazy!"

Gary and Judee Brone share a hug after the official announcement of the Class C boys' results. Photo courtesy of Mark Brone.

The C-FC boys' 1984 Wisconsin Class C state cross country championship team, October 27, 1984. From left to right, kneeling: Jeff Rich, Dan Lettner, and Mark Brone. Standing: Coach Gary Brone, Guy Todd, Scott Adler, and Paul Abts. Photo courtesy of Mark Brone.

A few seconds later, after the shock of the news subsided, my feelings were not of elation but relief even more profound than the relief I'd felt in Neillsville. I had served my teammates well enough and had not messed it up. Somehow, together and against the odds, we had pulled it off.

CHAPTER TWENTY-ONE

DAWN

The boom box played softly, and the mood in the Darlington van was tempered. Thirty-Eight Special's "Hold on Loosely" filled their ears during the ride back to the hotel in Reedsburg. On the one hand, the Redbirds had run a solid race, and a third-place finish was a notable accomplishment. They had achieved more than any other team in their school's history. On the other hand, the third-place finish left them without a trophy and with the familiar anonymity they had experienced in the 1983 season's third-place finish at the Prairie du Sac Sectional. Even though the effort had been solid, the team members felt they had not performed their best under the difficult conditions. Troy finished in seventh place, one spot shy of the podium. His career had ended, falling just short, along with the Redbirds' other magnificent seniors: Brian Whalen, Jay Stauffacher, Doug Dunham, and Tom Evenstad.

It was a different atmosphere than after other races. It was one of no pressure and no expectations, no next meet, no worry about sickness or injury. Arnie congratulated the kids on their efforts and accomplishments. It had been the best year in the program's history, and they had overcome many barriers. But for the second year in a row, Arnie looked around the van and wondered how those leaders could be replaced. The chance of replacing five of his top eight runners with the kids on the junior varsity seemed bleak. His JV squad was strong, but none had run under eighteen minutes, and none could replace Troy Cullen or Brian Whalen. For the moment, Arnie had to hide his disappointment so his squad could realize what they had accomplished and walk away with a sense of pride and satisfaction.

Through the rain, Ann drove the van carrying the Redbirds JV boys' team home. Though the young runners were disappointed with the outcome, they'd been filled with pride from the third-place finish. The trip to the state meet had shown them what might be possible if they set their minds to it. Todd Johnson had a quick intellect, and he was tossing possibilities around in his head. He knew their JV squad was good enough to have beaten many varsity squads. It also occurred to him that Brian Whalen had run exceptionally well as a senior, with only one season of training. If Brian could do that, perhaps there would still be enough time for their team to improve. Perhaps there was enough time for him to morph from a sprinter into a formidable distance runner. Within a couple of hours of watching his varsity teammates fall short of their goal, Todd's mood had already turned into one of resolve, and he spoke up during their ride.

"We can get to that meet again next year. We have a good enough group in our JV ranks to get there."

It was bold talk. Johnson had never run below nineteen minutes and had barely held onto the sixth spot on the Redbirds' JV squad. Yet he was talking as if he had been racing with the varsity earlier in the day, against the best talent in the state. Although only a junior, Johnson spent a good deal of time with Troy and Tom when they were not competing. Some of their magnetism had rubbed off on him.

Then Kent Ruppert chimed in and seconded Todd's statement.

"It will take a lot of work if we're gonna do it. We need to put in the miles next summer in order to have a shot. James, Bob, and Kirk will be back, but the rest of us have to step up."

The group chatted about their dream most of the way home and began plotting their course for the offseason. The conversation surprised Ann, and she smiled while she drove but did not interject.

Arriving home, Todd grabbed a sheet of paper and wrote down a new personal goal:

Who do you need to beat to become a varsity runner next season?

He posted the sheet in his room, where he could not hide from his commitment.

Back in Darlington, Tom was anxious. The wedding party had moved to the reception hall, and people were filing in. They began asking him how the team had done, and he could not give them an answer. Kirk had just arrived, but he did not know the result either, only that Troy had finished seventh, and he had crossed in thirty-first. There was no phone for Tom to call the guys at the meet. He had to wait and wonder. The buzz at the reception continued until fans carrying the news returned to town a couple of hours later.

As our van pulled out of the parking lot, a cassette tape clicked into the receiver of the boom box, and AC/DC's "Back in Black" fueled our euphoria. We had been "let loose" from mediocrity's "noose," and we were "running wild."

Our first stop was the drive-through of the nearby Burger King. Appetites were ravenous by then, and the school had given Gary a stipend for team meals. The van quickly filled with bags of burgers and fries. Mark topped us all, downing three Whoppers within a few minutes. Soon afterward, the tires hissed hypnotically on the wet roads, creating harmony with the boom box for the long trip. Guy sat in the seat next to me, his new medals hanging from his neck. The championship trophy was propped on his knees while he admired it. It was heavy and large, with a wooden profile of our native state set behind the golden figure of a runner. For a moment, his steely eyes were absorbed in thought, as if the artifact held a piece of him. He sensed my gaze and turned to look at me.

"That runner has your stride."

I smiled back.

"He moves about as fast, too!" I replied.

By the time the van approached the intersection of Highways 35 and 53 near Winona, we had burned through a dozen cassettes. Gary noticed flashing lights and a jumble of vehicles ahead and slowed down. We quickly realized it was the Fountain City Fire Department, along with several hundred fans gathered on the shoulder. The radio stations in Winona had broadcast the news before our team arrived home, and the district responded to the call. Members of the high school band were playing fight songs as our squad stepped out of the van. The girls' team joined us, and we climbed into an old pumper truck that served as our chariot for a ride over the Great River Road to a rally at the high school. Adversity threw its final tantrum, pelting rain in our faces. We did not care.

On the stage of the gymnasium, looking down at the rally, I spotted eight-year-old Jesse Brone standing next to one of his grade school buddies. Jesse's face beamed with a huge grin and cheerful eyes as he looked up with adoration at his dad and big brother, who were holding the trophy next to me. Our day was nearly done, but I knew that in that moment, the program had a future as bright as Jesse's face.

After the rally, Gary walked Paul to the van behind the school. Gary had used the remainder of the school stipend with a purpose in mind. He opened the door and handed Paul two bags of sandwiches and fries to take home with him.

The C-FC cross country team climbs aboard a fire truck with the championship trophy. Photo courtesy of Betty Rich.

Later that night, a soaked group of runners sat in the apartment above the hardware store in Fountain City, washing down pizza with cans of soda. As the rain fell outside, an incandescent glow radiated from within. The championship trophy gleamed as a temporary centerpiece on the kitchen table. We told jokes and reminisced about the events of the season. Judee Brone's laughter echoed off the walls of her comfortable nest, provoked by the teenagers in her midst. Our group savored the fleeting moment of youth while endorphins coursed through our veins.

The Redbirds arrived at their hotel in Reedsburg to shower and spend another night. Before supper, Arnie visited each room to thank his runners for their sacrifice. He reminded his seniors that they were the first team from their high school to make it to a state competition and that it was a significant accomplishment. He then went into James's room with Bob Cullen to talk with his two juniors who would captain their next season.

"Guys, it can't end this way. We can get back to state next year, but it is going to take an entire team effort, and you will be our leaders. We have to get new guys out and make sure that everyone puts in their summer miles. This is just the beginning."

The words painted hope on their faces, and both boys agreed that they would set the tone. But while Arnie tried to exude confidence, he was questioning himself the entire time. He walked out of their room wondering if what he had said was, in fact, just wishful thinking. For the moment, he was content to soak in the fantasy of possibility, and the Redbirds went to their last team dinner together to close the season.

That night, Arnie's sleep was restless again. The vision of Wadzy Martens' car leaving the parking lot kept replaying in his mind.

Time marches on. The 1984 Darlington cross country team shares a reflective, post-race moment. Photo courtesy of Arnie Miehe.

Early Sunday morning, my dad knocked on my bedroom door and entered with a copy of the *Winona Daily News*. As my eyes adjusted to the light of day, he tossed the paper on my bed and said, "Congratulations, state champ!"

The irony of the situation occurred to me in that moment. The school's gridiron team was also in the paper. They had ended their season with a 4–5 record. Our school's first state championship would not have happened had Scott and Dan continued with football. We would not have been celebrating if Mark had decided to quit three months earlier to battle on the gridiron. Our moment would have been lost if Paul had been failing in school or had not suffered on that ankle. Our program would have lain fallow if our coach had not volunteered for his role when asked by his son. Life had opened a door and allowed me to become part of a remarkable team formed from haphazard beginnings in an obscure school library.

Suddenly my old injury did not define me. The wound had been a blessing, not a curse. It was simply the disruption required for me to discover the trail of crumbs. I no longer felt compelled to prove my worth, finally reaching acceptance. For me, a new understanding of value had emerged. We needed each of us along the way, utilizing our combined gifts to conquer adversity. Bonds had formed, and selfishness had been temporarily suppressed, replaced with sacrifice for one another. Despite our differences, my teammates had paid a price for me, and I had done the same for them. The achievement was something that none of us could have realized alone because none of us was that exceptional on his own. That shared commitment was the real prize. Relief switched to appreciation for the journey and for my teammates.

At that same moment in Fountain City, a man was seen running along Highway 35. The rain had stopped, but spatter slung off his soles as he made his way south. He appeared distressed, and several drivers reduced their speed to see if he needed assistance. Tears were streaming down his face while he proceeded along the thoroughfare in the early light of day, sobbing. The runner was Gary Brone. The emotions of the fifteen-month journey had finally overcome him during his workout, and the motorists did not realize they were looking at a joyful man. Gary had united an aimless group of kids with talent they did not know they possessed. He had pushed through his own self-doubt and inspired them to reach for an improbable achievement. He had believed for them when they could not believe in themselves. They had all held together in the face of adversity. Starting from crumbs, his group had cleared a trail for the teenagers yet to come—a trail those runners could use to pave a legacy.

CHAPTER TWENTY-TWO
BREAKTHROUGH

On Sunday afternoon, Darlington turned out the fire engines for its team and paraded them down Main Street, pulling up to the school for a rally. It had been a long time since the community had a team to celebrate, and they were eager for an opportunity to share their pride. It was a salute to their first trip to a state tournament and the accomplishment of a third-place finish. A fine group of pioneering seniors who had run their last race relished the moment.

The seven varsity runners sat in chairs at center court for the ceremony. It was Darlington's first pep rally for a cross country team in the school's history. Tom sat in the stands, dressed for a *Guys and Dolls* performance that was scheduled after the rally. He looked enviably at his brother and buddies sitting on the gymnasium floor. He was happy for them and proud of them, but oh, how he'd longed to be at the state meet and on that floor. He knew he had been a part of the journey, and he knew that they knew. The sacrifice had been worth it, just to see them at center court, celebrated by their community.

The band stopped playing, and the cheerleaders knelt on the floor. Darlington's principal, Dave Chellevold, spoke first. Decades earlier, Chellevold had played football for Wadzy Martens, and he was the administrator who had hired Arnie.

"We're all here this afternoon because we care about hard work ...

The 1984 Darlington squad is paraded through town on fire trucks after finishing third at the state meet. Photo courtesy of Arnie Miehe.

because we care about perfection ... because we care about trying ... and because we care about togetherness."

He looked at the team seated before him. "Thank you for trying, for never giving up, and for being you!"

Each runner received acknowledgment and was given a chance to say a few words. The mood in the gymnasium was uplifting, but as Arnie looked at his departing seniors, the moment was bittersweet.

When it was his turn to speak, Arnie walked up to the lectern microphone to thank the assembly for their support.

"Cross country is a difficult sport. It's a little hard for the kids to keep going sometimes. They need that little boost at home, and I don't think they would be able to do it without you."

He went on to share moments from the season and finished with an acknowledgment.

"Teamwork. Teamwork is what it takes to have success in cross country—or any team sport. Perhaps that seems obvious on the surface, but I can guarantee you that it is not. It takes a group of people who dedicate themselves to a common purpose. We can all say we want the same thing. We can all dress up in the same uniforms. We can all ride the same bus. We can all attend the same competitions. That stuff is easy, that stuff is superficial, but that does not make you a teammate.

"A good team member shows up and works hard when there is no glory in it, when nobody is watching. A good teammate puts in the work when they're in the rain, when they're cold, when they're sick, and when they're in pain. They are dependable and dedicated in practice, not just words. A good teammate fills gaps; he or she 'plugs the dike' when there is a leak. A good teammate picks up the other fellow when he is down. A good teammate forgives the other and then helps him to become better. A good teammate knows his or her role, even if someone else gets the glory. Their shared purpose matters more than who gets credit. A good teammate does the right thing, even when it is the hard thing. In the end, if they meet their purpose, they will all share in the benefits."

Arnie's eyes scanned the crowd and fixed on Tom, who began to fidget in his seat as Arnie continued.

"I want to recognize someone who is here today and epitomizes the kind of teammate I just described. He is the type of young man we all would like to have as a teammate. He is as much a part of this team as myself or any of the seven guys sitting in front of you, but circumstances did not allow him to run yesterday. He deserves to share in this moment. Tom Evenstad, please come down and take your rightful seat on the floor with the other guys."

Applause thundered from the crowd, and Tom's face flushed. It was the only time he had been publicly recognized in any sport. He stepped down from the bleachers and sat next to his brother. He fought to keep his composure while he looked at Arnie and the crowd.

Ann spoke to Arnie that evening and shared the discussion she'd heard from the JV boys in the van on the way home from the meet. Arnie simply smiled, unconvinced that it would make a difference. He could not show his disappointment in front of the team or the community. He had buried his emotions after the meet and put on his best face. Arnie was glad his kids were dreaming of bigger things, but he had to remain realistic. Rationally, he could not see how his team could replace the seniors who had been lost, even if the younger kids worked hard to achieve their potential. It was just not going to be enough. Too much talent was gone. His seniors had forged the trail, and he had seen the opportunity before them. But he could not see who could carry the mantle forward. It was easier not to talk about it and set reasonable expectations.

Arnie coached the track team in the spring of 1985 and watched his runners' times improve. Troy Cullen qualified for the state final in the eight hundred meters and placed sixth. But Arnie was concerned about sophomore Kent Ruppert's progress—or lack of it. Ruppert had been the cross country team's alternate runner for the state meet at Christmas Mountain, and Arnie had hoped to see him improve during the spring. Any chance the team had in the fall would depend upon each runner's progress. Kent was small, but he was a tough kid and an excellent wrestler. He had earned his spot at the 106-pound weight class through "wrestle-offs" and solidly established himself in that varsity role. But when the tournament approached, Kent cut another eight pounds so that a heavier teammate could improve his chances to advance. As a result, his teammate captured a sixth-place finish at the state wrestling tournament. Kent's ravaged body paid the price for his selfless act. By the time track season rolled around, he was eating again, and his metabolism was struggling to adjust. Kent's face swelled and left him with "chipmunk cheeks." He did not run well during the track season, and Arnie became concerned.

An athlete's drive is rarely visible to others. An observer can easily ascertain size, strength, and speed, but the will to win hides within the athlete. Kent was not happy with his performance during the track season, and he began running daily to make Arnie's two-hundred-mile club during the summer. He had regarded Troy Cullen as the best distance runner in the history of Darlington High School, so Kent set a personal goal to beat Troy at the alumni meet in late August.

By midsummer, Arnie was still struggling to mentally prepare for a season that would not follow the same upward trajectory as the prior three. Then one day, as he was shopping for groceries, another patron stopped him in the aisle.

"Hi Arnie. How's the team going to be this fall?"

"I think we're going to be pretty tough," Arnie replied.

He didn't know why he said it. It was not rational, only instinctual, but his demeanor improved when the words came out of his mouth.

He asked himself, *Why not keep that perspective and drill an upbeat attitude into the team?*

A week later, on a muggy summer morning, Arnie got a phone call from another Redbirds quarterback. This time it was junior Dave Hirsbrunner on the phone. Like Brian Whalen, Hirsbrunner was popular in school and a physically gifted athlete. His peers called the strawberry-blond "Hirsh," and he had a tenacious attitude in competition. Dave's family lived on their farm outside of town, and he knew what hard work was. Like Brian, Dave wanted to go in a new direction with a winning team. During the spring track meets, Arnie had seen Dave setting records in the high jump. He knew Hirsbrunner could sprint but was unsure of his aerobic fitness. It did not matter; he wanted athletes to join his squad, so he welcomed Dave.

By the time practice started in August, Arnie had seven boys and one girl who had become members of the Mile Club over the summer. Each had run at least 250 miles in the heat during the ten-week period. The group included several former boys' JV runners who had ridden in the van with Ann after the state meet: James Schuetz, Bob Cullen, Kent Ruppert, Todd Johnson, and Pat Sonsalla. Johnson's body had matured, and he showed up with some new physicality for his senior year. They had not forgotten their conversation in the van after the meet at Christmas Mountain and had dedicated themselves to improvement during the offseason.

And there was something else. Forty-one boys and girls showed up for the first practice of the season. The numbers in Darlington's cross country program were swelling to include nearly 15 percent of the student body. The efforts of the prior seasons had made an impact. The traditional cookout after the first practice, the alumni meet, the homecoming torch run, the Mile Club, and the grade school distance meets had combined to elevate the program in the estimation of the community and among the students. The winning records had not hurt recruitment either. Being a part of the cross country program at Darlington had become an aspiration for many. "Arnie's Army" had arrived.

Once school started in late August, Dave Hirsbrunner was having second thoughts about joining the cross country team. The practices were harder than he had anticipated, and he dreaded lacing up his shoes when it was time for the next workout. There might still be time to rejoin the football team and make something out of his season.

In the locker room, he turned to Kirk and said, "I think I'm going to quit and go back to playing football. This running shit is just too damned hard."

Kirk looked stunned. "No, don't quit now! You're just getting started. Believe me, Hirsh. It will get better. Give it some more time."

Dave had another problem he didn't share with Kirk—his dad. George Hirsbrunner was an immense man, standing six feet, four inches tall, and weighing over 330 pounds. The years of farm work had swollen his fingers to the size of sausages. He spoke with a deep, resounding voice that matched his enormity. Big George had played football for Wadzy Martens as a young man and was the kind of opponent no one wanted to encounter on the gridiron. George wanted to see his son scoring touchdowns with the pigskin in his hands. After returning from the first night of cross country practice, Dave went to the barn to help finish milking. George raised his head and glared at him.

"If you're going to run with the sissies, then you're going to help with the morning milking!"

George had always given Dave a reprieve from the morning chores during football season. He wanted him to get his rest for football. But George was incensed by his son's decision and began rousing him out of bed at four-thirty each morning. Adding insult to injury, George forced Dave to watch each football game from the bleachers as the season got underway. He made Dave pay a penance for his dalliance with cross country. The pressure to succeed already had Dave in knots, and the season had barely started. He'd begun contemplating a switch back to football where he knew he'd be playing on Friday nights and where he'd regain his father's approval.

On August 31 the Redbirds ran in their annual alumni meet. Troy returned from his dorm on the University of Wisconsin–La Crosse campus to run in the race as a new alumnus. When it was over, the varsity defeated the alumni squad soundly. James had finished second in 17:23, and the next seven Redbirds crossed the line within the following minute, including Dave Hirsbrunner. When Dave joined the team, he secretly believed he could beat Kirk in a 5K. During the race, he moved up to Kirk's side and thought about pushing past him. But before the race started, Arnie had asked the pair to finish together. He felt it would build unity and strength for both, so Dave complied. The result was a confidence boost for the whole team.

Arnie's former JV squad had run together as a pack during the race and posted better times than the fifth varsity runner from 1984.

Troy had not run since graduating in the spring and had quickly adapted to college life. The entire Darlington varsity squad made him pay by crossing the line before him. After beating his former leader, Kent smiled at Troy with satisfaction. Troy smiled back and rubbed his belly.

"Too many beers!"

They no longer had a standout runner in Troy, but the Redbirds did have balance and numbers. The top eight runners stuck together during a race. It was a new equation, and suddenly Arnie's eyes perceived a trail of crumbs.

On the stage before their next practice, Arnie hinted to his team about their potential.

Kirk Evenstad finishes in the oppressive heat at the Darlington Alumni Meet on August 31, 1985. Photo courtesy of the *Republican Journal*.

"What is one plus ten?"

The squad looked around at each other for a moment, wondering if their coach was setting up a joke.

"Eleven," Kent blurted out.

"Yes, and what is four plus five?"

"Nine."

"That's right! Don't you see? You don't have to have the first runner in a meet to win a team race. You need the lowest combined score. If you have the best runner, that helps. But you can also do it with strong, fourth-, fifth-, and sixth-place finishers. We don't need to have the fastest runner; we need the fastest team."

Arnie liked to mix up the squad's workouts and was always looking for ways to inject some fun into the monotony. He came up with an idea for a new practice he called "One Club – One Ball." He introduced it to his team the night before one practice to let them know what he was planning.

"Tomorrow we're going to go to the golf course for practice, and I will split you into teams with one ball each. You will hit the ball and then run after it and hit it again until it goes in the cup. You're going to golf nine holes as a team. The winning team will be the one that finishes with the lowest combination of strokes and time. See you tomorrow!"

The next afternoon Arnie trotted up the stairs to the stage and looked at his grinning team before him. Sitting in the front was Todd Johnson, wearing a scarf, knickers, plaid socks, and a beret. He was chewing on a golf tee.

"So, when's tee time?" Todd said.

Arnie burst into laughter.

The Darlington squad poses for a photo before their "One Club—One Ball" workout. Todd Johnson is on the far left. Photo courtesy of Arnie Miehe.

Todd's times had improved dramatically enough to make the varsity squad as a senior. He also brought a new chemistry to the team. Todd had become a constant source of laughter on the bus rides to the meets and in the practices. Arnie was serious about his craft and generally wanted his kids to mentally focus on their task before a meet. When Todd had the whole bus in stitches for most of their rides, it didn't sit well with Arnie at first. Then the team started to pile up victories, arriving at their meets loose and in a good mood. Witnessing the results, Arnie decided to let it roll, sensing that Todd's humor lifted the other kids' performances.

That September, Scott Adler and I were living in a dorm on the University of Wisconsin– Platteville campus. Over the summer, Scott had gone through basic training in Fort Leonard Wood, Missouri. He had a new commitment one weekend each month as a medic in the Army Reserve. The tuition aid from the military was helping him pay for his education. I was nearly broke, having gathered just enough savings to attend my first year of college. We had made the journey to school together and were beginning our studies as undergraduate engineers. I was not prepared for the academic challenge. High school had come easily, but the pace of learning in my new field, the competition, and the social distractions made my first semester difficult. I found myself learning how to study with intensity and used the Karrmann Library on campus as a place to focus. Of course, the library was also filled with resources that could be used as a distraction. When I got the chance, I kept an eye on the sports pages.

Things had changed back home. The coaches' poll and the papers no longer mentioned the C-FC boys. Mark had returned to the squad as captain but only reluctantly. He had continued to harbor dreams of playing football his senior year. Gary and Judee would not sign his permission slip, which was required for the sport, and it had touched off a bitter discussion above the hardware store. By the time the season began, Mark was leading a fresh batch of underclassmen new to cross country. Dan had returned with him to mentor the younger kids. Mark developed a hip injury that he struggled with for much of the fall, and despite their efforts, the team was not competitive. It was a rebuilding season, but there was a new spark of interest in the student body, and greater numbers showed up for practice. The younger kids had witnessed the success, and the program was taking root.

I did see in the papers that Gary's girls' team was ranked among the top three teams in Class C. Heidi Stettler was leading the group again and had a new complement of talented runners with her. When it came to mental toughness, Heidi "walked the talk." She did not look like it, but she was as tough as they came. The girls were winning invitationals for the first time. Interestingly, Darlington's girls' squad was also ranked in the top five, and their boys' team was once again picked first by the coaches.

Gary's career path also changed again. He and Judee were struggling financially and trying to sell the hardware store. Judee was launching a program in Winona called Key Kids, which provided a safe place for kids after school, and she continued to direct plays in Fountain City. The additional modest income allowed Gary to go back to school and complete his teaching certificate. The experience of coaching kids had reinvigorated his interest in teaching.

SEPTEMBER 7, 1985

Arnie announced his starting seven for the Darlington Invitational on Friday, the day before the meet. Seniors James Schuetz and Bob Cullen had been selected as captains for the squad. Both had been running for the Redbirds since their freshman year, in Arnie's first season as coach. Both had run well at Christmas Mountain the prior fall. Both had responded to Arnie's request in the hotel room after the state meet and had been an example to the younger kids during the offseason, qualifying for the Mile Club.

Kent Ruppert, Todd Johnson, Dale Kelly, Pat Sonsalla, and Kirk Evenstad rounded out the varsity. Each was worthy of the honor. But Arnie suddenly faced a new challenge with his gift of balanced talent. After Arnie announced the starters, Dave Hirsbrunner confronted him in the locker room.

"Coach! Whaddya mean I'll be running on the JV? I held back in the alumni run because you told me to finish with Kirk! I could have been in the front seven."

Hirsbrunner was not about to take a back seat on the second-string unit after giving up the quarterback position to run for Arnie.

He had been a four-sport standout the prior year as a sophomore.

"Dave, settle down," Arnie retorted. "This is our first invitational of the year. You ran well during the alumni race, but the other guys finished ahead of you. You haven't had the training or experience yet. Give it some time. You'll get your chance, but you have to prove it during the practices and meets. These spots are earned, and you need to gain the respect of the other runners on the team, especially those who have been doing this for years."

"I don't have more time! Everybody in town hates me now. I could be starting for the football team!"

Dave stormed off.

The Darlington Invitational had grown from prior years and included seven teams from the southern portion of the state. It was humid on Saturday, and temperatures were in the nineties by race time. Nonetheless, the Redbirds varsity responded well and beat the runner-up team by thirty-two points.

Despite his mood, Dave showed up and won the JV contest, clocking a time that would have put him in Darlington's fourth spot in the varsity race. Big George had shown up to watch. When he saw his son cross the line in first place, pride overwhelmed him, and he began to tremble visibly. After just one race, George became a cross country fan.

A few days later, in a dual meet against Southwestern, Arnie rested most of his top seven and let his JV runners fill in for the varsity. Hirsbrunner crossed the line first in 17:43.

SEPTEMBER 14, 1985

Arnie could no longer ignore Dave's progress and potential as a distance runner. He entered Dave in the starting seven for the River Valley Invitational and bumped Pat Sonsalla to the JV. The field for the big meet was once again strong, with second-ranked Brookwood and third-ranked Boscobel participating. C-FC was also in attendance, having received the honor of an invitation to participate after the previous year's state title.

Dave was still learning how to pace himself during a race and had not tested himself yet. While the team was warming up, he asked Kirk for his advice.

"How fast do you think I can go? Who should I target during the race?"

Kirk smiled. "You're pretty fast, but don't get a big head. You can beat most of these guys, but don't try to stick with the Clark brothers from Boscobel. They'll run you into the ground."

Dave pressed the pace from the start and finished in seventh place, with a time of 17:24. He had run most of the race with his teammates James and Kent, eclipsing them near the finish line. Within a couple of weeks, he had improved his time by more than a minute to become the top runner for the Redbirds' formidable squad. Darlington crushed the field and took first place as a team. C-FC's young boys' team finished eleventh.

Standing near the chute, Arnie smiled as he witnessed the transformation. After receiving his placement card, James ran over to him, beaming.

"Coach! Did you see what Hirsh did? Holy cow!"

The reaction from Arnie's captain was remarkable and revealed James's character. Most teenagers would have responded with chagrin after being surpassed by another for the top spot on the team. But James realized that Dave's sudden progress had enhanced the potential for their squad. Arnie's expectations for their journey together were instantly elevated.

In October, Heidi had been voted onto the C-FC homecoming court. It was traditional for the girls to be selected first. Then, each girl would ask a boy to be her escort on the court. Drawing upon the example of the prior fall, Heidi asked a cross country runner to accompany her, and Mark agreed to be her attendant. However, when Heidi submitted her choice to the school officials, she was denied. Her escort would have to be a football player. The icy walls of exclusivity melt slowly, and at the time, the thaw from the recent state championship was not enough to bring about that change.

In mid-October, I was in the library at night, studying for an upcoming calculus exam. I'd had my fill of taking derivatives and solving for "x." I needed a break and started skimming through the sports pages on the newspaper rack. The regular season had ended for Wisconsin's high school cross country squads. Gary's girls' team was still doing quite well in the rankings. They held the second spot in the coaches' poll, right behind Fennimore, who had beaten C-FC and Darlington a month earlier at the River Valley Invitational. Darlington's girls were also listed, right behind C-FC.

The Darlington boys had held their number one ranking for the entire season with one noticeable improvement from the previous year. Their record was unblemished. Most notably, their victories included two triumphs over their old nemesis, the second-ranked team in Class B, Platteville. There was no doubt the Redbirds had become the team to chase in Class C.

OCTOBER 22, 1985

Darlington hosted the regional meet at their high school for the second straight season. But this time, they weren't shooting hoops in the gymnasium before the meet. They elected to maintain their

The Darlington pack leads a mid-season invitational. From left to right: Kent Ruppert, Todd Johnson, James Schuetz, and Dave Hirsbrunner. Photo courtesy of Arnie Miehe.

focus instead. Second-ranked Monticello-New Glarus was competing in the regional with them, and Arnie did not want any last-minute distractions or injuries. The varsity team was itching to race, having rested from their last competition nearly two weeks earlier.

The day was gray and cool, and the Redbirds got off the line to a strong start—perhaps too strong. Dave, James, and Kent were all among the top five runners early in the race, and the pace was faster than Arnie had hoped. They had a fox to chase. Hank DeHaan, Monticello's star, was a magnificent athlete and took a commanding lead. Even worse, DeHaan's next two teammates were competing neck and neck with Darlington's leaders. The pressure to perform was visible, and after the first mile, the lid popped off. Upon rounding a fencepost on the baseball field, Dave pulled up with a hip pointer and could not stay with James. The pain was so great that he had to drop out of the race.

James Schuetz makes a tight corner at the Darlington Regional on October 22, 1985. In close pursuit, Dave Hirsbrunner approaches the turn just prior to pulling up with a hip pointer. Photo courtesy of the *Republican Journal*.

A hip pointer can result from an impact or from overuse of the muscles attaching to the outside brim of the pelvic bone. It is an excruciating injury. As James passed the mile marker, he called out to Arnie.

"Coach, Hirsh dropped out!"

Arnie was stunned. He trusted James's report, but how could that be? Panic consumed Arnie's mind and sent him into a frenzy. His team had been cruising without a loss for the entire season, and suddenly the wheels were coming off. In an instant, their tournament prospects were fading. Monticello-New Glarus was not a team to be trifled with.

Arnie charged up and down the edge of the course, pleading with the other kids to "step it up." Kent realized something was wrong when he saw Dave drop and needed no prompting to push hard. But the Redbirds had to replace their top runner with a great performance from the rest of the squad if they were going to advance. When Bob and Todd passed Arnie, he made it perfectly clear to them that the team needed them more than ever.

The response he got was remarkable.

Without Dave, the Redbirds next four runners turned in their best times of the season. Kent placed second in the meet with James on his heels. Todd also responded with a feverish final charge to place thirteenth. But the effort Bob gave was extraordinary. He improved his personal record by thirty-six seconds to finish as the Redbirds' fifth runner. Bob had started as a skinny freshman in Arnie's first season as coach and had quietly held the seventh spot on the team the previous two seasons, logging hundreds of miles during the sticky summer when no one was watching. When his team needed him most, he answered the call.

Hank DeHaan crossed the line without a challenger. The calamity with Dave's hip had little effect on the team's result. Darlington soundly defeated Monticello-New Glarus by fourteen points. The Redbirds had delivered a clinic to the crowd about the value of teamwork.

But the unexpected injury put a scare in the Redbirds' psyche a few days before the sectional race in which the competition would be even tougher. Hip pointers can take weeks to heal, and Dave was in considerable pain when Arnie approached him. His concern only grew after he evaluated the hip, and Dave made a trip to the doctor the next morning.

The report that came back was bleak. Dave received a cortisone injection in his hip, and the physician said that running on the leg was out of the question for the sectional meet.

The common questions of grief rolled through Arnie's head. *Why Dave? Why now?* The sectional was only three days away, and who knew if Dave could run at the state meet—if they qualified. *Why did it have to be so difficult? Why were there always obstacles stealing his joy?*

Arnie called upon Pat Sonsalla to fill the seventh spot on his varsity squad for the sectional on Saturday. His teammates had placed the moniker of "Shmoo" on Pat. Despite putting in the hard work for several years, he remained on the periphery of the varsity squad. His time had come, and Pat filled the gap.

OCTOBER 26, 1985

On Saturday morning, the Redbirds were riding a bus to Rio High School in Columbia County, northeast of Madison. Temperatures were mild, and the sun was shining. They had high hopes of advancing to the state meet the following weekend, but without Dave, their minds carried more than a little trepidation.

In addition to number two Monticello-New Glarus, the Redbirds faced another tough field in the sectional. Number four Fennimore, number six Brookwood, and number seven Boscobel had all qualified for the meet. Boscobel had both Clark brothers and Greg Bell returning from their strong squad the previous year, and Brookwood had returned its best runners from their 1984 campaign. Although Darlington had beaten most of their sectional opponents during the regular season, the absence of Dave Hirsbrunner put the outcome in question.

When they arrived in Rio and started warming up, the Redbirds caught a break. Monticello-New Glarus's star, Hank DeHaan, was sidelined and unable to race due to a stress fracture he had developed during the regional meet in Darlington. The ferocious pace had taken its toll on more than Hirsbrunner. Monticello-New Glarus would not be able to stay in contention without their talented leader on the course. Still, the rest of the field was formidable.

The course was gentle, and the race was hotly contested from the start. Early on, Kent found himself near the front with a group of Boscobel and Brookwood runners pushing the pace. By the two-mile split, the swift tempo had taken a toll, and he was starting to feel himself slip. Self-doubt crept in, and the *I can't* mindset began to dominate his thoughts. Kent had reached his limit and ceded the pace. One opponent passed him, and another runner approached from behind his shoulder.

"Let's go, Roop!"

The sound of James's voice in that moment lifted Kent's spirits and gave his legs new hope. The pair overtook the runner who had passed Kent moments earlier. Kent's focus returned as they battled together, passing several other runners. By the time he and James finished, Kent had set a new personal record. He had given all he could. Without James's support, there was no telling how far Kent might have slipped over that last mile.

Boscobel's Richard and Kevin Clark finished first and second. Their teammate Greg Bell came in fifth. The Bulldogs' strong showing at the front of the race put a strain on Arnie's team, commanding them to push the pace faster than they had wanted. To make matters worse, Brookwood had placed all their scorers in the top twenty finishers.

Todd Johnson (obscured) pursues a runner from Brookwood on a slope at the Rio Sectional. Bob Cullen follows closely behind as Coach Arnie Miehe encourages his runners. October 26, 1985. Photo courtesy of the *Republican Journal*.

But the Redbirds responded to the challenge by setting three personal records. Kent and James each finished under seventeen minutes and within the top ten. All five of the Redbirds' scorers were in the top twenty, including Bob Cullen, who once again answered the bell for his team. His years of dedication and lonely runs had paid dividends. In the end, Darlington won a narrow four-point victory over Brookwood. Despite placing three individuals in the top six, Boscobel's team did not advance.

The members of the Darlington boys' cross country team display their 1985 Sectional Championship plaque. From left to right, kneeling: Todd Johnson, James Schuetz, Bob Cullen, and Coach Arnie Miehe. From left to right, standing: Kirk Evenstad, Kent Ruppert, Dale Kelly, and Pat Sonsalla. Photo courtesy of the *Republican Journal*.

On Sunday, October 28, the phone in my dorm room rang. When I picked up the receiver, I heard my mom's voice. She talked about the usual things a mother discusses when her child is away from the nest. My brothers had finished their football season, the neighbors were building a new house, the leaves needed to be raked, and she wondered whether I was getting enough to eat. But she also had an update for me from the sectional cross country meet in northern Wisconsin, where the C-FC girls had competed the night before. Fennimore was not in the same sectional in 1985, and the C-FC girls were the easy favorite. I had been waiting to hear how they'd done, hoping to attend the state meet in Madison the upcoming weekend. My mom told me that Heidi had fallen on the course one hundred meters from the finish line and could not finish.

Heidi was one of the most mentally tough people I knew, and she had suppressed her mind's argument so forcefully that she collapsed within sight of the chute. She crawled incoherently for a few more yards but lost control of her limbs and ended up flailing helplessly on the grass. Mark was watching near the finish when Heidi collapsed, and he sprinted onto the course. The sight unnerved him. Heidi's face was ashen, and her eyes would not track. He lifted her off the ground and carried her to a waiting ambulance, resulting in her immediate disqualification. Her sister Karen had traveled from Minnesota to watch the race and accompanied Heidi to the hospital, where she was treated in the emergency room.

The team's sixth runner could not close the gap, and the C-FC girls' squad missed their opportunity to advance, dashing their dreams. A matter of a few yards had transported their team from a distinguishing achievement to anonymity.

It made me sick to hear it. The thought of Heidi having something like that happen to her seemed so unfair. I had witnessed her hard work during our training. I'd seen her dedication to excellence as a teammate, as a student, and in the band. Heidi was among the very best runners in the state and would have likely stood on the state meet podium that year. But despite her talent, sacrifice, and determination, she would never get the chance to run at a state cross country meet. Instead, Heidi's legacy in the sport would be her episode at the 1985 sectional and its illustration of the grit many kids develop through cross country.

Dashed hopes and dreams are common in athletics—and in life. Neither Heidi nor Tom Evenstad was unique in that respect. Disappointment is an unwelcome emotion, but it offers a benefit. It holds the mirror up for self-reflection and growth. It provides the basis for resiliency and strength. Many are the exceptional athletes and teams that have fallen on the wrong side of the knife's edge, consequently cloaked in anonymity from illness, injury, or some other last-minute calamity. Life throws adversity in our paths. In time, failure and suffering find all of us. How we react to adversity is what matters. Do we let it have the final word, intolerably ruminating over the lost opportunity? Or, do we learn from the experience, tap into renewed determination, and focus on the next goal? Some of the toughest people I've ever met have been diminutive girls who ran cross country. Heidi's qualities made her exactly the kind of kid Gary was trying to attract to his program.

Heidi recovered and ran at the state track meet the following spring. She graduated high school with honors and marched in the Badgers band during her undergraduate career at the University of Wisconsin.

The last week of October in 1985 brought a shift in the jet stream across the center of the country. The winds aloft dipped deeply into the Gulf of Mexico, ushering air laden with moisture into the Upper Midwest. Cooler temperatures and soaking rains ensued. The state cross country meet was scheduled for November 2 at the Yahara Hills Golf Course in Madison, but the turf became a sopping mire, unfit for a foot race with hundreds of athletes. Schedules for fall sports have little room for flexibility with winter seasons hanging in the balance. Changes can have a domino effect of disruption, but the WIAA made the difficult and unprecedented decision to postpone the meet until the following Saturday, November 9. Under the conditions, they had little choice.

On Friday afternoon, Arnie was walking through the hallway of the school when a voice came over the intercom asking him to report to the office. When he got there, Dave Chellevold told Arnie the state meet had been postponed a week due to flooding on the course. It was another obstacle that created more stress in the young coach's mind.

Arnie was not alone. The delay caused all of the coaches and teams even more anxiety than they would normally carry on the cusp of a state competition. The struggle to maintain peak condition and focus was hard enough without last-minute changes in a schedule. The poor weather also hampered efforts to train. But Arnie saw a silver lining with the unexpected adjustment. Dave's hip was starting to heal, and he was mobile again. Arnie had kept him on a bicycle during their practices and pushed Dave to go through his core work with the rest of the squad in hopes he might compete. An additional week of rest might give the Redbirds a chance to have Hirsbrunner back in the starting lineup. Even if he were not 100 percent, having Dave's fierce presence on the course would be a psychological boost to the rest of the team.

The following Friday, Arnie assembled his team in his classroom. Pat Sonsalla, who had filled the gap when Dave was injured, joined

The 1985 Darlington varsity squad pictured with their bikes before a late-season workout. Photo courtesy of Arnie Miehe.

them as their alternate for race day. Arnie was all business while he covered their pre-race regimen. He had a topographical map of the Yahara Hills course drawn on the chalkboard so that the kids could see the elevation changes along the route. He discussed their strategy and approach to the race, what they should eat for supper that night, when they would leave in the morning, and what hotel they would stay at after the meet was over. He droned on intensely for a half-hour. When he had finished, he asked if there were any questions.

Todd Johnson raised his hand. "Who's bringing the prophylactics?"

The room howled with laughter, and Kent Ruppert rolled on the floor, unable to breathe from the stitch in his gut. They were all red-faced, with tears running down their cheeks. Todd sat with a straight face looking at his teammates on the floor. A minute later they were walking out of the classroom together, smiling, and unafraid of the challenge. Todd's audacious question had cut the tension and put everything back in perspective.

After they left, Arnie sat at his desk, surrounded by his pre-race notes, shaking his head and smiling. A little humor was exactly what they needed.

YAHARA HILLS GOLF COURSE, NOVEMBER 9, 1985

The Redbirds woke early on Saturday morning, prepared to go about their pre-race routine with their usual businesslike approach. As he had done the prior year, Arnie wanted the team to arrive in plenty of time to survey the course. Madison was only an hour's drive from Darlington. Arnie had opted to let the kids sleep in their own beds, rather than driving the night before and sleeping in an unfamiliar hotel. The team assembled at the high school and climbed into a Chevy Suburban. As they left the parking lot, light snow began to fall.

The ride there was tense and slower than Arnie had planned. The snow was getting heavier with each mile. The forecast had not been accurate, and it was the heavy, sticky stuff that comes early in winter when the temperatures flirt with the freezing point. The snow clung to the trees, and the roads were greasy. Arnie tried to make light of the conditions with his team, telling them that it was going to be fun to run in the snow. But the flakes kept getting heavier as they approached Madison. A long line of vehicles backed up for the turn into the Yahara Hills Golf Course, and suddenly the Suburban lurched forward with a thud. A sedan following them had slid into the back of the Redbirds' Suburban. The car's driver had cranked the wheel in an attempt to avoid a collision but tapped the SUV's bumper with its tire. The sedan ended up in the ditch. Arnie turned on his hazard lights and bolted out of the door to see if he could help. The occupants were shaken but fine. The car had grazed the Suburban's fender, but there was no visible damage. Additional help arrived to push the car out of the ditch, and the Redbirds proceeded to the Yahara Hills parking lot.

When Arnie parked the Suburban and stepped onto the pavement, two inches of snow had already accumulated. The squad walked to the clubhouse to get the latest word before their pre-race scouting tour. Race officials were already in a frenzy to adapt, but the meet had reached the point of no return. It was too late to reschedule with hundreds of runners and fans already arriving from around the state. Moments earlier, the WIAA officials had allowed a variance to the uniform code normally required in the tournament runs. Runners were obliged to wear bib placards for identification by officials, but they'd permit the contestants to wear whatever garments they felt necessary during the race to protect themselves from the elements.

Fans huddle in blizzard-like conditions waiting for the start of the 1985 Class C boys championship race. Photo courtesy of the *Republican Journal*.

266   DRIFTLESS RUN

Only once, in 1985, did the WIAA make this exception for a Wisconsin state meet.

While the Redbirds waited in the clubhouse, the team from Menominee Indian walked in and stood nearby. Upon seeing them, the Darlington runners became silent. Menominee Indian was back for the second straight year with a veteran squad. Arnie had been concerned about them ever since seeing their sixth-place finish at the 1984 state meet and from their consistent ranking in the top five all season. He had little reassurance for how his kids would match up during the meet. As a result, after the sectional race, Arnie forced his squad to memorize their names and targeted the Menominee club as the team to beat.

Brookwood's veteran crew was also standing in the clubhouse. Darlington had to face them once again after narrowly defeating the Falcons a week earlier.

A few minutes passed, and the Redbirds walked out the door to tour the course. The Yahara course was fine ground for a state meet under normal conditions. The turf was groomed routinely, and the course was set up in three loops. Each loop was roughly a mile in length, making it easy to divide the race into equal segments and measure performance during competition. But the sod had been soaked in the rains the week before, and it was now covered with sticky snow. Cleats were of little value on top of that blanket. Each stride demanded concentration to avoid a fall.

The roads became so treacherous that several Redbirds fans turned their vehicles around and went back to Darlington. But while the team was scouting the course, a spectator bus from Darlington finally arrived. After it was emptied, the team walked over to the bus to utilize its extra space and change into their uniforms. Arnie kept a calm outward appearance for his team, but inside, he was upset with himself for not having the contingency covered. They had left their cold-weather gear behind in Darlington. His team had no tights, no gloves, and no long-sleeved T-shirts to wear under their jerseys. When he looked at his kids, their eyes did not reflect his concern. The weather was just one more obstacle in a list of many they had encountered on their journey. They calmly rummaged through their duffel bags looking for articles of clothing to add to their attire. They managed to scavenge an assortment of stocking hats for their heads. The boys found short-sleeved T-shirts they had stashed for casual wear and put them on under their jerseys. Extra tube socks were fashioned into makeshift gauntlets to cover their hands and forearms. It looked silly, but they did it anyway.

Arnie reminded his team how they had gotten to this point. He called on them to remember the last two seasons in which they had reached new heights, only to fall just short of their goals. James, Bob, and Kirk had run at Christmas Mountain, and the rest had attended the meet. Arnie opened the old wound of disappointment and let it fester with his team. He reiterated their "beat it or eat it" mantra and said that they just needed to go about their usual business to achieve their objective.

"I want you guys to run a smart race. Get out in good position, but stay relaxed over the first loop. On the second loop, lay the groundwork for moving up. By the time you begin the third loop, you need to be picking off other runners. If there is a runner in front of you to beat, then beat him! And for God's sake, watch your footing out there. We can't afford to have falls in this stuff!"

When they moved to the starting line, it became apparent that the Redbirds were the only team with their jerseys visible to the contestants. The rest of the runners wore sweatshirts with hoods, sweatpants, and varying attire. Their teams were indistinguishable. The Darlington kids would be targeted, and they'd have no idea who their nearest competitors were representing.

The boys' Class C race was the final contest of the meet, and it was well after noon when the squads lined up. The chalk line was no longer visible under five inches of accumulated snow, and the wind had picked up. By the time the gun cracked, it was snowing harder than it had been all day. The teams skidded out of their lanes, and the ragtag figures disappeared into a shroud of white. It was snowing so hard the runners could not see from one flag to another on the course. Runners from the University of Wisconsin, who knew the course well, had been placed as "rabbits" along the route. They navigated for the pack. Arnie positioned himself near the end of the loop so he could sense how his runners were placed. As they reached the first mile, their split times were horrendous, as they were for all of the contestants. The snow had required shorter strides, and the footing was awful. Arnie wanted his kids to ease into the race, but despite the slow pace, his Redbirds were farther back in the pack than he'd hoped. Dave was racing for the first time in weeks. Arnie had no choice but to let Dave attempt the race but was unsure how he would fare. Once Dave was on the course, he settled into the middle of the pack and fought to suppress the biting pain. It became obvious that he had not fully recovered. Arnie's nerves started to eat at him, and he pleaded for each runner to pick up the pace as he passed by.

James Schuetz (#621) attacks a hill in blinding snow at the 1985 State meet. Photo courtesy of the *Republican Journal*.

As Kent passed the first-mile marker, the official called out his split, nearly a minute behind his normal pace. The whiteout conditions made it hard to ascertain his position, but he knew his split time could only mean he was way behind where he should be. The blinding snow pelted Kent's face, and he cocked his head to the side. He closed his forward eye and squinted through the other to see where he was going. The coping mechanism allowed him some limited vision, but he could not see the next runner ahead of him. Just the same, he picked up the pace and began passing opponents. When he could see them, Kent followed tracks in the snow to stay on the course. Hundreds of ghostly fans lined the route, barely visible through the shroud that surrounded him. Their shouts and screams served as an aural beacon, guiding his path. As Kent neared the second-mile split, he pulled up behind a small group of runners. He was prepared to pass the group but halted his attack as they entered a sharp turn. The race official standing nearby motioned to the runners to keep them on the course. Kent then realized that the pack in front of him was the lead group, and he changed tactics. He was so blinded by the snow that he did not think he could lead a race and stay on the course. It was better to follow closely and not make a wrong turn. Kent was in a good position to score well for his team, and he braced himself for the last mile.

After the second mile, the Redbirds were not in position to win. Arnie shouted at his kids to pour out everything they had. He surmised from prior state meets that his scorers needed to place within the top thirty runners, or a title would be out of reach. A total score under fifty points would provide that assurance, and they were nowhere close. Arnie sprinted in the opposite direction of the runners so he could position himself halfway on the final loop and call to them one more time.

Wearing gauntlets fashioned from tube socks, Todd Johnson ascends a slippery rise during the 1985 state meet at Yahara Hills. Photo courtesy of the *Republican Journal*.

With one thousand meters left in the race, James and Dave were in better position. When Todd passed his coach, five meters behind his teammate, Dale, they were too far back in the race to give the Redbirds a chance.

Arnie cried out to both of them to charge forward. "Todd! You've got to go! We're in trouble!"

Upon hearing his coach's anxious voice, Todd's eyes locked on Arnie, and his posture lifted. He surged forward and began to pass Dale. By that point, Dale was struggling with his hands. Both had been stinging from the cold by the end of the first mile. After two miles, they had become dead weights, opposing his will. As Todd pulled up next to him, Dale's spirits lifted, and he increased his gait. Arnie watched them disappear, side by side, into the cloak of snowflakes.

All of the contestants' times were dismal, but Kent ended up in seventh place, tying the spot Troy Cullen had secured the previous year. James ran remarkably well and finished thirteenth. Dave battled on his bad hip to cross the line in twenty-third. Their first three scorers had crossed in good position, but the Redbirds' fate would be determined by the legs of Todd Johnson and Dale Kelly.

An exhausted Darlington squad dons their warm-ups after the race. Photo courtesy of Arnie Miehe.

The Darlington runners exited the chute in wretched shape, soaking wet and exposed. During the race, Dave's uncovered skin developed purple blotches. One of the Darlington fans covered him in an embrace for a couple of minutes to restore some warmth to his body. Kent immediately retrieved his sweats, but he could not feel his hands. After he failed to dress himself, one of his classmates stepped in and helped dress him.

After walking back to the chute, several Darlington fans asked Arnie if he'd seen Todd and Dale finish. He shook his head. The Redbirds fans along the final straightaway had witnessed the pair unleash a furious charge. They passed more than a dozen runners together before crossing the line.

Snow laden and soaked, James Schuetz recovers after exiting the chute at the Yahara Hills course. Bob Cullen searches for air in the background. Photo courtesy of the *Republican Journal*.

Arnie walked up to Ann. She had collected the Redbirds' placement cards from the kids after leaving the chute, and he asked her what their score was.

"Fifty-four points."

Arnie's gaze dropped to the ground, and his heart sank.

"It's not going to be enough, Ann. I'll turn in our cards to the officials if you could take care of things on the bus. I'll meet you there in a few minutes."

Arnie collected himself for a moment and began walking to the RV where the race officials were tabulating the results. He opened the RV's door and stepped inside the small shelter. Standing nearby was Brookwood's coach, John Smith.

Arnie glanced at Smith and asked, "How'd you guys do?"

"Not worth a shit!"

Arnie kept probing for any information he could get from Smith.

"Did you hear how the other teams did? What's the word?"

"Sounds like Bayfield had a good race."

Arnie was stunned. Bayfield was from the far northern part of the state, on the shores of Lake Superior. The Trollers were not a familiar squad at state cross country meets. They'd barely broken into the top ten in the coaches' poll late in the season and had not shown up on Arnie's radar. His heart skipped a beat as he recalled the surprise C-FC had given him the prior fall.

The door on the RV creaked open, interrupting their conversation with a draft of cold air. The Bayfield coach poked his head inside and handed John Smith an envelope containing the Trollers' placement cards. He had mistaken the Brookwood coach for one of the WIAA officials working inside. Smith looked over the placement cards and calculated Bayfield's total. He then passed them along to the officials and turned to Arnie.

"Bayfield scored fifty-five."

Arnie's heart skipped another beat, and he handed Darlington's placement cards to the same official. She rifled through the pack and looked up at the Redbirds' coach.

"Your team's score is seventy-six."

Arnie gave her a frustrated glance.

"That can't be right! Check that again."

The official took back the cards and scanned them another time.

"Oh, I missed this one! Your score is fifty-four."

Ann's count had been correct.

John Smith turned to Arnie with his hand extended and said, "Congratulations!"

Darlington had won its first state championship, in a driving snowstorm, by a single point. Arnie's throat thickened at the news, and he turned to walk back to the bus. Somehow it did not seem possible. Only a few months earlier he was mentally preparing himself for a rebuilding season. He had lost all those seniors from the 1984 squad, the squad that he thought would win a state title. Yet he knew his young runners had worked hard enough, and he had believed in their potential. The events of the last four seasons washed over him as he slowly made his way toward his squad in the snow. The sweltering runs in the sun, the untimely injuries, the heartache of narrow defeats, the seniors lost to graduation—all of it came to him at once. The team title had dropped suddenly into his lap when he had least expected it, and he was overcome with emotion. He was nearly speechless as two figures approached him through the snow.

Ann had returned from the bus with Deb Hauser, the school's athletic director, to see if Arnie had learned the result. The head coach looked ragged walking toward them, with drenched, tousled hair topping his scalp.

As they met, Ann noticed the stunned look on Arnie's face and asked, "How'd we do?"

Arnie struggled to summon an audible voice. "Oh my gosh. We just won!"

The trio embraced, soaking in the unfamiliar feeling, along with the snow. They collected themselves for a moment before resuming their walk toward their entourage.

After exiting the chute, the Redbirds runners had gone back to the bus. By then, it was nearly full of the fans sheltering inside. The squad pulled off their soaked shirts and put their warm-ups back on. Their cheeks were rosy, but the mood was dripping with anxiety. The vapor from their bodies fogged the windows as the team sat with their followers, wondering about their fate. James wiped the condensate from his window so he could see the activity outside the bus. The menacing sky was extinguishing the last light of the day, and after a few minutes, he saw Arnie approaching.

The bus door squeaked open, and the first person Arnie saw was Dale Kelly. Dale was standing by the bus's front heater, warming his hands and wearing a grimace. He stepped aside to let his coach pass. Arnie did not know it at the time, but Dale's fingers had suffered frostbite on the course. When Arnie reached the top of the stairs, the nervous chatter ceased. All eyes turned to the stoic face at the front. Arnie said nothing and strolled to the center of the bus. Spellbound heads pivoted toward him, silently seeking an end to the suspense.

"Bayfield scored fifty-five points; they were second. We're state champs!"

The bus exploded with screams and started rocking on its tires.

Todd Johnson leapt from his seat and bear-hugged his coach, no longer able to control his deadpan face.

In the melee that ensued, Arnie spotted senior Bob Cullen sitting quietly in his seat, overwhelmed by the news. The unassuming kid who, as a freshman fifth runner in 1982, had fallen short of giving the Redbirds a conference title was fighting to restrain his emotions. Bob never complained about his role and had steadily improved during his career. The advance of the entire program overshadowed his progress, and he had barely held onto his varsity position. For four years, he had steadfastly performed his duty while others received the accolades. But from that moment on, Bob would always be a state champion. In that breathless instant of affirmation, joy spilled from Bob's eyes.

The awards ceremony took place at Madison's La Follette High School auditorium. Kevin Clark of Boscobel captured the individual crown. Not a single Redbirds runner stood on the podium with him. But they had something more special. They had a cohesive team. When the Class C team title was announced to the crowd, the WIAA officials draped a gold medal around the neck of each Redbirds runner. Arnie walked up and accepted the championship trophy. He immediately handed it to Bob and Todd, who hoisted it above their heads and faced the cameras. Arnie stepped aside and watched.

From the awards stage, the coach looked upon the rows of spectators seated before them. He spotted John Schuetz and Joe Ruppert, next to the center aisle, one sitting directly in front of the other. Both had worked tirelessly for years dairy farming. They had each toiled to make payments and provide for their families. The wear was evident on their leathered hands and faces. Arnie knew their struggle was unrelenting, but both had taken time away from their chores to attend their sons' meet. And there they were, before the stage, in an unfamiliar environment. Their eyes were welling with pride as they witnessed their boys claiming the first state title for their high school. The sight would remain etched in Arnie's mind.

After the ceremony, the team stepped into the lobby for some photos with parents and friends. Then Suzy Favor, the future Olympian from Stevens Point, walked by. She had just won her fourth straight individual title.

Dave called to her, "Hey, Suzy! Would you mind joining us for a photo?"

Favor trotted over to the Redbirds to memorialize the moment. The farm boys had become rock stars.

The Darlington Redbirds stand on the stage at the 1985 state meet award ceremony holding their championship trophy. From left to right: Kent Ruppert, James Schuetz, Dave Hirsbrunner, Todd Johnson, Bob Cullen, Kirk Evenstad, Dale Kelly, alternate Pat Sonsalla, and Coach Arnie Miehe. Photo courtesy of the *Republican Journal*.

When the cameras stopped clicking, Arnie's squad climbed into the Suburban. The skinny squirts who had run on the JV with Tom Evenstad two years earlier had reached the pinnacle of their sport.

After a moment, Dave settled into his seat and exclaimed, "Dammit!"

"What's wrong?" asked Arnie.

"Today is my dad's birthday, and I forgot to get him a gift."

The guys patted him on the back, the smile returned to Dave's face, and they resumed their chatter. The boom box was in the back seat, and they popped a cassette into the receiver. Aldo Nova's guitar whined through the speakers, and the Redbirds reveled in "Fantasy."

Kent Ruppert was sitting in the middle of the front seat beaming with a smile that had not left his face for several hours. The guys in the back were handing the championship trophy to each other and soaking in the music. When the trophy reached the front seat, Kent propped it on his lap. It was as tall as his torso, stretching from his thighs to his chin. Kent looked at it for a moment, and the smile fled.

He turned to Arnie and asked, "Is this all we get?"

"Yes. Why?"

"If I knew that, I would not have gone out for cross country!"

His teammates roared with laughter and pounded Kent on the head.

The next day Darlington turned out the fire engines and paraded its team down Main Street to celebrate their first state championship. Like the year before, the community filled the school's gymnasium for their pep rally.

The Darlington community fills the high school gymnasium to celebrate their first state championship team. Photo courtesy of Arnie Miehe.

Dave Chellevold started the ceremony by announcing, "Ladies and gentlemen, I give you the 1985 state champions!"

Arnie's squad marched into the gymnasium to a standing ovation, and the pep band belted out the school song. After the crowd was seated, each runner was introduced and got a moment at the microphone. Arnie went last and walked up to the podium with the championship trophy.

"I'd like to start by wishing a happy belated birthday to George Hirsbrunner."

Big George had shown up at the state meet to watch his son run. At the rally, he was sitting in the top row of the gymnasium's bleachers with his back against the wall.

As all eyes turned to George, Arnie continued, "George, with everything going on yesterday, Dave forgot to get you a gift. I know it's a little late, but we thought we'd bring back this trophy for you instead!"

The crowd erupted. Tears of delight rolled down George's cheeks, and he waved to the audience.

CHAPTER TWENTY-THREE
THE MATRON
August 30, 2015

The heat of the August day pulled my mind back to the present as I scanned the family photos on the table. There was a photo of Gary in his classroom at C-FC, where he had been hired after getting his teaching certificate. There were photos of Judee directing the Fountain City River Players at the historic auditorium in town. Her community theater productions had become well-known. Several cast and crew members were scattered in the line as we all waited.

Other pictures showed the Brones at their shop with customers and friends who had purchased bikes. The business had flourished for years after the hardware store closed. Cyclists came from all over the Upper Midwest for Brone's Bike Shop's specialty products and for Mark's technical skills. With Judee selling coffee and ice cream from a counter in the back, it became a place to meet old friends. Brone's Bike Shop jerseys became a common sight at time trials and road races in the region. The Brones continued to share their love of endurance sports through their work in that shop. Nothing lasts, but some things never change.

Then there were the photos of Gary and Judee with their grandchildren. Mark had married. He and Shelli had a girl and a boy, Haili and Mason. The pictures captured joyful moments for their family and made me smile.

On the next table were the pictures of Jesse. The smile fell, and my eyes watered upon seeing them. In 1997, the Brones lost their youngest son to a workplace accident. He was twenty-one years old, and his death was a tragedy for the entire community. In my mind, I could still see him on his bike and on the Little League diamond catching my pitches. Jesse became an excellent cross country runner like his older brother and represented C-FC at the state meet during high school. He was popular with his peers and became the first cross country runner at C-FC to be voted homecoming king. After graduation, he ran cross country for the University of North Dakota. One of the largest annual races in the region is the Jesse Brone Invitational, held on the C-FC course.

The loss of their child devastated Gary and Judee, as it would any parent. It was a smothering grief, the type so severe that it can steal life's purpose and eviscerate the soul. Gary was driftless for a time after Jesse's death. He quit teaching. During that period of suffering, Gary rediscovered his purpose by coaching kids and found that he could still make a difference in their lives. The extended family he and Judee had nurtured through the years gave him a reason to carry on. He found opportunity amidst adversity, yet again. He found a way to persevere, yet again. He found a way to love through sacrifice, yet again. And even with his suffering, he could find joy, yet again.

He became anchored once more, thanks to the program he had pioneered with his family, which managed to survive despite its uncertain early years.

Sitting near the line was Brian Semling, one of the program's best runners from the early 1990s. He was in grade school when I ran at Christmas Mountain. Brian's dad had been my science teacher in junior high, and I introduced myself to him. Brian had heard the stories of that first team from Gary and Mark. We shared

Gary and Jesse Brone. Photo courtesy of Mark Brone.

memories of better days while I waited in line.

At the front of the line I spotted Guy Todd giving Gary a hug. It had been twenty years since we'd seen each other, and he left before I could speak with him. As elusive as ever, he was too far ahead of me to catch.

Many of them were there, sprinkled amongst the crowd of community members. The Pirate harriers had come home, standing once again in the chute. They were waiting to be received, somehow still hoping that they would emerge to have lipstick smacked on their cheeks. There had been hundreds of them since that first season in 1983. Hundreds had heard her say, "Always do your best!" They'd come to pay their respects to a woman who had become another mother to them when they were teenagers. Our dear Judee had passed unexpectedly, her big heart having given all it could. There was no more bright smile for us. No more cheery greetings with an offer of coffee when we stopped by the bike shop to check in with "the family." There was a new gap for the team to fill. But those of us there could not fill it, and I knew the hole would never close in our hearts. Her life had mattered. It was a painful pilgrimage of gratitude for all of us.

A year later, on a sunny Saturday afternoon in October, a group of middle-aged alumni joined the C-FC High School cross country team for a run on our home course. We had gathered to honor Judee's life and assisted Gary with placing a memorial stone and a tree on the site. It was a place where she had cheered the Pirate runners for over thirty years. Several of the original team members were there to support Gary and run with Mark. Paul, Scott, Karen, and Heidi finished on that familiar trail, their times naturally slower than in high school. I was there too, but I could not run. A knee replacement required that I cheer them on instead. Despite the loss of our dear Judee, it was a moment filled with old stories and laughter. She would have loved that gathering. The bonds we formed as teenagers were still there. After decades of separation, it was as if we were never apart. We were all still part of Gary and Judee's extended family.

"The greatest moments in life are not concerned with selfish achievements but rather with the things we do for the people we love and esteem."
—Walt Disney

Several members of the 1983 C-FC cross country team in October 2016 at the Judee Brone Memorial Alumni Run. From left to right, kneeling: Jeff Rich, Mark Brone, and Heidi Stettler. From left to right, standing: Coach Gary Brone, Paul Abts, Scott Adler, and Karen Stettler. Photo courtesy of Mark Brone.

CHAPTER TWENTY-FOUR
LEGACY

The small family dairy farms of Wisconsin have withered into obscurity, merging into larger operations. A drive through the country reveals the bones. Skeletal barns and lonely silos now dot the landscape. Automation has replaced the need for much of the hard labor. Yet the land continues to bear fruit for some of those resilient families, and the heartbeat still throbs. The natural beauty of the area remains.

More Wisconsin schools now field cross country teams than in the 1980s. The advancement of technology has made the meets much easier and more thrilling for spectators to view. Darlington and C-FC are just two examples of small school cross country programs that have achieved notable success. In recent decades, other small schools in southwestern Wisconsin, including Albany, Boscobel, Brookwood, Fennimore, La Crosse Aquinas, and Lancaster, have each produced multiple championship teams. The sport has become a source of pride in many communities of the Driftless Region.

Darlington captured consecutive boys' state team championships in 1985 and 1986. In their senior year, Dave Hirsbrunner, Dale Kelly,

Kent Ruppert, and Kirk Evenstad led the way. Their program went on to achieve remarkable success. The Darlington boys' team has qualified for the state meet twenty-two times since 1984, including eight state titles. The Redbirds had a consecutive run of six titles between 2011 and 2016, a string of distinctions that only two schools in Wisconsin history have achieved. The Redbirds have also claimed five state runner-up trophies. Their boys' team record stands unmatched for small schools in the state. The Redbirds girls' teams have qualified for the state meet seventeen times since 1989, with one state title and one state runner-up trophy. Both the boys' and girls' teams won state championships in 2016. In 2005, Arnie Miehe was inducted into the WCCCA Association Hall of Fame. He was named the 2015 National Coach of the Year by the National Federation of High School Coaches Association.

Arnie Miehe and Ann Smith developed into a great coaching team for the Redbirds' cross country squads. Ann was a role model for the runners and hosted countless team meals for the teenagers. She was Arnie's assistant for decades, coached the junior high program, and served as a reliable and sensible advisor during difficult moments. Ann and Arnie became a couple and were married in 1987.

They had four children, two girls and two boys. As might be expected, the Miehe's kids developed a love for running and the work ethic to excel as endurance athletes. Carly, Hana, Kent, and Tyson became cross country runners for Darlington High School. All four became team captains for the Redbirds. All four became team MVPs. All four were named to all-conference teams. All four represented Darlington at state cross country meets. All four were designated as WIAA Scholar Athletes. Kent and Tyson were members of the Darlington Boys' State Championship team in 2011. Tyson became a three-time individual state champion. He also became a Division I runner for the Big Ten champion Wisconsin Badgers and

Arnie and Kent Miehe, October 2022.
Photo by Jeff Rich.

was inducted into the WCCCA Hall of Fame in 2020. Hana and Kent became cross country coaches themselves. In 2022, after forty-one seasons, Arnie Miehe finished his final season as the varsity coach for Darlington's cross country program. His son Kent became the new head coach for the team.

Many of the program's traditions that Arnie introduced in his first season still exist, and he has started new traditions as well, such as the Run Across Wisconsin, which is held in conjunction with the county Relay for Life. The Redbirds start at Lake Michigan and conduct a two-day run to the Mississippi River. This tradition has raised over $28,000 for cancer research in twenty years.

Several hundred people stop by the school to watch the annual alumni race in late August each year. Most years, James Schuetz runs on the alumni team, finishing with a time that is not too far off from his high school days.

During recent decades, the consolidation of dairy farms into larger operations around Darlington has provided a new opportunity. The need for rural labor to support these businesses has attracted immigrant families from Latin America to the area. The school district has used an inclusive approach with these new residents. Today, nearly a third of the cross country team is comprised of students of Latino descent. The staff has used a multilingual approach to coaching, banquets, and other functions to ease the transition and welcome new families. Participation in the program has continued to thrive.

Arnie and Ann's leadership has impacted hundreds of teenagers who have stepped forward in life, stronger from the experience of running cross country for the Miehes. They've also inspired more than a dozen former runners to become coaches.

There is another truly remarkable legacy for a small high school. Since Darlington's first state meet trip in 1984, the school has produced four state championships in football and another in boys' basketball. Through the work of administrators, coaches, faculty, and students, all of their athletic programs have flourished alongside the rise of the cross country program. The small school has built a culture of excellence around athletics that carries into the community. Wadzy Martens saw the potential in 1984.

"A rising tide lifts all boats."
—John F. Kennedy

The Darlington High School trophy case in 2021, featuring the team's state championship and runner-up trophies from multiple sports since 1985. Photo by Jeff Rich.

People at the state meet in 1984 could not pronounce our school's name and had never heard of it before. That was about to change, and Cochrane-Fountain City became a familiar name on the cross country scene. After the 1984 meet at Christmas Mountain, Gary Brone was honored as the District Three Coach of the Year by the WCCCA for his team's Cinderella performance in achieving their first state championship.

Throughout Gary's career, the C-FC boys' teams have qualified for the state meet ten times, with one individual champion and five team championships, including a consecutive string from 1993 to

1996. In each of those four years, the Darlington boys were the state runners-up.

The C-FC girls' teams have qualified for the state meet six times, winning four team titles and producing four individual champions. In 1996, both the boys' and girls' teams won state team championships, a feat only six schools have accomplished in the state's history, one of which is Darlington. That same year, Rachel Earney was the individual state champion, and her sister, Selina, was the runner-up in the girls' race. In his final season, on October 29, 2022, Gary coached his girls' squad to a state championship. On that same day, C-FC's Addy Duellman and Wesley Pronschinske captured the girls' and boys' individual titles. It was the first time in the history of the Wisconsin state cross country meet that a girl and a boy from the same school won individual titles in the same season. Like Darlington, the Pirate trophy case is filled with hardware from those decades of teams. Most impressively, the Brone family has made a positive impact on hundreds of young lives over that four-decade span.

In 2003, Gary was honored with his induction into the WCCCA Hall of Fame. At the banquet, Arnie Miehe introduced Gary to the crowd. At the time of this writing, in 2022, Gary Brone was seventy-nine years old and had just completed his fortieth and final season as the cross country coach at Cochrane-Fountain City. He and Arnie have paralleled each other on their remarkable coaching journeys in so many ways, even finishing at the same time, with nine team state championships each.

The crowd gathers at the C-FC course for the Jesse Brone Invitational. September 2021. Photo by Jeff Rich.

What a joy it is to run! The naïve arrogance of youth blinds most of us to that fact, but to the elderly and to those who have known the loss of their legs, it is painfully obvious. All that is needed for validation is a moment watching grade schoolers. Kids run everywhere, regardless of necessity. Time robs us of our capacities during the journey of life. We cannot see it in our youth, or it is opaque to the few who can comprehend its effect at an early age. Our first few decades are consumed by annual growth and acquisition. There is an upward trajectory that tricks the mind into believing it will always be that way, and each successive year will bring greater capability. We begin to believe physical or mental loss is something others endure, yet it will somehow not be the case for us. We do not see our future selves and the decline for all who trek far enough along life's journey. I yearn to run again, but I know now I never will. I dream about it still. If I concentrate, I can recreate what it felt like in my mind, the freedom of propelling forward with ease and speed, covering great distances with the breeze through my hair.

Our moment forty years ago was unique to those of us who lived it, but the story line is not unique in the world of sport. It is one Cinderella story among thousands of similar stories across the spectrum of athletics throughout the years. The story is not remarkable in that sense; our feats of athleticism are not unprecedented, and our victories are not that consequential. We were not heroes and did not risk our lives to confront the horrors that others have faced. The story is only worth telling for the lessons it illustrates. Team sports should be teaching us about life and each other. In today's world, those lessons seem lost to selfish pursuits. For my teammates and me, cross country placed an unexpected opportunity at our feet. It was a time when we each faced struggles and setbacks. We had started as individuals for our own reasons, but we were required to make personal sacrifices for the benefit of others. It seemed as if there was a recipe that included something divine mixed with our own determination. The product was personal growth. The journey was our instructor, with a lesson plan that read:

- Opportunities exist amid adversity.
- Action turns opportunities into achievement.

- Greatness is achieved with bold goals and risk.
- Growth is forged through adversity.
- Perseverance overcomes many barriers.
- Sacrificing for one another is the embodiment of love.
- Shared sacrifice yields benefits that the individual cannot attain.
- We can affect our destinies.

Stories of victories and championships fade with time, and all glory slips from our fingers. Names and feats are lost to history. Like the leaves of autumn, we wither and crumble as athletes, forgotten by the next generation. However, we can continue to hold the lessons of life with us and apply those when we have the chance. We can share them with others. The lessons are more precious and enduring than any accolades. For my part, I have an old injury, a coach, and my teammates to thank for helping me learn these lessons. I have carried them in my heart since 1984 when I ran through those Driftless hills with my mates, whom I still love.

To this day, Gary Brone keeps the individual medal intended for his 1984 team's seventh runner in a case at his home. Occasionally, he holds it and reflects on that fragile moment. It marks the last time a Wisconsin title was captured by a team with fewer than seven

Coach Arnie Miehe and Coach Gary Brone. February 4, 2023. Photo courtesy of Karen Rich.

runners. It reminds him of the strength in unity. It whispers depth in small numbers. It attests that in scarcity, there is abundance in this world. We just need to have the vision to see it.

"Flee not from your hardships for they hold treasure to plunder."
—Jeff Rich

Photo by Jeff Rich.

EPILOGUE

Interaction enables much of our advancement in life, both personally and within society. None of us achieves much of significance without aid from others. Our society emphasizes the accomplishments of individuals while often dismissing the sacrifices of the others who made those individual accomplishments possible. We like the allure of a hero saving the day when, in fact, it is usually more than one person who makes things happen. Life's everyday distractions draw our attention inward, and we tend to focus on our self-interest. We aspire to do things together but primarily serve ourselves. When we fail to reach a goal, we commonly withdraw with frustration rather than honestly confront ourselves. We miss the chance to learn from the failure and then make another attempt. Withdrawal waives the prospect of working with others who can offer solutions we cannot deliver on our own. We miss our chance to see who or what might emerge and change our circumstances. Withdrawal limits our growth, and the individual then chooses to live within their constraints.

Team sports provide moments for personal insight during our youth. They offer opportunities for interaction and a way to confront meaningful challenges without the consequences of adult life. But we frequently rush past those moments in sports that would provide a chance for reflection. We fail to pause, placing priority on the scoreboard or clock instead. Of course, results matter, but results will be short-lived without growth and learning.

It seems that in recent decades, our society has framed team sports as a launching pad for the individual. Entertainment and hero worship have somehow superseded the life lessons and character development athletics can offer. The media glorifies individual superstars, money, and other entrapments of fame. Families sacrifice to chase the dream that their child can become the next superstar. In reality, almost none of them will earn a living through sports. Even the most talented will finish their athletic careers in their early twenties. Barriers such as injury, superior competition, or other real-life consequences will force a conclusion. Why do we attach our identities so strongly to this pursuit, as I did in my youth? What benefit are we seeking through the dedication of so much time and treasure?

Our need to label our self-image as a "winner" pushes us to deny a fundamental fact of life. We will all lose at some point. There will be financial failures, failed relationships, career failures, failing health, and above all, the loss of our lives. To say that we "never lose" is a falsehood. Cycles of failure and learning are how humans develop. It is the primary way we better ourselves. Coping effectively with setbacks builds resourcefulness, resilience, and character. That is not to say we should be happy with failure or accept it as the end result. Life is competitive, so sports can offer us a window into how to compete wisely. After all, most of our goals are commendable, and we should strive toward their achievement. The disappointment from our failures should earnestly drive us to learn from the experience. In fact, those who learn best from their hardships and can pull together as a team tend to win the most. But to deny that we fail is a feel-good fantasy that imprisons us within our own walls of immaturity. Fulfillment and gratitude will only come from the success borne through adversity. One of the best gifts a parent can give a child is to let the child safely struggle through a challenge. Without the rain, the sun will not shine as brightly.

Lessons gained through the experience of team sports can be applied throughout life. If we are paying attention, we do not need to win a championship to learn from the experience of team competition. Both the C-FC and Darlington teams faced adversity in similar ways during their respective journeys. Each squad struggled through setbacks, accepted risk, and learned to work together. There were some striking parallels between the two programs that illustrate some of these lessons:

OPPORTUNITIES EXIST IN THE MIDST OF ADVERSITY.

Both teams had athletes who were willing to walk away from the gridiron's lure in the eighties culture. There were various reasons for their decisions, but each had to wrestle with the pushback that resulted in order to achieve something new and exceptional.

ACTION TURNS OPPORTUNITIES INTO ACHIEVEMENT.

Both teams dedicated themselves to a higher standard of work during the offseason. That commitment to personal improvement yielded stronger team performance and a new level of excellence in their programs.

GREATNESS IS ACHIEVED WITH BOLD GOALS AND RISK.

Both schools had to overcome losing cultures. In order to win, we must first believe that we can win. Each team found that it could win a big meet against strong competition.

Both coaches celebrated incremental individual and team achievements to positively reinforce their improvement. Both coaches fostered self-esteem within their runners along the journey. They helped them to believe in themselves, which bolstered their self-confidence.

Both coaches set aggressive—but realistic—goals for their individuals and teams. Each coach understood the limitations and growth potential of their personnel. If a goal is unbelievable, then it will be easy to shed expectations and accountability. A goal is often realistic but requires extraordinary commitment, toil, and innovation to achieve. When that is the case, a good coach will present evidence and reasoning to support the authenticity of the goal, as both coaches did. Arnie and Gary repeatedly built confidence in their runners to help them keep their objectives in focus. Both coaches developed and maintained close personal relationships with the individuals on their teams. That insight provided them with an understanding of how to properly motivate each kid without destroying the fragile confidence of the teenage ego. Above all, a good coach will not let a setback derail a goal and will foster a positive culture within the team's ranks. The tone starts at the top and flows down through the upperclassmen.

PERSEVERANCE OVERCOMES MANY BARRIERS.

Both C-FC and Darlington suffered dejection after their 1983 sectional race. Both had prospects of making it to the state meet that season, and the path forward looked murky after falling short. C-FC had to overcome inadequate numbers in a sport that demands depth. Darlington had to overcome the loss of talented seniors to graduation. Neither threw in the towel, and despite challenges, both squads continued on their paths forward.

GROWTH IS FORGED THROUGH ADVERSITY.

Both teams battled inclement weather. Both skirmished with hills regularly during their training. Both teams had key individuals suffer serious injuries at critical points. Yet, they did not withdraw from competition and worked through the pain to achieve their goals. Both teams had kids who struggled in school or with issues at home. Both teams became familiar with adversity and how to handle it successfully by supporting one another.

SACRIFICING FOR ONE ANOTHER IS THE EMBODIMENT OF LOVE.

Runners on both teams rose to the occasion to cover an individual's weakness. This allowed a sixth or seventh runner to shine or a junior varsity member to rise. Sometimes in life we need to play a role on a team. That role is often not that of the star or one that brings individual accolades, yet it is no less significant to the team's fortunes. It provides the opportunity for role players to find purpose, grow, and gain self-confidence. It offers an opportunity to gain respect from teammates for the value they can bring.

SHARED SACRIFICE YIELDS BENEFITS THAT THE INDIVIDUAL CANNOT ATTAIN.

The more experienced runners on both squads treated the underclassmen respectfully and viewed them as important contributors to the program's future. Teenagers, like adults, are motivated by the need to belong and to feel important to a team's success. That inclusive attitude creates a level of commitment that taps into unseen potential. At C-FC and Darlington, inclusivity fostered a positive culture that led to continued championships at both schools.

Both teams learned to run as a pack during the heat of competition, often finishing in a cluster. The method eased their pain, bolstered their confidence, and discouraged their opponents. This trait was developed through many hours of training, suffering, and laughing together. Neither school had an individual champion running on its squad. Each team's strength and success came through their unity. They found that they could still win without a superstar if they responded like a "super team."

WE CAN AFFECT OUR DESTINIES.

In 1982, nobody would have predicted that Arnie Miehe or Gary Brone would ever coach cross country, much less that each would earn nine team state championships during his forty-year tenure with the sport.

WHERE ARE THEY NOW?

Bob Cullen lives with his wife in Hadley, Massachusetts. They have two sons. Bob has been a math teacher for thirty-two years and currently teaches high school math in Windsor, Connecticut. Bob continues to enjoy running and bicycling. He finished the New York City Marathon in 1991 and completed a cross country bicycle tour from Seattle, Washington, to Asbury Park, New Jersey, in 1995. He has also completed various self-contained bicycle tours around the country.

Troy Cullen graduated with a BS in education from the University of Wisconsin–La Crosse. He is married and lives in Appleton, Wisconsin. Troy teaches mathematics at Kimberly High School, where he was also the girls' head basketball coach until May 2022. During his twenty-two years as the varsity coach, he led the Kimberly girls' program to 414 wins. His coaching record places him in thirty-fifth place, among girls' basketball coaches in the state.

Doug Dunham earned his PhD in physics from the University of Wisconsin–Milwaukee and is currently a professor and the director of the Materials Science and Engineering Center at the University of Wisconsin–Eau Claire.

Kirk Evenstad graduated from the University of Wisconsin–Platteville and runs his family's farm with his older brother, Tom. Together, they host the Great Holland Road Run each autumn for the Redbirds.

Tom Evenstad graduated from the University of Wisconsin–Platteville and currently runs the family farm with his brother, Kirk. He has remained active in the cross country program as a community member. Although Tom never got the chance to run at the state meet, his dedication was rewarded as a parent. Three of Tom's four children ran for Darlington at the state cross country meet. His son Tanner was a member of three championship teams during Darlington's six-year consecutive string. Tom's son Taylor played football as a lineman and was named to the Wisconsin High School All-Star Football Team. Tom has stated that the Evenstads will always host the Redbirds cross country team for the Great Holland Road Run each year, as long as there is a Miehe coaching.

Dave Hirsbrunner graduated with a degree in education from the University of Wisconsin–Platteville, where he competed in cross country and was a multi-event competitor for the track-and-field team. After graduation, he had many successful years coaching high school cross country teams in Monroe, Wisconsin. Dave married his high school sweetheart, Cory, and has two children, Jake and Jordan, both of whom became accomplished athletes and received scholarships to compete for the University of Wisconsin. The family resides in Waunakee, Wisconsin.

Todd Johnson lives near Blue Mounds, Wisconsin, where he is a mail carrier.

Dale Kelly is a product support engineer for Promega Corporation. He lives with his wife, Jennifer, in Fitchburg, Wisconsin.

Kent Ruppert graduated from the University of Wisconsin–Platteville with a degree in agricultural business. He is married and lives in Maquoketa, Iowa, where he owns his own tax and financial consulting business.

James Schuetz and his wife, Michelle, have two adult sons. He owns Destiny Motors, a successful small-engine repair business in rural Hazel Green, Wisconsin. James still shows up and runs in the Darlington Alumni Meet each August.

Jay Stauffacher graduated from the University of Wisconsin–Platteville with a degree in business and finance. He lives near Darlington, Wisconsin, where he is the co-owner and general manager of his family's business, Highway Dairy Farms of Darlington. Jay has also served as a board member of the Wisconsin Milk Marketing Board. He has two adult sons who live in the Darlington area.

Brian Whalen graduated with his buddy Troy from the University of Wisconsin–La Crosse. He currently works in maintenance for the Gibraltar School District. He lives in Baileys Harbor, Wisconsin.

Paul Abts finished a twenty-year career in the Navy and completed his associate degree. He is married, has two daughters, and lives in Fountain City, Wisconsin, where he works for the U.S. Army Corps of Engineers.

Scott Adler graduated from the University of Wisconsin–Platteville with a degree in mechanical engineering. He served in the U.S. Army as a reservist and built a successful career as an engineer. Scott retired in 2022 and lives with his wife in Green Bay, Wisconsin. They have two adult children. Scott maintains his love of endurance sports as a CrossFit enthusiast and a cross country skier. Among his achievements, he successfully completed the Wisconsin Ironman triathlon in 2011 and continues to compete in the American Birkebeiner ski race each February. To this day, his 1984 patellar tendon injury needles him after a workout.

Mark Brone graduated from the University of Wisconsin–Stevens Point, where he played basketball. He owns Brone's Bike Shop and resides in Trempealeau, Wisconsin, with his wife and two children. As an adult, he has distinguished himself as a coach, an amateur cyclist, and a custom bicycle technician.

Dan Lettner graduated from Saint Mary's University in Winona, Minnesota, with a degree in education after serving in the Marine Corps. He currently resides in Houston, Texas, where he teaches science to elementary school students.

Jeff Rich graduated from the University of Wisconsin–Platteville with a degree in mechanical engineering. Before retiring in 2019, he spent twenty-nine years working in the manufacturing, healthcare, and clean energy sectors. He lives with his wife in West Salem, Wisconsin, and they have three adult daughters.

Heidi (Stettler) Frey received her undergraduate and post-graduate degrees from the University of Wisconsin–Madison where she played trumpet in the marching band. She went on to become a certified athletic trainer and received her master's degree in exercise science and biomechanics. She worked as an athletic trainer with the volleyball and rowing teams at the University of Washington–Seattle and the University of Wisconsin–Madison for many years and continues working in various roles in the health and wellness field. She is married and lives near Cannon Falls, Minnesota.

Karen (Stettler) Wilson graduated from St. Olaf University in Northfield, Minnesota. She lives near Fountain City, Wisconsin, on the farm where she grew up. Karen is married and has two children.

Guy Todd lives in Maple Lake, Minnesota, with his wife. They have an adult son.

ACKNOWLEDGMENTS

As a novice writer and author, I could not have finished this project without significant assistance from a large group of people who provided feedback and advice. Memories become blurry after forty years. Multiple perspectives provide a more balanced and accurate piece of nonfiction. I'm extremely grateful for the help I've received on this journey and hope the result is instructive and entertaining.

First, I'd like to thank my wife, Karen, who had to endure countless hours of watching me buried in my laptop, hammering on the keyboard and retelling old stories. Love is patient, and I'm grateful for your support as I've undertaken this project. You've been a great sounding board when I needed someone to talk with about my doubts on this journey. I could not ask for a better partner in life.

Part of my purpose for writing this book was to honor two legendary coaches, Gary Brone and Arnie Miehe. Athletes, coaches, and leaders can draw wisdom from their example. I hope that retelling this story concurrently, rather than focusing on a single team, honors the sport and makes it a more compelling account. The ironies, trials, similarities, and lessons are easier for the reader to distinguish. Thanks to both of you for your unselfishness, humility, and partnership. We are better together!

Gary, I cannot thank you enough for your commitment to the community, the C-FC School District, your former runners, and to me personally. Your positive attitude, engaging personality, and zest for life are contagious. Many have looked to you as a model friend, neighbor, and coach. You've made a difference in my life, and I'm forever grateful. You were my inspiration to pick up the pen.

Arnie, thank you for the countless hours of meetings, phone calls, and review as I worked with you on gathering the Darlington story. I am so happy that you answered the phone when I first gave you a call, and I've come to value your counsel and friendship. Your commitment to your community and students is admirable. Your example of servant leadership is something everyone can learn from. Your impact is obvious, and the culture that exists at Darlington High School is truly special. I hope that this book meets your expectations. I did my best to recreate the Darlington perspective without the benefit of actually having lived it with you. In some ways, I now feel that I did live it with you, and we ran side by side the whole time. Thanks also to Ann and your entire family, who have been so generous to me.

Thanks to my former teammates Paul Abts, Scott Adler, Mark Brone, Dan Lettner, Karen (Stettler) Wilson, and Heidi (Stettler) Frey, who shared memories and reviewed drafts as I reconstructed our story from so long ago.

Thanks also to my teammates who were pioneers in those first years: Vicki Blank, Janet Brommer, Dana Duellman, Tracy Duellman, Todd Farrand, Teresa Jumbeck, Korey Klink, Becky Lettner, Mary (McCamley) Yazvec, Guy Todd, and Valerie Wantoch. Without you, our program would have never launched.

To my former competitors from Darlington, whom I now call friends: Troy Cullen, Bob Cullen, Doug Dunham, Tom Evenstad, Kirk Evenstad, Shawn Hauser, Dave Hirsbrunner, Todd Johnson, Dale Kelly, Kent Ruppert, James Schuetz, Jeff Schuetz, Jay Stauffacher, and Brian Whalen. Thank you for speaking with me and reviewing my drafts so I could attempt to tell your story. We had a shared experience at a young age, and I now realize how similar our paths really were. Your input was invaluable, and I look forward to sharing more memories with you in the years to come.

Thanks to my many friends, colleagues, and contacts who reviewed my work and provided constructive feedback to me. Many helped, but in particular: Dave Adams, Ashley Duellman, Jim Engels, Karen Engels, John Massey, Gina Kenyon, Randy Kenyon, Randy Knecht, Chris Petersen, Darren Pokorny, Michelle Petersen, Betty Rich, Dick

Rich, Kevin Rich, Brian Semling, Scott Sievert, Greg Sutton, and Tony Thelen.

Thanks to coach Donn Behnke of Stevens Point Area Senior High School, who took the time to speak with me and provide contacts as I sought to publish my work. The insights you provided make it easy to see why you've had such a successful career as a coach. I'm so impressed with the legacy you've created in Stevens Point.

Thanks to the staff of the *Republican Journal* in Darlington, Wisconsin, and *Lee Enterprises, Inc.* (publisher of the *Winona Daily News* in Winona, Minnesota) for allowing me to share their material. The old articles and photos helped to accurately recount the events and color the story for the readers.

I'd like to thank Mitchell Austin, Darlington High School principal, the Darlington school board, and Troy White, Cochrane-Fountain City High School superintendent, for the permission to use the school logos. Your help has made this story easier for the readers to follow. Both districts can be proud of their programs' positive impact on young lives.

Thank you to the WIAA and the WCCCA for the results archives and historical references that provided me with additional details on these past events. Your organization and support of the fine sport of cross country is very much appreciated.

Thank you to my friend, Morgan Lynn Haun, for creating the scene on the title page.

Thank you to my editor, Susan Murray, who helped me shape a rough manuscript into a more suitable product. I have come to admire your wisdom and professionalism. Your experience as an educator shines through, and your kindness makes learning a joy.

In conclusion, a special thank you to my friends Kristin Mitchell, Shannon Booth, and Kristin Gilpatrick at Little Creek Press. I am so grateful to have had your guidance and expertise on this journey. You've helped me navigate the complex task of getting published and I could not have done it without you. Everyone needs the support of others to be successful in life and I was very fortunate to find the great team at Little Creek Press.

JEFF RICH

ABOUT THE AUTHOR

Raised on the banks of the Mississippi River and the oldest of three brothers, Jeff Rich absorbed high school athletics from the perspective of a coach's son. That early experience created a strong connection with sports and the outdoors. However, at the age of sixteen, a traumatic football injury triggered a shift to a new sport and some valuable life lessons.

After high school, the author graduated from the University of Wisconsin–Platteville with a degree in mechanical engineering. Before retiring in 2019, he spent twenty-nine years working in the manufacturing, healthcare, and clean energy sectors.

An avid outdoorsman, Jeff spends much of his time combing the hills and trout streams of the Upper Mississippi's Driftless Region. He and his wife, parents of three adult daughters, reside in West Salem, Wisconsin.

Printed in the United States
by Baker & Taylor Publisher Services